To

_____

_____

From

_____

_____

Date

_____

HOPE
for each
MORNING

JOANNA TEIGEN

CHRISTIAN ART PUBLISHERS

Published by Christian Art Publishers
PO Box 1599, Vereeniging, 1930, RSA

© 2021
First edition 2021

Designed by Christian Art Publishers

Cover designed by Christian Art Publishers

Images used under license from Shutterstock.com

Scripture quotations taken from the Holy Bible, New International Version®,
NIV® Copyright © 1973, 1978, 1984, 2011 by Biblica, Inc.® Used by permission.
All rights reserved worldwide.

Set in 12 on 15 pt Cronos Pro
by Christian Art Publishers

Printed in China

ISBN 978-1-4321-3119-7 Faux Leather
ISBN 978-1-4321-3487-7 Hardcover

21 22 23 24 25 26 27 28 29 30 – 10 9 8 7 6 5 4 3 2 1

To Rob

For nearly 30 years, you have shown the love of Christ
in your love for me and our family.
It has been a joy to follow the Lord by your side.

January

JANUARY 1

Remembering God's Love

*I will remember the deeds of the LORD; yes, I will remember
your miracles of long ago. I will consider all your works
and meditate on all your mighty deeds. You are
the God who performs miracles; you display
your power among the peoples. PSALM 77:11-12, 14*

Are you afraid you'll go hungry tomorrow? No, because you've had food each day of the year. Do you worry the sun won't come up in the morning? No, it's risen in the sky from the beginning of time. Do you knock and introduce yourself when you arrive at home? No, because you remember who loves you and where you belong.

God knows we need to remember him too. Fear and trouble come out of nowhere and we don't know what to do. In those times, the Bible says to remember. Remember God's power. Remember his love. Remember the way he answered prayers and stayed by our side. When we remember God's faithfulness in the past, we find peace for today and courage to face the future.

Can you remember how God has taken care of you? How he has guided your steps? Forgiven your sins? Provided what you needed? Healed and helped you, over and over?

When we're sad or afraid, let's remember God and trust him. " ... for [the Lord's] compassions never fail. They are new every morning; great is your faithfulness" (Lamentations 3:22-23).

Lord, may we remember your power, love,
and blessings through the year ahead. Amen.

JANUARY 2

The Father's Kindness

"I led them with cords of human kindness, with ties of love.
To them I was like one who lifts a little child to the cheek,
and I bent down to feed them." HOSEA 11:4

God is mighty, powerful, and all-knowing. He's the ultimate warrior and Judge. He's so huge, heaven is his throne and the earth is his footstool (Isaiah 66:1). As the great I AM, he reigns over all things. We serve an awesome, almighty God.

God deserves our submission and awe. Yet it's his gentle kindness that draws us close. It's like a little girl who follows her mother or father because she expects to be cared for. If a small boy feels scared, hurt, or hungry, he'll run to the parent who loves him. Little ones know who will tenderly give them what they need.

God is the most loving Father of all. He's all powerful, but he uses his strength to protect you. He's the King of Kings, but he uses his authority to command angels to guard you. He knows everything, not so he can name your mistakes but so he can know your heart. We can run to him when we're afraid, hurting, or guilty of sin. "There is no fear in love. But perfect love drives out fear, because fear has to do with punishment" (1 John 4:18). In God's kindness, we find compassion and forgiveness. He leads us by his love.

Lord, you are loving and kind, and you care for us in every way.
Help us to trust you like children. Amen.

Be More Considerate Online

*Remind the people to be subject to rulers and authorities,
to be obedient, to be ready to do whatever is good,
to slander no one, to be peaceable and considerate,
and always to be gentle toward everyone.* TITUS 3:1-2

To be considerate means to consider what we say and do before we do it. We ask ourselves, *Have I obeyed the people in charge of me? Am I doing the right thing? How will my choices affect other people? Will my words be helpful or hurtful?* We pause and think how our words and actions might impact the people around us.

It's especially challenging to be considerate when we go online. Social media makes it easy to criticize our leaders and tear people down. People can throw out feelings and opinions without any fear of consequences. Yet gossip, insults, and rude remarks do lasting damage to our hearts. It's just as important to love like Jesus online as it is in person.

Let's commit to pleasing God in the way we use our devices. We can reach out to message those who feel lonely or left out. We can respond to pictures and posts with kindness instead of criticism. We can choose videos and content that build up our minds and spirits. We can even "unplug" if we're tempted to hurt instead of help. God's Spirit will help us to be considerate at all times to everyone.

> Lord, give us wisdom to use our devices in loving ways.
> We want to be considerate and do what's right. Amen.

The Money Trap

"No one can serve two masters. Either you will hate the one and love the other, or you will be devoted to the one and despise the other. You cannot serve both God and money." LUKE 16:13

Money can buy lots of fun. It's the ticket to movies, theme parks, and concerts. It'll get all the gadgets you dream of at the store. It pays for travel to exciting destinations. A bank account full of cash could buy whatever our hearts desire.

Money offers security, too. It meets our need for food and clothing. Bills get paid and the house and vehicle stay in good repair. A generous supply of money keeps many worries away.

With the good that money can do, our hearts are tempted to love it too much. We can depend on it for happiness or trust it to keep us well and safe. It becomes a hard master, driving us to gain more and more. Before long, we find no amount of money will ever be enough.

God knows serving money will keep us from loving him. We can't run after money and follow Jesus, too. We'll become discontent, selfish, and fearful of losing it all. The gifts of God's peace and abundant life will slip away. Today, let's remember the Giver of all our money. His love is free, and it's better than anything money can buy.

Lord, we want to serve you. Guard our hearts
from the love of money. Amen.

JANUARY 5

Come Out of Hiding

*Then the man and his wife heard the sound of the LORD God
as he was walking in the garden in the cool of the day,
and they hid from the LORD God among the trees
of the garden. But the LORD God called to the man,
"Where are you?"* GENESIS 3:8-9

Every time we sin, we want to hide. We get rid of the evidence so we don't get caught. We make excuses to explain it away. Instead of taking responsibility, we lay blame on other people. Sin leads to lying to deny or cover up what we've done. In our guilt and shame, we hide from God and those we've hurt or disobeyed.

God loves us too much to leave us hiding in the darkness. He sent Jesus "to seek and to save the lost" who need rescue from their sin (Luke 19:10). His Spirit wakes up our conscience to remember what's right. His Word holds his promises to forgive and show mercy. He invites us to come out of hiding, confess our sin, and receive a clean heart.

Are you hiding today? Do secret sins weigh you down with guilt and steal your joy? Is God speaking to your heart and asking, "Where are you?" Today, let's come into the light. Let's tell the truth about what we've done. In turning away from sin, we can turn back to God. He'll set us free so we never have to hide again.

*Lord, we thank you for coming to find us
in our sin. Your love is our life. Amen.*

A Comfort We Can Share

*Praise be to the God and Father of our Lord Jesus Christ,
the Father of compassion and the God of all comfort,
who comforts us in all our troubles, so that we
can comfort those in any trouble with the comfort
we ourselves receive from God.* 2 CORINTHIANS 1:3-4

Nobody is too young or too old to suffer hard things. But no matter how hurt or disappointed we might feel, God is good. He's faithful to help us and get us through to the other side of our problems. But he doesn't stop there! He pours so much love and comfort into our hearts that we can share it with others who are hurting.

Do you know how it feels to be lonely and left out? Now you're able to reach out to someone who needs a friend. Have you had to try, try, and try again to accomplish your goals? You can encourage someone who's ready to quit. Have you overcome sin that brought guilt and trouble to your life? You're able to share the good news of Jesus' love and forgiveness with the world.

God will never waste our pain. He'll answer our prayers for help and hope so we discover how great his love truly is. Then, we get to take the comfort he's given and pay it forward. His love goes on and on.

Lord, thank you for meeting us in the middle of our problems. Show us how to comfort others with the comfort you give to us. Amen.

Grace Is Not Earned

*For it is by grace you have been saved, through faith—and
this is not from yourselves, it is the gift of God—not
by works, so that no one can boast.* EPHESIANS 2:8-9

At school a strong report card comes from studying hard to achieve good grades. At work a paycheck or weekly allowance is earned through finishing each day's job. We try to look good, act nice, and please people to make friends. If we become successful or popular, it's tempting to feel proud of what our efforts accomplished.

Yet no matter how we try, we can't earn God's love. Following the rules, sharing with others, and going to church won't make us more welcome in heaven. Our salvation isn't paid for by our good behavior—it's a free gift from God.

Is there a penalty for our sins? Yes. Can we do enough good to cover our sins? No. Our sin-debt was fully paid by Jesus' death on the cross. God invites us to receive the gift of life by trusting in Jesus. Instead of bragging about our goodness, we praise God for his free gift of life and love.

Are you trying to earn God's kindness by your own hard work to be perfect? Are you scared God will turn away if you mess up? Rest in his generous love that never ends.

Lord, thank you for your grace and the gift of salvation.
Your love is wonderful! Amen.

Walk the Talk

*Suppose a brother or a sister is without clothes
and daily food. If one of you says to them,
"Go in peace; keep warm and well fed," but
does nothing about their physical needs,
what good is it?* JAMES 2:15-16

When you were young your mom might have said, "Good night! Sweet dreams!", and tucked you into a comfortable bed. You had cool sheets in summer and fuzzy blankets when it was cold. Your head rested on a soft pillow. You knew you were safe as you drifted off to sleep.

But if your mom said, "Good night," but put you on the hard floor, you wouldn't have a good night at all. You'd think she didn't care if you were cold or woke up stiff and sore. Her words would say one thing, but her actions would say the opposite.

Kind words are important, but giving and helping mean so much more. Visiting a lonely neighbor is better than waving hello from across the street. Bringing groceries to a food pantry provides a meal that satisfies. Giving money helps a mother pay the bills when she's out of work. Donations provide clean water, medical care, and schooling for kids in poor countries. We can show Jesus' love in what we say and in what we do.

It grieves our hearts to see people hungry, hurt, or alone. Let's show Jesus' love and do all we can to help.

Lord, help us to make a difference in the world around us. Amen.

Break Down Your Tower

*They said to each other, "Come, let's make bricks
and bake them thoroughly." ... Then they said,
"Come, let us build ourselves a city, with a tower
that reaches to the heavens, so that we may make
a name for ourselves; otherwise we will be scattered
over the face of the whole earth."* GENESIS 11:3-4

In the city of Babel, the people wanted to build something awesome. Their tower would show off their advanced technology, money, and power to everybody. It would stand as proof they could do anything. They couldn't wait to stand out in the world and "make a name for themselves."

We all want the same thing, don't we? It feels good when people say we're smart, good-looking, talented, or successful. The problem is, winning the game, getting a promotion, or feeling popular with our friends can become too important. We try so hard to build ourselves up—just like that tower—that we forget how much we need God.

Let's check our hearts today. Do we want praise and attention for ourselves, or do we want to bring God glory? Are we working hard on our own, or are we depending on God for help? Who is the builder of our lives today?

Lord, you say apart from you we can't do anything (John 15:5).
Teach us to be humble so we stay close to you
and learn to love like Jesus. Show us how to make
your name great in everything we do. Amen.

He Opens Our Eyes

*And even if our gospel is veiled, it is veiled to those
who are perishing. The god of this age has blinded
the minds of unbelievers, so that they cannot see
the light of the gospel that displays the glory of Christ,
who is the image of God.* 2 CORINTHIANS 4:3-4

Have you opened the refrigerator, but couldn't see your snack sitting right on the shelf? Maybe you tried to show someone a bird, but they couldn't tell which branch you pointed to. On a foggy morning, you can hardly see the road ahead as you drive. Sometimes we can't see what's right in front of us.

God has shown himself so everyone can see him. The wonders of nature tell of a Creator. God revealed his "invisible qualities—his eternal power and divine nature" through all he made (Romans 1:20).

God sent his own Son, Jesus, into the world from heaven. Jesus came to make his Father known and make a way to him (John 1:18).

God gave his Word—"the very Scriptures that testify about me"—to show himself to all who read it (John 5:39).

Yet with all the evidence, not everyone can see God. Sin and Satan have blinded people's eyes, plugged their ears, and confused their thinking. Yet God wants the world to know he exists and loves them. " … whenever anyone turns to the Lord, the veil is taken away" (2 Corinthians 3:16). He opens our eyes so we can believe.

Lord, open the eyes of the lost ones we love. Amen.

JANUARY 11

Worldwide Worship

*"Who will not fear you, Lord, and bring glory
to your name? For you alone are holy. All nations
will come and worship before you, for your
righteous acts have been revealed."* REVELATION 15:4

Every person will worship someone or something. If we traveled the globe, we'd see people bowing down before statues. We'd hear prayers and chants to other gods. Skyscrapers and monuments would glorify money and power. We'd see libraries filled with books of human wisdom in every language. The human heart looks for truth and love in every corner of the earth.

God is the answer to every need. Jesus promises, "I am the way and the truth and the life. No one comes to the Father except through me" (John 14:6). Yet many choose to ignore our holy and loving God. They worship what God has created instead of the Creator himself. It's heartbreaking to see a lost world denying the One who can save and give eternal life.

Yet someday, the whole earth will worship him. "It is written: "'As surely as I live,' says the Lord, 'every knee will bow before me; every tongue will acknowledge God'" (Romans 14:11). Even now, believers are sharing the Gospel around the world. All people will see Jesus' glory as the King of Kings at his return. As we wait for that day, let's be faithful to pray and tell the world about Jesus.

Lord, we long for the day when all people will exalt your holy name.
Trust and love are found in you alone. Amen.

God Is Our Superhero

*Do not be far from me, for trouble is near
and there is no one to help.* PSALM 22:11

We all love a good superhero story. Invincible strength, special powers, and high-tech gadgets overcome danger and doom. Good triumphs over evil and saves the day.

We'd welcome a superhero if our car slid into a ditch or a threatening storm was in the forecast. Who wouldn't welcome the chance to fly when stuck in a traffic jam? Parents dream of seeing through walls to keep an eye on their kids. We wish we could summon a hero any moment we're in trouble.

What do we do when problems crash into our lives? In the middle of a crisis, who can we call for help? Who will come close when we're scared and alone? Our Lord is better than any superhero we could imagine. He's real. With him, all things are possible (Matthew 19:26). He is able to do more than all we ask or imagine (Ephesians 3:20).

Our powerful, unstoppable God is full of love. He listens to our prayers when we cry for help. He's always close and holds us in his hands. Nothing we face is too difficult for him to handle. He overcomes the darkness. We can find peace knowing he's always on our side.

Lord, "yours is the greatness and the power and the glory
and the majesty and the splendor, for everything in heaven
and earth is yours. In your hands are strength and power
to exalt and give strength to all" (1 Chronicles 29:11-12). Amen.

JANUARY 13

Singing Songs of Joy

*"The LORD your God is with you, the Mighty Warrior
who saves. He will take great delight in you;
in his love he will no longer rebuke you, but
will rejoice over you with singing."* ZEPHANIAH 3:17

Singing and celebrating go hand in hand. When you turn a year older, you have "Happy birthday to you!" sung to you. Christmas carols play nonstop during the holidays. Graduates march to "Pomp and Circumstance" to receive their diploma. A wedding is filled with music as the bride walks down the aisle and the couple shares a dance as Mr. and Mrs. A party isn't a party without music. Through singing, we rejoice in God's blessings in our life.

Did you know God celebrates you and me when we believe in Jesus? "There is rejoicing in the presence of the angels of God over one sinner who repents" (Luke 15:10). When we turn from unbelief to faith, from darkness to light, and from sin to obedience, God rejoices with singing.

God isn't just celebrating our good choices. He's rejoicing that we've "crossed over from death to life" (John 5:24). We've been adopted as his children. We'll be together for all of eternity. Our sin brought pain and suffering, and our salvation brings joy and peace. Since God loves us, he rejoices with singing over the life we find in him.

Lord, give us joy that sings as we love and obey you always. Amen.

Depend on God's Power

*His pleasure is not in the strength of the horse, nor his delight
in the legs of the warrior; the LORD delights in those who fear him,
who put their hope in his unfailing love.* PSALM 147:10-11

A racehorse could outrun a cheetah on the track, and a draft horse can pull thousands of pounds. A race car speeds across the finish line with hundreds of horsepower under its hood. Soldiers train for precision and arm themselves for battle to protect their land. Arenas fill with fans eager to watch their favorite monster truck roll over its opponent. We cheer on for the quarterback as he breaks through the defense to make a touchdown. In this world we celebrate power, strength, and speed.

Do we try to be powerful, too? Are we practicing, training, and working to be the best? Are we striving to be invincible? Do we avoid failure and weakness at all costs? With a combination of hope and fear, we do all we can to feel safe and successful.

While God wants us to be wise and careful, he's not impressed by our strength. Our brains, our muscles, and our bank account won't earn trophies in heaven. He's most pleased when we depend on his power instead of our own. Let's stop trying to solve our own problems. We can admit we're tired, scared, or don't have what it takes. If we ask God to love and help us, he promises to make his power perfect in our weakness (2 Corinthians 12:9).

Lord, you are our strength and our song.
We put our hope in you. Amen.

JANUARY 15

Always Keep Growing

We ought always to thank God for you, brothers and sisters,
and rightly so, because your faith is growing more and more,
and the love all of you have for one another
is increasing. 2 THESSALONIANS 1:3

Kids grow a little taller every day. They learn more in school each year. Practice pays off, and they grow in strength as athletes, artists, or musicians. They grow in independence as they learn to do more on their own. It's exciting to watch kids grow up into the people God created them to be.

Eventually, kids reach their full height. They graduate from school. The goals and dreams they hold will run their course. Yet God says we can still keep growing every day of our lives—we grow in faith and love as we follow Jesus.

Faith grows as we receive God's answers to our prayers. It grows as we see him keep every promise in his Word. Our faith grows as we trust him to help us and take care of our needs. Our belief in Jesus' love becomes more confident and brave as he proves it over and over.

As faith grows, love grows too. God's Spirit fills us with kindness and mercy toward other people. He teaches us to be generous and eager to help. We forgive just as we've been forgiven for all our sins. The longer we know and love God, the more love we have to share with the world. Let's keep growing in faith and love as we follow Jesus forever.

Lord, grow us in the ways that matter most. We want bold faith
and love that grows deeper every day. Amen.

JANUARY 16

A Wife Is a Treasure

*He who finds a wife finds what is good and receives favor
from the Lord. A wife of noble character who can find?
She is worth far more than rubies. Her husband
has full confidence in her and lacks nothing of value.
She brings him good, not harm, all the days
of her life.* Proverbs 18:22, 31:10-12

Family was God's idea. He says children are a blessing to their parents (Psalm 127:3). A husband cares for his wife like Jesus. A wife is a gift from God to her husband. A loving, godly family shows the world God's kindness, his faithfulness, and his love.

A wife is a blessing to her husband. She encourages and builds him up. A wife helps to create a peaceful home in this crazy world. She prays faithfully. A wife gives her husband joy as she loves their children. She shows respect and honors him as a leader. A wife is a treasure to her family.

Yet a loving wife isn't just a gift to her husband. She shows the church how to love Jesus. She serves her family, just like we're called to serve our family in Christ. Her humble heart teaches us to honor the Lord. As she opens her home in hospitality, we learn to "offer hospitality to one another without grumbling" (1 Peter 4:9). In all she does, she uses her strength and gifts for good.

Lord, you filled my home with your love. Use me and my family
to show what it means to follow you. Amen.

JANUARY 17

Running from God

"Go to the great city of Nineveh and preach against it,
because its wickedness has come up before me."
But Jonah ran away from the LORD
and headed for Tarshish. JONAH 1:2-3

Some of God's assignments are difficult. He might ask you to make friends with a difficult person. You might have to give your hard-earned money to someone in need. You may have to work instead of taking time to relax. You have to submit to those in charge, even if they haven't earned your respect. You might have to take no for an answer. We all should love and forgive our enemies. God's way isn't the easy way. We can be tempted to run in the opposite direction.

Do we ignore God's Word when it's hard to obey? Do we avoid the person we're told to love? Instead of giving, do we grab on to our money and possessions more tightly? Do we lie or make excuses for running from God? Today, let's turn our feet around and run toward him instead. He'll give us strength and power to obey when we feel too weak (Isaiah 40:29). He'll stay with us wherever we're told to go (Joshua 1:9). His love will change our hearts so we love and trust him through it all.

Lord, you say if we love you, then we'll obey your Word.
Grow your love in our hearts. Amen.

My Strength and Shield

The LORD is my strength and my shield; my heart trusts in him,
and he helps me. My heart leaps for joy, and with my song
I praise him. The LORD is the strength of his people,
a fortress of salvation for his anointed one. PSALM 28:7-8

Is trouble coming at you hard and fast? Maybe you are having relationship problems. Or doctors can't help you feel better. Your work feels overwhelming, and you wonder how you'll do it all. You're criticized and put down no matter how hard you try. Money is running out, but expenses keep on coming. The decision you face feels impossible. You feel trapped. Tired. Confused. You have no shield to protect you from harm.

Do you wish you could run away and hide? God says he's like a fortress built around you. He shields you from enemies who want to hurt you. He holds you up when you feel like you're falling. God brings relief by promising to give what you need. He stands in front of you, defending you and keeping you safe.

Today, let's pray for God's help. Let's be honest about our struggles and fears and tell him all about it. By trusting him, we can step away from the battlefield and let God fight for us. He'll give us strength and fill our hearts with joy. In the end, we'll praise him for what he's done.

Lord, you're our shield in the battle of life.
Help us to trust in your love. Amen.

Get to Work

A sluggard says, "There's a lion in the road,
a fierce lion roaming the streets!"
How long will you lie there, you sluggard?
When will you get up from your sleep? PROVERBS 26:13, 6:9

What were you supposed to do today? Did you manage to complete your to-do list? Which responsibilities were the most difficult?

It can be a challenge to finish our work. We're easily tired, bored, and distracted. We'd rather quit so we can relax and enjoy ourselves. If lazy choices leave our work undone, we have a choice: admit our mistake or make excuses.

Have you heard the funny excuse that says, "The dog ate my homework"? We're more likely to say, "It's not my fault!" Or, "I'll do it later. I'm too busy. This job is too hard. It's not fair." It's hard to admit the real problem is inside you and me.

God gave us work as a gift. He knows a clean and organized home is healthy and peaceful. Completed studies lead to greater knowledge and skill. A job well done earns respect and rewards. In his love, God is always working for us. He guides, protects, and helps us every day. Jesus said, "My Father is always at his work to this very day, and I too am working" (John 5:17). Let's be like Jesus and work as his servants every day.

Lord, keep us from lazy habits so we can serve and love like you. Amen.

Guiding the Way

*"If your brother or sister sins, go and point out their fault,
just between the two of you. If they listen to you,
you have won them over."* MATTHEW 18:15

God says we can use our words to guide each other to something even better. We can talk about our sins and help each other do what's right.

When we see our friends and family falling into sin, it's serious. Sin hurts. It leads to painful consequences. It fills us with guilt and shame instead of joy and peace. Sin can be addictive or create habits that are terribly hard to break. Every time we choose our own way over God's way, we damage our relationship with him and others.

God's love shows us what to do when our loved ones are struggling with temptation or bad choices. Instead of tattling or pointing fingers, we show we care. In a private, respectful conversation we can point out the sin we see. We share our concerns and God's offer of forgiveness. The truth in our words can help others repent and make a fresh start.

Lord, you set us free from the power of sin. Show us how to help each other walk in obedience to you all the time. Amen.

JANUARY 21

Choose Your Friends Well

Do not be misled: "Bad company corrupts good character."
1 CORINTHIANS 15:33

Our work and recreation mimics those around us. We start to look like the company we keep, the things we immerse ourselves in. A friend's bad attitude will rub off on us. The language we hear becomes the words we speak. We work and play like those around us. We take on the habits, the plans, and the point of view of the people closest to us.

How would you describe your friends? What is their attitude toward others? Do they work hard or do the bare minimum? Would you say they respect the rules, tell the truth, and express a patient and grateful attitude? What do you admire most about your friends and hope to imitate?

God cares about your heart. He wants to help you have a strong character so you can think, act, and love people like Jesus. Let's surround ourselves with those who bring out our best.

> Lord, give us wisdom in choosing our friends. Surround us
> with people who encourage our spirits and help
> us do what's right. Amen.

Make Everyone Feel Welcome

*"But when you give a banquet, invite the poor, the crippled, the lame,
the blind, and you will be blessed. Although they cannot repay you,
you will be repaid at the resurrection of the righteous." When one
of those at the table with him heard this, he said to Jesus,
"Blessed is the one who will eat at the feast
in the kingdom of God." LUKE 14:13-15*

Do you feel excited when someone puts a party invitation in your hand or your mailbox? Have you ever walked into a room and had a friend move over to make space for you to join them? It feels good to be invited and made welcome. For that moment you feel like you're special. You're wanted and you belong.

Jesus makes everyone feel wanted, no matter how rich or poor, popular or lonely, strong or limited they might be. He wants everyone to believe in him and become part of his family. Jesus' love and compassion are free gifts to every person who wants to receive them.

When we follow him, he wants us to love everybody, too. How can we show kindness, making others welcome without asking for anything in return? Let's pray for God to show us who needs love and friendship most of all.

Lord, thank you for inviting us to become part of your kingdom family.
Show us how to love others in your name by making
them welcome in our lives. Amen.

JANUARY 23

Encourage Your Loved Ones

If an enemy were insulting me, I could endure it; if a foe
were rising against me, I could hide. But it is you,
a man like myself, my companion, my close friend,
with whom I once enjoyed sweet fellowship
at the house of God, as we walked about among
the worshipers. PSALM 55:12-14

A parent, sibling , or a best friend knows us well. They know our strengths and the struggles we've overcome. They hold a front-row seat to our ideas and personalities. They've prayed for us and celebrated our victories. We put our heart in their hands.

Because of this, mean words and put-downs hurt the most from people we love. We take their insults to heart. We feel betrayed. Embarrassed. Rejected. We become insecure and wonder if their words are true. The closeness we share is torn apart.

We're called to "encourage one another and build each other up" (1 Thessalonians 5:11). With our words we honor each other as God's creation, made in his image (Genesis 1:27). Before pointing fingers at mistakes, we patiently overlook the offense (Proverbs 19:11). We commit to "slander no one, to be peaceable and considerate, and always to be gentle toward everyone" (Titus 3:2).

Lord, let us love each other through our words. Amen.

Running for the Crown

I have fought the good fight, I have finished the race,
I have kept the faith. Now there is in store for me
the crown of righteousness, which the Lord,
the righteous Judge, will award to me on that day—and
not only to me, but also to all who have longed for
his appearing. 2 TIMOTHY 4:7-8

God compares our life as believers to running a race. It's not a race to reach the finish line first—it's a race of endurance to finish at all! On this "track" we run, we face obstacles before the finish line of heaven. We're tripped up by sin. We can become lost following false teachers or bad influences. In tough times, we grow tired or doubt God's love. He knows how hard it is to run with the world against us.

How do we keep going when we want to quit? We remember the rewards God has waiting at the end. It's not a cheap trophy to put on the shelf. God will put a crown of righteousness on our heads. He holds heavenly treasure for each of his children. He wants "the eyes of your heart [to] be enlightened in order that you may know the hope to which he has called you, the riches of his glorious inheritance in his holy people" (Ephesians 1:18).

Let's encourage each other to keep running for the crown—loving God every day without giving up.

Lord, help us to run the race of faith until we see your face in heaven.
Amen.

Put God First

"You have planted much, but harvested little ... You put on clothes, but are not warm. You earn wages, only to put them in a purse with holes in it. You expected much, but see, it turned out to be little ... Why?" declares the LORD Almighty. "Because of my house, which remains a ruin, while each of you is busy with your own house." HAGGAI 1:6, 9

Have you tried to dig a hole at the beach, but it filled with sand as fast as you could scoop it out? Did you reach the last page of a book, but a cliffhanger ending left you wanting more? Have you worked and saved, only to spend it all in one shopping spree? Our efforts don't always last or give the results we hope for.

When we work hard to get a lot for ourselves, we're always disappointed. But when we seek to grow God's house—his kingdom of believers in the world—we gain blessings that last forever. We build God's house by sharing the good news of Jesus. We obey him in everything—we love our neighbor. Use our spiritual gifts. Give and help to show Jesus' love in action. We let our light shine so everybody will see our good deeds and glorify God (Matthew 5:16).

We have a choice. We can work a lot to gain little. Or, we can "seek first his kingdom" and trust God to give us all we need (Matthew 6:33).

Lord, help us to build your house by loving and serving you. Amen.

From Coveting to Gratitude

"You shall not covet your neighbor's house. You shall not covet your neighbor's wife, or his male or female servant, his ox or donkey, or anything that belongs to your neighbor." EXODUS 20:17

New clothes eventually fade, stain, or grow too snug. Our best dishes chip and our prized possessions fade. Technology moves forward so our devices seem obsolete. Nearly everything we buy will eventually wear out or fail to keep us happy. When that happens, we're tempted to crave something new.

God knows how jealousy works its way into our hearts. We keep score of who has the biggest and best. Instead of celebrating others' blessings, we feel angry inside. We think, *Don't I deserve what they have? Is God holding back good things from me? It's not fair!*

The cure for coveting is gratitude. When we start to compare our lives with others', we can remember all God has done. He's kept us safe, fed, and warm. He provided loving family and friends. Our days are filled with purpose and meaning. We've received his own Son as our Savior. He has "blessed us in the heavenly realms with every spiritual blessing in Christ" (Ephesians 1:3). Nothing on earth can compare with our treasures in heaven. We've been given more than we ever deserve.

Lord, guard our hearts from coveting. Fill us with gratitude for every blessing you've given. Thank you for your love. Amen.

A Thirst for God

Jesus answered, "Everyone who drinks this water
will be thirsty again, but whoever drinks the water
I give them will never thirst. Indeed, the water
I give them will become in them a spring of water
welling up to eternal life." JOHN 4:13-14

Every living organism depends on water to live. You've seen flowers wilt and grass grow brown and dry with no rain. Our bodies are made up of 75 percent water—we could only survive a few days without it! You know how thirsty you become after working out or spending time outside on a hot day. We feel thirsty and even sick if we wait too long for a drink.

Jesus created this world, designing it so every plant, animal, and person requires water for life. The cups of water we just drank won't satisfy our thirst for very long. Yet he offers another kind of "water" that lasts forever.

When we put our trust in Jesus for salvation, we receive the Holy Spirit. The Spirit is "a river of living water" flowing from within us (John 7:38-39). He satisfies our thirst for God once and for all. We 'drink' from an unlimited supply of hope and joy, knowing we'll live for always as part of God's family.

Lord, our hearts feel thirsty for more of you today.
We want the living water Jesus promised us through
believing in him. Fill us with your Spirit. Amen.

JANUARY 28

What Is Truly Fair

For the LORD gives wisdom; from his mouth come knowledge and understanding. Then you will understand what is right and just and fair—every good path. PROVERBS 2:6, 9

Some people make the mistake of thinking "equal" is the same thing as "fair." Equal means to be exactly alike, but fair means each person gets what they need.

If God treated us equally, we'd have too much or too little. In his wisdom he sees each of us as one of a kind. He knows how to take care of us and help us grow. He knows exactly what to give or take away for our good.

We can pray and ask God to share his wisdom with us. He'll teach us what's truly fair and right in our unique situation. If we're jealous or frustrated, he'll help us to patiently trust in his love. "For the LORD God is a sun and shield; the LORD bestows favor and honor; no good thing does he withhold from those whose walk is blameless" (Psalm 84:11).

Lord, your ways are higher than ours. In your love you give us exactly what we need. Help us to trust you are right and fair. Amen.

JANUARY 29

Amid the Fires of Adversity

*If we are thrown into the blazing furnace, the God
we serve is able to deliver us from it, and he will deliver
us from Your Majesty's hand. But even if he does not,
we want you to know, Your Majesty, that we will not
serve your gods or worship the image of gold
you have set up.* DANIEL 3:17-18

It takes courage to follow Jesus! We feel the heat when the enemy attacks our faith and tempts us to sin. We know "everyone who wants to live a godly life in Christ Jesus will be persecuted, while evildoers and impostors will go from bad to worse, deceiving and being deceived" (2 Timothy 3:12-13). As we love and obey, we pick up our cross and suffer with Jesus in this world.

In the middle of that bad news is the best news of all. We might be rejected by the world, but we're accepted by God. We may be insulted, but we're honored by the King of kings. "Our light and momentary troubles are achieving for us an eternal glory that far outweighs them all" (2 Corinthians 4:17).

God can keep us safe and secure, no matter how the fires rage around us. Even if he lets us feel the pain, we know whose we are. We have hope of eternity with all the love, joy, and peace God has in store.

Lord, make us faithful to you through the fire.
Our hope is in you. Amen.

Hope in Times of Grief

Be merciful to me, LORD, for I am in distress;
my eyes grow weak with sorrow, my soul and body
with grief. Let your face shine on your servant;
save me in your unfailing love. PSALM 31:9, 16

In this broken world, we will hurt and suffer. Dreams die and we feel the pain of disappointment. Death separates us from friends, pets or loved ones. We say goodbye to those we cherish the most. When we're sad and grieving, we feel we're in the dark. In that darkness we can feel lost and alone. We wonder if we'll be happy and whole again.

Even in our hurt, we can hold on to God's promises. He says, "I will never leave you nor forsake you" (Joshua 1:5). "He heals the brokenhearted and binds up their wounds" (Psalm 147:3). "Now is your time of grief, but I will see you again and you will rejoice, and no one will take away your joy" (John 16:22). God will shine his light of love into our darkness.

God is a loving Father. He counts our tears, hears our prayers, and wants to hold us close. You and I can ask him hard questions and tell him how we hurt. He loves us so much he'll stay close through it all. He'll do whatever it takes to heal our hearts.

Lord, you say "weeping may stay for the night,
but rejoicing comes in the morning." Help us
to know your love even when we're sad. Amen.

JANUARY 31

Stand Firm

Put on the full armor of God, so that you can take your stand against the devil's schemes. For our struggle is not against flesh and blood, but against the rulers, against the authorities, against the powers of this dark world and against the spiritual forces of evil in the heavenly realms. Therefore put on the full armor of God, so that when the day of evil comes, you may be able to stand your ground, and after you have done everything, to stand. EPHESIANS 6:11-13

Just as it's difficult to hold our footing on a slippery sheet of ice, it's hard to stand firm in life. We get knocked down by doubt—*is God really here? Is he good? Will he answer my prayers?* We fall to temptation, pleasing ourselves instead of God. We're pushed and pulled by other people's opinions. Anger and fear keep us from steady thinking. The enemy uses every kind of attack to trip us up.

How do we stand firm no matter what comes our way? We accept salvation through Jesus that sets us free from evil's power. We trust in God's love. We study the Bible's truth that never changes. We pray for help and strength. If we trust God, we'll never fall.

Lord, dress us in your armor so we stand firm in every struggle.
Give us faith in you and your Word. Fill us
with your power and strength today. Amen.

February

God's Love Is a Sure Thing

It always protects, always trusts, always hopes, always perseveres. Love never fails. 1 CORINTHIANS 13:7-8

Not much lasts forever in this world. Our gas tanks run out of fuel. Shoes wear out or go out of style. Seasons come and go. Our full stomachs feel hungry after a few hours. Addresses, jobs, acquaintances and certain pursuits are left behind in time.

Yet in God's Word, we read the word "always" over and over. His love is one sure thing for all of eternity. He promises to listen when we pray, help us when we cry to him, and finish the work he started when we first believed. He loves us too much to give up or walk away. Even if we fall into sin or doubt, "he remains faithful, for he cannot disown himself" (2 Timothy 2:13).

God's love teaches how we're to love each other. We do all we can to protect one another from harm. We expect the best of each other and trust we're growing every day. If we mess up or cause hurt, we forgive and offer another chance to get it right. We keep on loving day after day, year after year, believing we'll share life together forever with Jesus.

Lord, thank you for love that never fails. May we always love each other the way you love us. Amen.

The Blessing of Children

*Children are a heritage from the LORD, offspring a reward
from him. Like arrows in the hands of a warrior
are children born in one's youth. Blessed is the man
whose quiver is full of them.* PSALM 127:3-5

When babies and young children are little, parents do all they can to care for them and meet their needs. They provide food, clothing, an education, medical care, and a loving home. It gives a mom and dad great joy to help their kids grow, learn, and thrive.

As both children and parents grow older, that love and care goes both ways. God uses kids to bring great blessing to their family. As kids grow in their faith in Jesus, they can pray for their parents and encourage their faith in God.

Children are a heritage and a reward from God. Cherish them and watch God work in them as they grow. Look out for the ways they encourage you to grow more like Christ.

Lord, thank you for children. They are a priceless blessing.
Show us how to love and care for each other in every way. Amen.

Offering Sympathy

*When Job's three friends … heard about all the troubles
that had come upon him, they set out from their homes
and met together by agreement to go and sympathize
with him and comfort him. Then they sat on the ground
with him for seven days and seven nights. No one said
a word to him, because they saw how great
his suffering was.* JOB 2:11, 13

The Bible says, "In this world you will have trouble" (John 16:33). We know how it feels to say goodbye. To suffer with pain and sickness. To lose and fail and feel like giving up. Our most precious things become broken or lost. When someone we love is hurting in their trouble, how do we help?

Do we offer advice, a quick fix, or a long list of solutions? Will flowers or gifts offer real relief? Do we urge them to put on a brave face and get over it? Do we tell our own stories of when we struggled, too?

The best kind of sympathy is a listening ear. If we sit quietly, we can pray for God to bring help and comfort. We can hold their hand and let them know they're not alone.

God has compassion for our pain. He counts our tears and listens when we pray (Psalm 56:8). He never leaves our side. As he loves us, we learn to love each other.

Lord, show us how to love others in their sadness. Amen.

Salt of the Earth

*"You are the salt of the earth. But if the salt loses its saltiness,
how can it be made salty again? It is no longer good
for anything, except to be thrown out
and trampled underfoot."* MATTHEW 5:13

A salty bag of chips or popcorn is hard to resist. Salt turns bland vegetables, meats, and eggs into tasty meals. Without salt, we'd want to get up and leave the table.

Salt is also a kind of medicine. It kills germs and prevents infection. It can soothe a sore throat and clear a stuffy nose. Salt is able to keep us healthy.

Salt is used to keep food from spoiling. A steak will rot and smell if it's left out of the freezer for too long. Yet if that meat is cured in salt, it's safe and good to eat for a long time.

Salt is a good gift from God. Just like salt, believers in Jesus are to be a blessing to the world. We can make the world a happier place. Because of Jesus' love, we have complete joy in our hearts (John 15:11). We bring peace to our community by living God's way. We serve and give to others, and we respect the law. Since Jesus lives in us, we bring him wherever we go. Jesus shines his light in the darkness through our lives.

Lord, make us salty so we share your love with the world. Amen.

Love That Erases Fear

There is no fear in love. But perfect love drives out fear,
because fear has to do with punishment. The one
who fears is not made perfect in love. 1 JOHN 4:18

Nobody likes to get in trouble. If we make a mistake, we're tempted to lie and cover it up. We're afraid to get caught and face the consequences.

When you sin or fail, do you steer clear of the person you let down? You might wonder, *Will they be mad at me? Am I in big trouble? Can they tell I feel guilty inside? Do they already know what I did?* Instead of feeling close and happy, your sin and guilt are keeping you apart.

We can let our sin separate us from God, too. Instead of trusting in his love, we stop praying. We avoid the Bible and its truth. Assuming he's angry or disappointed, we keep our distance.

God is not a harsh, angry Father. Because of his love, we don't have to be afraid. He's ready to forgive the moment we confess what we've done. Jesus took the penalty for our sins on the cross, so nothing stands between us and God's love.

Are you feeling afraid of God today? Remember how much he loves you. He gave his own Son so nothing will separate you ever again. Let him create a pure heart in you, and give you back the joy of your salvation (Psalm 51:10, 12).

Lord, make us sure of your love so we're free from fear. Amen.

The Best Choice

"Now fear the LORD and serve him with all faithfulness.
Throw away the gods your ancestors worshiped
beyond the Euphrates River and in Egypt,
and serve the LORD. But if serving the LORD
seems undesirable to you, then choose for yourselves
this day whom you will serve ... But as for me
and my household, we will serve the LORD." JOSHUA 24:14-15

God chose you to be his child before the world was made. He loves you 100 percent. He gave his only Son to die so you could live. God always forgives when you confess. He listens to every prayer and cry of your heart. He keeps every promise he's made to help you, guide your way, and make you more like Jesus. Our God promises that if you're his, no one can snatch you from his hand (John 10:28).

God asks for the same kind of love in return. He calls us to choose him as our Lord and King. We depend on him instead of money. We aim to please him instead of people. We trust him for salvation instead of our own good behavior. We hold to the Word as truth instead of the world's opinions. We choose him to be our everything.

Let's go all-in with God and put him first in our hearts today and always.

Lord, we want to answer your call to "love the Lord your God with
all your heart and with all your soul and with all your strength"
(Deuteronomy 6:5). We choose you today. Amen.

Listening to God's Words

In the past God spoke to our ancestors through the prophets
at many times and in various ways, but in these last days
he has spoken to us by his Son, whom he appointed
heir of all things, and through whom also he made
the universe. HEBREWS 1:1-2

God has made a way for us to hear him since the beginning of time. In the Bible's Old Testament, we read stories of men and women called by God to tell what he had to say. God would "put his words in [their] mouth" so they could share everything he commanded (Deuteronomy 18:18). Through the prophets, his people heard God's plans, his directions, and his heart of love.

When Jesus was sent to the world from heaven, he brought a message from God. Jesus announced, "The Spirit of the Lord is on me, because he has anointed me to proclaim good news to the poor. He has sent me to proclaim freedom for the prisoners and recovery of sight for the blind, to set the oppressed free, to proclaim the year of the Lord's favor" (Luke 4:18-19). Jesus came to tell God's plan to save the world—and you and me—from our sins.

When Jesus and the prophets told God's words, people could listen or deny what they said. Today, let's listen to Jesus' words, do what he says, and become blessed in what we do (James 1:22, 25).

Lord, thank you for speaking so we can listen,
obey, and know your love. Amen.

Be Generous

One person gives freely, yet gains even more;
another withholds unduly, but comes to poverty.
A generous person will prosper; whoever refreshes
others will be refreshed. PROVERBS 11:24-25

Imagine trying to empty a big bowl of water one spoonful at a time. Using a small spoon to move a lot of water can feel frustrating. Each spoonful hardly makes a difference. Trying to fill the bowl little by little would make anyone want to quit. When you switch to a bigger cup, the job could be finished in no time.

This idea is true with whatever we're giving. If we only share little by little—keeping as much in our own 'bowl' as we can—the giving is no fun at all. But when we give generously, we find out we can make a real difference. Our joy in the giving grows bigger and bigger, too.

Let's think of ways we can be generous right now. What could you give a teacher or colleague to say 'thank you' for all they do? Who is lonely and needing the gift of friendship or attention? Who might need a helping hand? How can we make a big difference to someone in need?

If we choose to give our love away, we'll experience more of God's love than we've ever known before.

Lord, make us a generous family, just as you give freely to us. Amen.

FEBRUARY 9

What Our Hearts Love Most

*Do not love the world or anything in the world. If anyone
loves the world, love for the Father is not in them.
For everything in the world—the lust of the flesh,
the lust of the eyes, and the pride of life—comes not
from the Father but from the world.* 1 JOHN 2:15-16

The rows of candy by the cash register stir up cravings for a treat. The commercials during our favorite show make us want to run out and go shopping. A job opening stirs up a competitive spirit to win no matter what. In this sinful world, we're tempted to please ourselves every chance we get.

We only have one heart that can only hold one true love. It can love what we see and enjoy in this world. Or, it can love our Father God. Today, do we feel jealous of others? Is it hard to feel content or satisfied? Do others say you're a sore loser or a bragging winner? Have I cheated or manipulated to get what I want? Our words and actions show what our hearts love most.

If we love the world, it won't love us back. Yet God promises to love us always. He'll save us from sin, fill us with joy, and give us a new heart. We can leave the world behind and receive what's best of all. His love is life forever.

Lord, we love you more than anything in the world. Amen.

Bite Your Tongue

*"If you play the fool and exalt yourself, or if you plan evil,
clap your hand over your mouth! For as churning cream produces
butter, and as twisting the nose produces blood,
so stirring up anger produces strife."* PROVERBS 30:32-33

If we're not careful, our words can shake people up and start a fight. You know how frustrated you feel when others try to get all the praise and attention for themselves. You've felt hurt or angry when someone tried to get you in trouble. Gossip leaves you feeling embarrassed and even betrayed by your friends. Lies and cruel words create all kinds of conflict. It's hard to repair a friendship that's been damaged by an angry fight.

Today, let's remember to think before we speak. We should ask ourselves if our words will help or hurt. Will they build others up or tear them down? Are we trying to make ourselves look good or honor other people, too? Are we making peace or shaking things up until they explode in a fight? If in doubt, choose to be quiet and say nothing at all. Let's be peacemakers like Jesus. We can use our words to love each other all the time.

Lord, help us to close our mouths when we're tempted
to stir up anger around us. Show us how to keep the peace
at wherever we go every day. Amen.

Bless Others with Your Gifts

*We have different gifts, according to the grace given
to each of us. If your gift is prophesying, then prophesy
in accordance with your faith; if it is serving, then serve;
if it is teaching, then teach; if it is to encourage, then
give encouragement; if it is giving, then give generously;
if it is to lead, do it diligently; if it is to show mercy,
do it cheerfully.* ROMANS 12:6-8

If you want to give a gift, you shop at the store to find that special something. You wrap it carefully and label it so everybody knows it's just for your friend. Once opened, your friend chooses a place to use and keep the gift she has received.

When God gives a gift, he creates a special ability made possible by his Spirit. He places the gift inside of you, the one he's wrapped in exactly the size, shape, and personality he's designed. God's people get to "open" the gift in you. They receive the blessing of that gift every time you use it.

No believer is left out when God is giving his gifts. You'll discover if you can teach the Word or lead, help or serve. You might encourage the downhearted or give to those in need. The one thing we know for sure is that your gift will bless the people of God.

Lord, show us your gifts and teach us how to use them.
Let us build your church with the gifts of your Spirit. Amen.

FEBRUARY 12

Asking for Forgiveness

*If we claim to be without sin, we deceive ourselves
and the truth is not in us. If we confess our sins,
he is faithful and just and will forgive us our sins and
purify us from all unrighteousness.* 1 JOHN 1:8-9

It's so hard to admit we made a mistake! Human nature tries to hide our sins in the dark. We don't want to get in trouble or feel embarrassed by what we've done. Sometimes we even lie to ourselves, saying "It's not my fault." "It wasn't that big of a deal." "Nobody found out, so it doesn't matter." But the only way to receive forgiveness and have a clean heart is to tell what we did—to confess.

God loves us so much, he wants us to find freedom from guilt and shame. He doesn't want hurt and anger to separate us from the friends and family we care about. Sin is destructive, keeping us from the joyful, abundant life God offers through Jesus. The peace of a clean heart is ours for the taking if we confess our sins in prayer.

God will never say "no" if we ask for forgiveness. No matter what we've done, we can tell God all about it. Instead of hiding, we can bring all our sin to him and receive the gift of a fresh start. He'll give us courage to be honest and make things right with others, too.

Lord, we've sinned against you and one another. We chose
to please ourselves instead of you. Please forgive us
and purify our hearts. Amen.

A Contrite Heart

*You do not delight in sacrifice, or I would bring it; you
do not take pleasure in burnt offerings. My sacrifice,
O God, is a broken spirit; a broken and contrite heart
you, God, will not despise.* PSALM 51:16-17

Our sins break God's heart. In Luke 19, we read how Jesus wept over the city of Jerusalem. They would commit the ultimate sin of rejecting him and nailing him to the cross. He knows sin leads to trouble, pain, and separation from him. He wants us to have the joy and peace that come from obeying him in every way.

The Bible makes it clear that none of us is perfect. "All have sinned and fall short of the glory of God," and "there is no one righteous, not even one" (Romans 3:23, 10). Every time we lie, disobey, or lose our temper, we have a choice: we can deny what we've done or feel sorry and anxious to make it right.

To be "contrite" is more than feeling guilty or embarrassed for what we've done. It's the feeling of a broken heart—just like God—over our sin. This kind of sadness opens the door to forgiveness and a new start. "Godly sorrow brings repentance that leads to salvation and leaves no regret" (2 Corinthians 7:10). When we go to God with our broken heart, he puts it back together and makes us new.

Lord, forgive us for our sins today. Make us truly sorry
when we disobey and give us a new heart. Amen.

God's Infinite Love

*And I pray that you, being rooted and established in love,
may have power, together with all the Lord's holy people,
to grasp how wide and long and high and deep is the love
of Christ, and to know this love that surpasses
knowledge—that you may be filled to the measure
of all the fullness of God.* EPHESIANS 3:17-19

Is it hard to wrap your mind around the size of God's love? His love doesn't come and go—it lasts forever. His love is a free gift. It's unconditional, since he loved us while we were still his enemies (Romans 5:8). His love is forgiving and patient, kind and tender-hearted. In his love for us, God gave his only Son so we could live forever. God is love, and all the love we have comes from him.

Imagine if we had a greater understanding of God's love. We'd be free of guilt and shame, since "perfect love drives out fear" of punishment (1 John 4:18). We would follow God with joy and courage, since we'd trust that his love holds him right by our side. We would no longer be defined by our looks, our success, or people's opinions. Instead, our identity would be secure as loved children of God (1 John 3:1). If we could fully grasp God's love, we would love others without holding back. His love changes us from the inside-out.

Lord, help us to know how much you love us. Amen.

What Are Your Riches?

Jesus looked at him and loved him. "One thing you lack,"
he said. "Go, sell everything you have and give to the poor,
and you will have treasure in heaven. Then come,
follow me." At this the man's face fell. He went away sad,
because he had great wealth. Jesus looked around
and said to his disciples, "How hard it is for the rich
to enter the kingdom of God!" MARK 10:21-23

Do you think you're rich? Some of your friends might have lots of money in the bank. Others are rich in friendship and fun. A creative person could be rich in talent for music or art. Some have a wealth of intelligence to solve tough problems. Athletes may hold skill and strength to win. In whatever way we're rich, we can feel like we've got it all.

While talent, money, and success are wonderful blessings, they put us at risk. We're tempted to depend on ourselves instead of God. We seek the riches of the world instead of "treasures in heaven" that last (Matthew 6:20). We put our identity in what we have instead of who we are as children of God.

Let's love the Giver more than his gifts to you and me. If we love God with all our heart, soul, mind, and strength, we'll gain what's best of all. Nothing is better than God's love.

Lord, you are our greatest treasure. Amen.

FEBRUARY 16

The Real Thing

But mark this: There will be terrible times in the last days.
People will be lovers of themselves, lovers of money,
boastful, proud, abusive, disobedient to their parents, ungrateful,
unholy ... having a form of godliness but denying its power.
Have nothing to do with such people. 2 TIMOTHY 3:1-2, 5

We can put on running gear and lace up our shoes. We can stretch and warm up like we're going to run a marathon. But if it's all for show, we'll get tired and quit by the first mile. We have the "form" of a runner without the strength and power to do it.

Are we "dressing up" like Christians or do we have the real power of God in our lives? Are we just religious, or are we reborn as God's children? The answer is found in who we love.

Lovers of self want praise and attention. Greedy and stubborn, they do whatever it takes to get their way. Lovers of self might play the part of a Christian, but God's power over sin and hate is missing from their lives.

Are we satisfied with a form of godliness or do we want the real thing? If we believe in Jesus as our Savior, the same power that raised him from the dead is ours! We have victory over sin. The Spirit fills us with the love of God. Our prayers are answered and lives are changed.

Lord, fill us with your power so we can live and love like Jesus. Amen.

Finding Hope After Loss

*"I will repay you for the years the locusts have eaten—
the great locust and the young locust, the other
locusts and the locust swarm—my
great army that I sent among you."* JOEL 2:25

A sharpener can turn a pencil to sawdust in no time. A single match can start a forest fire. Giant waves can wash away a sandy shoreline. A locust, or grasshopper, can eat its own weight in food each day. When millions swarm together, they consume and destroy farmers' fields. The people who depend on the crops for food are left with nothing. In ancient times, a locust plague brought terrible hunger and starvation.

God knows our world is broken and full of sin. He can see the pain that comes from losing everything. People lose loved ones. Jobs and homes. Health and strength. Dreams die and hope is disappointed. Suffering is real and sad. Because God loves the world so much, he offers hope.

God promises great joy for his children. No matter what we lose in this world, we gain treasures in heaven forever. Jesus is preparing a place where "'He will wipe every tear from [our] eyes. There will be no more death or mourning or crying or pain, for the old order of things has passed away.'" He will make everything new (Revelation 21:4-5).

Have you lost what's most important to you? Find hope in God's promise to love you and bless you forever.

Lord, our hearts can be broken. Restore us with your love. Amen.

Peace Between Siblings

Joseph ... was tending the flocks with his brothers, ... and he
brought their father a bad report about them. Now Israel
loved Joseph more than any of his other sons, because
he had been born to him in his old age; and he made an
ornate robe for him. When his brothers saw that their father
loved him more than any of them, they hated him
and could not speak a kind word to him. GENESIS 37:2-4

Tattling. Favoritism. Jealousy. Nothing turns brothers and sisters against each other like feeling second best. In ancient times, a robe was a sign of honor or royalty. Joseph's robe said, "I'm number one!" Competition and favoritism created terrible jealousy and anger in their family.

Ten to one you have experienced sibling rivalry or seen it in action between your own children. It's important to make everyone in the family feel important. All of us have been made in God's image and we're "fearfully and wonderfully made" by his design (Psalm 139:14). Each member of your family is a chosen, cherished, and priceless gift from God. Do what you can to show love to each one today.

Lord, keep jealousy and anger out of our house.
Teach us how to love each other like you do. Amen.

Messengers of Hope

How beautiful on the mountains are the feet of those who
bring good news, who proclaim peace, who bring good tidings,
who proclaim salvation, who say to Zion,
"Your God reigns!" ISAIAH 52:7

Every person in the world is desperate for hope. The news tells sad, scary stories every day of people fighting or getting hurt. People we love become sick or struggle. Loved ones move away or let each other down. The future can look dark for those without anything to look forward to.

Since you know the good news of the gospel, you have a message of hope for everyone you meet. You can tell a lonely person that Jesus wants to be their friend. A guilty person who's made terrible mistakes can find forgiveness. The sick, injured, or weak can find strength and healing. No matter the disappointment or heartbreak someone has suffered, they can find life and hope in Jesus.

We're never more beautiful than when we carry God's message of peace and salvation. We can tell how Jesus came into the world "to seek and to save the lost" (Luke 19:10). We share our own stories of finding forgiveness and help from the Father. God's gift of love is the best news anyone will ever hear.

Can you name who needs hope today? Pray for them and be ready to share the good news of God's peace and salvation.

Lord, thank you for bringing the good news of Jesus
so we can be saved. Give us "beautiful feet" that carry
your message of hope to everyone. Amen.

Being a Peacemaker

Without wood a fire goes out; without a gossip
a quarrel dies down. As charcoal to embers and
as wood to fire, so is a quarrelsome person
for kindling strife. PROVERBS 26:20-21

If I forget to water a plant, it will wither and die. If I don't charge its battery, my phone will lose power. If we don't get enough sleep at night, our energy fades the next day. A campfire needs a steady supply of logs to keep burning.

The Bible says a fight is fed like that fire. Anger is sparked by disrespect. A rude word. A broken promise. A selfish act. You're offended, and tempers flare. The argument will burn out quickly if you apologize and work it out. But it will blaze even hotter if others get involved.

A gossip will spread word of your fight so others take sides. They'll tell you to take revenge and get what you deserve. They'll push you to keep fighting for the last word. You'll want to forgive and move on, they won't let it die. Their words are like wood on anger's fire.

The next time we're in an argument, let's keep it to ourselves. And if we see other people fighting, let's mind our own business. We can obey God's wise Word to "be careful to do what is right in the eyes of everyone. If it is possible, as far as it depends on you, live at peace with everyone" (Romans 12:17-18).

Lord, teach us to be peacemakers. Amen.

Sharing a Table

*"Here I am! I stand at the door and knock. If anyone hears
my voice and opens the door, I will come in and eat
with that person, and they with me."* REVELATION 3:20

When we celebrate a special day, spend time with people we love, or get to know new friends, it almost always involves sharing a meal together. Bible history shows a tradition of feasting to celebrate the Lord. We look forward to a "wedding feast" when all God's people join him in heaven. By God's design, gathering around the table is a symbol of happiness and love.

God wants to share a table with you and me. He wants a close connection where we share our lives with him. Just as we fill our stomachs with food, our spirits feast on Jesus. He said, "I am the bread of life. Whoever comes to me will never go hungry, and whoever believes in me will never be thirsty" (John 6:35). Imagine feeling completely satisfied and loved at the table with God!

Yet God doesn't break down the door and grab a plate. He "knocks" on our hearts to see if he's welcome. If we listen to his voice and his Word and believe, he comes into our hearts and stays with us forever. Let's open the door to him today.

Lord, we want to share our table with you now and forever in heaven.
Come into our hearts and lives. We love you. Amen.

FEBRUARY 22

Finding Contentment

I know what it is to be in need, and I know what it is to have plenty.
I have learned the secret of being content in any and every situation,
whether well fed or hungry, whether living in plenty or in want.
I can do all·this through him who gives me strength. PHILIPPIANS 4:12-13

Sometimes we receive a gift or card that makes us feel loved and important. At other times, though, we can feel we're missing out. Our favorite things become broken, lost, or boring. The budget leaves no room for extras. We grow tired from dealing with hard work or difficult people. Our burdens feel too heavy to carry.

Whether we're celebrating or struggling, God whispers a secret in our ear. He says we can feel peaceful and satisfied through all of life's highs and lows. The key is prayer—we give thanks for his gifts and ask for help in our troubles. As we reach out to God in every situation, we learn to trust him. We find he's always there. His love never changes. Our problems are cut down to size because he's more than enough. Our richest blessings don't compare to God's love. Through prayer we can be content all the time.

Lord, let us depend on you so we can be content.
Give us peace, strength, and joy every day. Amen.

The Ultimate Treasure

"The kingdom of heaven is like treasure hidden in a field. When a man found it, he hid it again, and then in his joy went and sold all he had and bought that field. Again, the kingdom of heaven is like a merchant looking for fine pearls. When he found one of great value, he went away and sold everything he had and bought it." MATTHEW 13:44-46

When we discover the love of God, we find the ultimate riches. His treasure chest holds forgiveness. Salvation through Jesus. Freedom from sin and fear. It holds a new name as we're adopted into his family. We find help and hope in our struggles. We receive his Spirit to guide and encourage us along the way. It holds "the way, the truth, and the life" so we can dwell with God forever (John 14:6).

What would we give to make God's kingdom our own? Would we sacrifice all we have to follow Jesus? Could we give up our popularity? Our plans for the future? Our money, time, and comfort? Our sin and pride? Nothing we give up compares to the treasure he holds for his children.

Today, let's give all we have to follow Jesus. Let's love him as he loves us. He is worthy "to receive power and wealth and wisdom and strength and honor and glory and praise!" (Revelation 5:12)

Lord, may you be our greatest treasure of all. Amen.

Growing in Faith

Like newborn babies, crave pure spiritual milk,
so that by it you may grow up in your
salvation, now that you have tasted
that the Lord is good. 1 PETER 2:2

Babies depend on milk—it's their perfect food with all the nutrition they need to grow and thrive. As they're cuddled and fed, they feel secure in the arms of their mother. They grow strong in mind, body, and heart as they're fed, loved, and cared for.

We're like spiritual babies when we first put our trust in Jesus. For us to grow up as believers, we need the "milk" of the Bible, prayer, and the habit of doing what's right. The Word helps our minds to grow in wisdom and understanding of who God is. Prayer puts us right in God's arms as we share our feelings, needs, and questions with our Father. Practicing obedience makes us strong when we're tempted to sin. God gives all we need to become "mature and complete, not lacking anything" (James 1:4).

What are we choosing to eat today? Are we craving nourishing spiritual milk? Or, are we swallowing the world's "hollow and deceptive philosophy" that leaves us spiritually weak and hungry? (Colossians 2:8) Today, let's receive the pure milk from God. We will taste and see he is good.

Lord, we want more of you. Grow us in your love. Amen.

Stop Pretending

One person pretends to be rich, yet has nothing; another pretends to be poor, yet has great wealth. PROVERBS 13:7

I can try to look like I have it all together. I wear a smile even when I'm down. I dress my best or clean the house to make a good impression. I could use big words or quote educated people to seem smart. An expensive car could imply that I'm rich. If I care what others think, I can pretend to be somebody else.

If I act like I'm more than I am, it's pride. Pride wants attention and popularity. Pride doesn't like to change or be corrected. At its core, pride wants to be better than everybody else. It makes me say, "I don't need you and I don't need God."

Yet if I pretend that I'm not blessed, I'm hiding God's goodness from everyone. Every dollar, strength, and talent I have is a gift from him. If I deny what he's done, my praises go silent. Others can't see his kindness and generosity in my life.

Let's be honest about our needs and blessings. If we need help, we can ask God because he loves us. If he gives to us in abundance, we can thank him for his grace. All we have and do should make his name great.

Lord, keep us from pretending to be
someone else. We are yours. Amen.

FEBRUARY 26

Justified by Faith

*So we, too, have put our faith in Christ Jesus
that we may be justified by faith in Christ and not
by the works of the law, because by the works
of the law no one will be justified.* GALATIANS 2:16

It's human nature to try to use our outer behavior to make us right with God. Yet in doing so, we shut him out of our heart. We hide our sin and the ugly, broken places in our life. Trying to save ourselves through our own goodness leaves us guilty and lost.

Instead, we can put our faith in Jesus. His death on the cross paid the penalty for every failure and sin we commit. Instead of trying hard to be good enough, we can trust in his perfect goodness and love. Through faith in Jesus, we're justified—declared innocent and righteous by God—and accepted as his children forever.

Are you working hard to earn God's love today? Believe in Jesus and let him fill your heart with peace.

Lord, through Jesus' death and life, you take away our guilt.
Thank you for making us your own. Amen.

More Than Just a Race

*Better one handful with tranquility than two handfuls
with toil and chasing after the wind.* ECCLESIASTES 4:6

I'd love to hike down a winding trail through the woods with a loved one. We might see flowers and shiny rocks to collect in our pocket. We'd hear birds singing and small creatures rustling in the leaves. A sparkling stream might invite us to dip our toes in the water. What a peaceful, refreshing time we could share together.

Imagine if we turned our hike into a race. With feet pounding down the path, we'd face forward until we reached the finish line. We'd ignore the sights, sounds, and fragrance of the natural beauty around us. We might gain first place, but we'd lose our chance to relax and make memories.

God wants our lives to be more than a race to the finish. We might spend all our time working for money and success. After achieving one goal, we could strive for even more. In our push to win, we'd be stressed and weary all the time.

If life turns into a race, we'll ignore our need for rest. We'll miss quality time with the ones we love. Ignoring God's Word, we won't make time to pray and seek his face. We might gain trophies, fame, and money in the bank, but we'll lose what matters most.

Let's follow our Shepherd to green pastures and quiet waters so he can refresh our souls. (Psalm 23:1-2) He'll save us from toil and give us joy.

Lord, give us your peace as we follow you. Amen.

FEBRUARY 28

Give God the Credit

This is what the LORD says: "Let not the wise boast of their wisdom or the strong boast of their strength or the rich boast of their riches, but let the one who boasts boast about this: that they have the understanding to know me, that I am the LORD" … For it is not the one who commends himself who is approved, but the one whom the Lord commends. JEREMIAH 9:23-24, 2 CORINTHIANS 10:18

Let's be honest—winning feels good! An 'A' on a test, a win on the scoreboard, and a blue ribbon for excellence make us feel strong. A well-earned bonus or promotion makes us feel good. We tackled a challenge and earned a well-deserved reward for our hard work.

Yet success comes with some risk. We're tempted by pride that says we're better than everybody else. We can feel invincible, believing we can win on our own without any help. Our hearts can crave attention and praise so we show off to anybody who will listen. God calls this "boasting," and it's a clue our hearts are in the wrong place.

Let's give God credit for all we can do. He gives physical health for exercise and intelligence to learn new things. He offers courage to get up on stage and the talent to perform. God provides the money and support that meets our needs. Let's use every gift and opportunity he gives to make his name great instead of our own.

Lord, show us how to use our strengths for you.
You are the greatest reward we'll ever receive. Amen.

God Marks Out Our Road

*Give careful thought to the paths for your feet
and be steadfast in all your ways. Do not turn to the right
or the left; keep your foot from evil.* PROVERBS 4:26-27

If a tightrope walker loses his balance, he'll tumble into the net before reaching the other side. A cross-country runner memorizes the course so she doesn't become lost and lose the race. A rock climber tests the rope, harness, and anchors for safety and sure footing on the climb. You and I step carefully and hold the railing when we take on a steep set of stairs. We know the danger if we miss a step.

God wants us to walk in step with his Spirit. If we walk with him, we'll bear spiritual fruit like love and kindness, goodness and gentleness, patience and self-control (Galatians 5:22-23). If we decide to turn away to mark our own path, we'll become disobedient to the Word. Instead of loving, we'll hate. Instead of making peace, we'll fight and argue. We'll give in to all kinds of temptations until sin takes hold of our lives.

In his love, God marks out a road for our feet. It's a path of peace and blessing, joy and safety as we obey him in everything. Best of all, it's the way to eternal life. When we believe in Jesus, trust in his Word, and keep going on his path of obedience, he leads us home.

Lord, keep us from turning from you. Amen.

March

Whiter Than Snow

Have mercy on me, O God, according to your unfailing love;
according to your great compassion blot out my transgressions.
Wash away all my iniquity and cleanse me from my sin.
Cleanse me with hyssop, and I will be clean; wash me,
and I will be whiter than snow. PSALM 51:1-2, 7

Do you remember that mistake you made? Everybody knew. People laughed. You might have been in a lot of trouble. Now, it's the story that's told over and over because nobody lets you forget what you did. Your shame is like an ugly stain that you can't wash away.

If anyone knows what we've done, it's God. "The eyes of the Lord are everywhere, keeping watch on the wicked and the good." (Proverbs 15:3) He even knows our secret sins which haven't been found out. We can't hide our thoughts, our words, or our actions from his sight.

Yet God doesn't point his finger in blame. He's not planning revenge. He doesn't laugh or make us feel small. Instead, God shows mercy. He takes our confession and forgives all we've done. He washes the stain of guilt away forever.

Today, do you feel embarrassed? Do you wish for a second chance? Are you keeping guilty secrets in your heart? Go to God in prayer. Tell him all about it. In his love, he'll wash you whiter than snow.

Lord, forgive our sins and wash us clean. Amen.

Peace Through Jesus' Blood

*In him we have redemption through his blood, the forgiveness
of sins, in accordance with the riches of God's grace that
he lavished on us. For God was pleased to have all his
fullness dwell in him, and through him to reconcile to
himself all things, whether things on earth or things
in heaven, by making peace through his blood,
shed on the cross.* EPHESIANS 1:7-8, COLOSSIANS 1:19-20

Our heart is a muscle that pumps blood through our body. The beating of our heart can tell us if we're busy or sleeping, worried or relaxed. Most of all, it lets us know we're alive!

When Jesus went to the cross, he was wounded in terrible ways. His heart stopped beating and his body died. Yet three days later, the power of God brought him back to life! He was breathing, walking, and talking with his heart pumping blood through his veins as strong as before.

Why did Jesus have to suffer, bleed, and die? It was the only way to make peace between people and God. He took the punishment for our sins so we can be forgiven. By rising from the dead, he conquered death so we can live forever. By accepting Jesus as our Savior, God accepts us as his children. Our sins don't count against us. We have a hope and a future in heaven. We receive all the grace and love God is eager to give.

Lord, Jesus' life has made us alive with him. Thank you
for saving us from our sins and loving us forever. Amen.

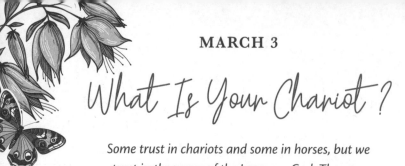

What Is Your Chariot?

*Some trust in chariots and some in horses, but we
trust in the name of the LORD our God. They are
brought to their knees and fall, but we rise
up and stand firm.* PSALM 20:7-8

In ancient times, a chariot with horses was the best technology you could take into battle. It offered speed, protection, and an advantage over the enemy. A soldier going into battle would feel invincible, trusting his chariot to carry him to victory.

Today, everybody is trusting in something to get them through the battles of life. A rich bank account can make a person feel secure. Working out and eating healthy foods can build hope for strong days ahead. Chasing after fame or popularity is a way to avoid feeling lonely or unwanted. Working long, hard hours can be a defense against failure or a lack of purpose.

In time, we find out we can't avoid problems forever. All the money, friends, or doctors in the world can't keep us from hard times. If we trust in people or things to protect us, we'll find ourselves disappointed. God invites us to trust in him—in his strength, power, and love—to take care of us. He's the One we can count on to get us through.

Who or what are we depending on today? Let's take our needs and worries to God and put our faith in him alone.

Lord, we're thankful we can depend on you all the time.
Keep us from trusting in what will only let us down.
Be our source of strength and help in every situation. Amen.

Everything We Need

*His divine power has given us everything we need for a godly life
through our knowledge of him who called us by
his own glory and goodness.* 2 PETER 1:3

God calls you and me to love him with all of our heart, soul, and strength. Loving him like that means we always trust and obey him, and we love others too. On our own, we just can't do it. Yet God promises to give every single thing we need for a godly life.

The moment we believe, we receive the Holy Spirit. He helps us to pray and prays for us too (Romans 8:26). He gives understanding of the Bible. He grows new things in our hearts and minds—love, joy, peace, forbearance, kindness, goodness, faithfulness, gentleness and self-control (Galatians 5:22-23). By the Spirit's power, we stand firm against sin and the enemy.

God also gave his Word. It's living and active, changing us from the inside out. The Bible is "useful for teaching, rebuking, correcting and training in righteousness, so that the servant of God may be thoroughly equipped for every good work" (2 Timothy 3:16-17).

Another part of God's "recipe" is each other! He created the church so we could find encouragement and spiritual family to share life with. We're stronger together.

Following Jesus is not the easy road, yet it's the way to joyful life forever. God loves us so much he gave all we need to walk with him each day.

Lord, thank you for giving us everything we need
to know and love you. Amen.

Marked with God's Seal

*And you also were included in Christ when you heard
the message of truth, the gospel of your salvation.
When you believed, you were marked in him with a seal,
the promised Holy Spirit, who is a deposit guaranteeing
our inheritance until the redemption of those who are
God's possession—to the praise of his glory.* EPHESIANS 1:13-14

Do you have fears about God? You might wonder if he hears your prayers. You could be afraid of his anger if you disobey. If you're bullied, criticized, or left out, you wonder if God really likes you too. When you're hurting or sad, you question if God cares. Does he love you no matter what? What could you do that is so bad, he'd turn his back on you?

God wants us to know that once we are his, we belong to him forever. Our sins from the past, the present, and the future are forgiven. Jesus promises, "I give them eternal life, and they shall never perish; no one will snatch them out of my hand. My Father, who has given them to me, is greater than all; no one can snatch them out of my Father's hand" (John 10:28-29).

To prove we're his, he gives his Spirit. He dwells in our hearts like a seal that says, "You're mine." Today, we can have joy knowing we'll live in God's love for eternity.

Lord, we trust you will love and keep us always. Amen.

A Life of Worship

*Therefore, I urge you, brothers and sisters, in view of God's mercy,
to offer your bodies as a living sacrifice, holy and pleasing to God—
this is your true and proper worship.* ROMANS 12:1

How do you show someone that you love them? You tell her with your words. You give her presents and fun surprises. You make memories by spending quality time together. You hold her hand and put your arms around her. If she is hurt or needs help, you do whatever it takes to keep her safe and well. You make her your top priority.

How do we tell God we love him? Some people think it's singing religious songs and going to church every Sunday. They say loving God is following rules, praying the right prayers, and memorizing the Bible. It's as if hard work will prove we love him.

God wants far more than your good behavior. He wants your whole self! Worship is giving God your goals and hopes for tomorrow. Your money and time to use as he wants. It gives your strength to serve him. Worship is loving both your friends and your enemies. It's forgiving as you've been forgiven through Jesus. Worship invites God into every part of your life.

Jesus sacrificed his life on the cross so we could live. Are we willing to sacrifice all we are and all we have for our God?

Lord, we offer ourselves to you because we love you. Amen.

MARCH 7

An Instrument of Righteousness

*Do not offer any part of yourself to sin as an instrument
of wickedness, but rather offer yourselves to God
as those who have been brought from death to life;
and offer every part of yourself to him as an
instrument of righteousness.* ROMANS 6:13

A hammer can shatter glass or hammer a nail. A horn can blast a warning from your car or play a beautiful song. A shovel can ruin a flourishing garden, or it can prepare a place for a beautiful flower to grow. A tool or "instrument" can help or hurt by how it's used.

You and I are instruments, too. God will use us for good when we place ourselves in his hands. He'll fill our minds with "whatever is true, whatever is noble, whatever is right" (Philippians 4:8). Our mouths will praise him and speak words of hope. Our hands will serve and help. Our feet will carry the good news of salvation to everyone (Isaiah 52:7). Our arms will reach out to the hurting. God can use every part of us to do good things.

What kind of instruments are we today? Do our words build others up or tear them down? Are we generous or taking more for ourselves? Are we ashamed of the gospel, or do we share Jesus with boldness? Do we love like God loves us? Let's remember whose we are. As children of God, let's be tools of goodness and love.

Lord, make us instruments of righteousness.
Take us and use us today. Amen.

MARCH 8

Be More Sensitive

A happy heart makes the face cheerful,
but heartache crushes the spirit. PROVERBS 15:13

What we feel on the inside often shows on the outside. Our facial expressions, our posture, and even how fast or slow we're talking or breathing give clues about our emotions. If we pay attention to those clues, we can know how to care for each other every day.

If someone looks tired or stressed, we can talk a little more quietly and save our questions for later. When one of us is excited and happy, we can give our full attention to hear their news and share the fun together. Sadness and tears need a gentle hug, and frustration and anger call for a listening ear or a little space to calm down. Giving each other room to have all kinds of feelings will help us understand each other better. We'll feel loved just the way we are.

Have you been missing a loved one's clues about their feelings? Can you share your ups and downs with the people in your life? Ask someone close to you to share one of their worries, hopes, frustration, or a praise with you. With prayer and practice, God will help you become more sensitive and caring to others.

Lord, you created us to have all kinds of emotions.
You know how we feel before we even say a word.
Show us how to take care of each other's hearts
and love each other well. Amen.

Unhealthy Cravings

*"The L*ORD *heard you when you wailed, 'If only we had meat
to eat! We were better off in Egypt!' Now the L*ORD *will give
you meat, and you will eat it. You will not eat it for just
one day, or two days, or five, ten or twenty days, but
for a whole month—until it comes out of your nostrils
and you loathe it—because you have rejected
the L*ORD*, who is among you … "* NUMBERS 11:18-20

Imagine if we received everything we craved and whined for! Unlimited chocolates would make us sick to our stomachs. Piles of shoes and clothes would crowd your room until there was no space to move. Hours of TV and binge watching would steal our sleep and make us exhausted.

God knows whining comes from a doubting, ungrateful heart, "for the mouth speaks what the heart is full of" (Matthew 12:34). The Israelites wailed for meat because they didn't trust God to feed and care for them. We fuss for what we want because we doubt God's goodness, too. Forgetting all the ways he's loved us in the past, we complain about today and worry about tomorrow.

What is the "meat" we're craving today? Is there a need or a desire you carry in your heart? Let's take our requests to God and trust he'll give us what's best at the perfect time.

Lord, you care for us every day. Make us thankful as we trust you.
Amen.

Signs Pointing to God

*And God placed all things under [Christ's] feet and appointed him
to be head over everything for the church, which is his body,
the fullness of him who fills everything in every way.* EPHESIANS 1:22-23

Even though we can't see Jesus with our eyes, we know he's alive in heaven. He wants to show himself to the world through his people, the church. Since we received the Spirit of God, we take him with us wherever we go. He's adopted us into his family. Everybody gets a look at Jesus when they see his church living and loving like him.

How can we show Jesus to people today? He's revealed by our "love, joy, peace, forbearance, kindness, goodness, faithfulness, gentleness and self-control" (Galatians 5:22-23). We can show patience and choose to forgive. Every time we choose to help each other out, to give thanks instead of complaining, and to be caring and gentle, we look like him. A humble attitude that shows respect and puts others first is just like Jesus, too.

Our home and our church family are like beautiful signs, pointing people to God. Let's be bold by obeying the Bible and doing what's right in front of everybody. Our love will help others find God's love too.

Lord, fill us up with your love. As your church, we want to show Jesus
to the world as we look more like you every day. Amen.

Take the Right Path

*"Very truly I tell you Pharisees, anyone who does not enter
the sheep pen by the gate, but climbs in by some other way,
is a thief and a robber." Therefore Jesus said again, "Very truly
I tell you, I am the gate for the sheep."* JOHN 10:1, 7

Everybody wants to enter God's kingdom. It holds heavenly treasures that last forever. It's filled with light instead of darkness and evil. It promises no more death, crying, or pain (Revelation 21:4).

In the kingdom we're part of God's family. We're safe and loved. Redeemed and forgiven. We have life that never ends.

We enter God's kingdom through believing in Jesus. His death paid the penalty for our sins. His life makes us alive. We turn from sin to trust and obey. We belong to God, and nothing can snatch us from his hand (John 10:28).

Some want to enter God's kingdom another way. They don't want to trust in Jesus. They believe that good works or religious traditions will open the door. If they trust in a shortcut, they lose everything. And worse, they steal the truth of Jesus from those who need him.

Are we climbing the fence into God's kingdom? Are we working hard to earn God's love instead of trusting in his grace? Today, let's put our faith in Jesus. He's the way, the truth, and the life (John 14:6).

Lord, our life and hope are found in Jesus. Amen.

Trust God's Generosity

*Everyone had gathered just as much [bread] as they needed.
Then Moses said to them, "No one is to keep any of it
until morning." However, some of them paid no attention
to Moses; they kept part of it until morning, but it was full
of maggots and began to smell.* EXODUS 16:18-20

God surrounds us with every kind of good thing. We have food to eat and clean clothes to wear. Friends and family make us feel loved. We have the opportunity to work, learn, and try new things. God has proved himself faithful to his promises, "for he satisfies the thirsty and fills the hungry with good things" (Psalm 107:9).

Sometimes we forget our God is generous. We want to control what we get and when we get it. We worry about tomorrow instead of trusting him to take care of us. Rather than wait for him to provide, we try to grab more than we need.

Our selfishness and lack of faith spoil our joy in the Lord. We miss out on his best gifts. Let's remember how God is good to us every day. We can trust him for all we'll need for tomorrow.

Lord, teach us to trust you day by day.
You are faithful and your love never fails. Amen.

Filling Up on the Lord

*While they were worshiping the Lord and fasting,
the Holy Spirit said, "Set apart for me Barnabas
and Saul for the work to which I have called them."
So after they had fasted and prayed, they placed
their hands on them and sent them off.* ACTS 13:2-3

Today's verses describe how God chose Barnabas and Saul for a special assignment. How did they know where to go and what to do? Big questions needed big answers. They spent time fasting and praying, asking God to show them the way.

Fasting is giving up food or activities to help you pay attention to God. It creates space in your life that God can fill up with himself. If I'm hungry for food, I can ask him to fill me with Jesus, the "bread of life." If I want more stuff, I can pray to be satisfied with his love. If my day is quiet and still, I can listen for God to speak. If I'm craving chocolate, I can "taste and see that the Lord is good." (Psalm 34:8) Fasting makes us open and ready to hear what God has to say.

Are you waiting on God for answers today? Do you have a problem to solve? Pray and fast, and be confident God will give you what you need.

Lord, we need to hear your voice. Show us what to set aside
so we can have more of you. Amen.

The Greatest Rescuer

*But when the kindness and love of God our Savior appeared,
he saved us, not because of righteous things we had done,
but because of his mercy.* TITUS 3:4-5

Firefighters answer the call to rescue people from danger. Police officers and soldiers stand in the line of fire to protect the innocent. Teachers work long hours to help kids learn and grow. Doctors and nurses bring care and healing to the sick and injured. We're served by all kinds of helpers in our community.

Their help doesn't depend on your money, your talents, or your personality. You don't have to pass a test or win a vote to be protected or cared for. Our public servants bring help out of duty and compassion.

Jesus is the greatest rescuer of all. You and I were "dead in [our] transgressions and sins" (Ephesians 2:1). We were "harassed and helpless, like sheep without a shepherd" (Matthew 9:36). We were lost and blind to the light of the gospel (2 Corinthians 4:4). We were "without hope and without God in the world" (Ephesians 2:12). Because of God's mercy, Jesus gave his life so we could live. He called us out of darkness into his wonderful light (1 Peter 2:9).

We did nothing to earn God's love. Our salvation is a free gift because of his mercy. God has a heart of compassion for you and me.

Lord, your mercy and grace give us life. We love you. Amen.

MARCH 15

Building Your House

*By wisdom a house is built, and through understanding
it is established; through knowledge its rooms are filled
with rare and beautiful treasures.* PROVERBS 24:3-4

A house provides safe shelter from the weather. Closets, cabinets, and shelves give places to keep our belongings. Sinks and tubs keep us clean, and rooms with chairs and tables allow us to gather together. A house is built so we can eat, rest, and live in comfort together.

God created our family and provided the home we share. He wants to make our house like a beautiful palace, filled with treasures that last. Each truth in God's Word is a priceless brick for the foundation of our home. He gives wisdom so our family can know what's right. The Spirit fills us with love so we can care for each other. Knowledge of Jesus teaches us to forgive and serve like him. Knowing our future is in heaven, our home will be filled with precious hope and peace.

We could work to fill our house with more stylish decor, fashionable clothes, and the latest tech. A decorator could update the look to the latest fashion. Yet in the end, all our possessions will pass away. Let's build our house on the wisdom of the Bible. As we know and love God more and more, our home will hold the greatest treasures of all. His love will fill these rooms and our hearts forever.

Lord, build our house upon your wisdom.
Fill it with the rare treasures of your love. Amen.

MARCH 16

Choose Your Words Carefully

*A perverse person stirs up conflict, and a gossip separates
close friends. A gossip betrays a confidence; so avoid anyone
who talks too much.* PROVERBS 16:28, 20:19

Friends are a gift from God. They lift us up when we feel down and discouraged. We share laughter and celebrate our most happy occasions together. Friends help us out when we need a hand. A loyal friend who loves us just as we are is truly special.

Yet just as germs or a virus can damage our health, gossip can ruin a friendship. Telling secrets or spreading lies breaks trust. Talking behind our friend's back creates hurt feelings. Our words have the power to wreck others' reputations and get them in trouble. Gossip takes a destructive hammer to a friendship. The damage can be impossible to fix.

Are we the kind of friends who keep our promises? Do we choose our words carefully to show respect and kindness? Can our friends count on us to say what's true and helpful all the time? Are we careful to avoid those who gossip? Do we serve as God's peacemakers wherever we go? By treating our friends as we want to be treated, we love them like Jesus.

Lord, we know how gossip can hurt feelings and break friendships
apart. Teach us to show wisdom, integrity, and love in all we say. Amen.

Turn to the Great Healer

*Is anyone among you sick? Let them call the elders of the church
to pray over them and anoint them with oil in the name of the Lord.
Therefore confess your sins to each other and pray for each other
so that you may be healed. The prayer of a righteous person
is powerful and effective.* JAMES 5:14, 16

It's miserable to be sick in bed. Tired, achy, and bored, you wonder when you'll feel better again. You miss your friends and you get behind in your work. You want to enjoy the outdoors and share time with your family.

For some, they must face the fear and loneliness of a hospital stay. Their disease or injury is serious and the future is uncertain. While their body hurts, their heart hurts too as they face pain and suffering.

In our sickness, we look for strength. We ask, "Where does my help come from?" (Psalm 121:1). God is ready to help us when we pray. He has the power to cure our body and heal our spirits too. If we feel guilty for secret sins, we can confess and be forgiven. If we've been stubborn and refused to obey, we can surrender to Jesus. He will make us clean and new.

Do we need to be healed, inside or out? Do we trust in God's love and mercy? Let's pray for each other and invite our church leaders to pray for us too. We'll be changed as we surrender our lives to Jesus.

Lord, use our sickness to show us your power and love. Amen.

The Most Valuable Thing

For you know that it was not with perishable things such as silver or gold that you were redeemed from the empty way of life handed down to you from your ancestors, but with the precious blood of Christ, a lamb without blemish or defect. 1 PETER 1:18-19

What is the most expensive thing money can buy? A mansion on your own private island? A spacecraft to travel to Mars? Precious jewels mined from deep below the earth's surface? Famous paintings or ancient artifacts? The things money can buy could take our breath away.

Yet in this whole world, nothing is more valuable than you. God created mankind with his own hands, giving us life with his breath. The Bible says we're made in the likeness of God. The people he made are so important, he refused to let us go. He sent his Son Jesus to come into the world as a human himself. While he lived among us, he taught, served, and loved everyone. When he died, he died to save us all. He redeemed us—or bought us back from death—by the blood he shed on the cross.

Since we have been redeemed by Jesus, we're not our own. He says we "were bought at a price" (1 Corinthians 6:20). Let's remember how Jesus gave himself for us and give ourselves to him.

Lord, we were lost in sin with no hope for life.
Thank you for redeeming us to be
your children forever. Amen.

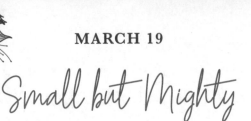

Small but Mighty

*We all stumble in many ways. Anyone who is never at fault
in what they say is perfect, able to keep their whole body
in check. Likewise, the tongue is a small part of the body,
but it makes great boasts. Consider what a great forest
is set on fire by a small spark.* JAMES 3:2, 5

One little word can hold a great deal of power. If someone tells a lie in court, an innocent person could lose their freedom. One word of gossip can tear apart a close friendship. A politician's words can win the election or lose the vote. Saying "I do" will join a bride and groom together for life. Each time we say "yes" or "no", we change the path of our life.

Since our words are small but mighty, we must use them wisely. Without God's help, we're sure to hurt people's feelings. We'll lie or exaggerate the truth. We might damage someone's reputation or ruin our own. We'll boast that we're smarter and stronger than we really are. We need the Spirit to guide us in all we say.

God revealed his love through words—the Word of the Bible. If we pray and abide in Jesus, our words will be a blessing. Our voices will speak truth, wisdom, and love to everyone.

Lord, teach us what to say to be a blessing. Amen.

MARCH 20

A New Home Address

*For, as I have often told you before and now tell you again even
with tears, many live as enemies of the cross of Christ.
Their destiny is destruction, their god is their stomach,
and their glory is in their shame. Their mind is set on earthly
things. But our citizenship is in heaven.* PHILIPPIANS 3:18-20

Where is home? The citizens of a country speak the same language. They share the same holidays, food, music, and history. A country's people cheer for their athletes, struggle side by side during natural disasters and war, and cherish their heritage. Home is where we feel we belong.

Once we're adopted into God's family, we receive a new home address. We become "foreigners and strangers on earth," and "fellow citizens with God's people and also members of his household" in heaven (Hebrews 11:13, Ephesians 2:19). Our house in this broken world is just a temporary stay before God takes us home forever.

Do you feel a little homesick today? As God's child, do you feel like you don't fit in around here? Are you excited to walk the streets of heaven? Can you imagine your Father's house, where Jesus is preparing a place just for you? (John 14:2). Hold on to hope—he's coming soon!

Lord, we thank you for the hope of heaven. Give us faith and patience
as we wait for you to bring us home. Amen.

The Miraculous Savior

Jesus performed many other signs in the presence of his disciples,
which are not recorded in this book. But these are written
that you may believe that Jesus is the Messiah, the Son of God,
and that by believing you may have life in his name. JOHN 20:30-31

The Bible's stories about Jesus are better than any superhero movie—and they're true! He had the power to give sight to the blind. He got the lame and paralyzed up on their feet. The deaf could hear, lepers were made clean, and incurable diseases were healed.

Jesus held power over nature, too. He could round up a school of fish for the biggest catch ever. He turned water into wine. He stopped a leafy tree from growing and bearing fruit. With just a word, he made stormy seas as smooth as glass.

These miracles, or signs, proved Jesus wasn't just an ordinary man. He was the Son of God who came to save the world. Jesus' signs helped people know he was the Messiah they were waiting for.

God recorded Jesus' signs in the Bible. Not only are they exciting stories, they build our faith. If we need healing, we know Jesus can do it. When we're afraid in the storms of life, Jesus gives peace. If we're in need, Jesus can take the little we have and make it more than enough. Jesus' miracles show he holds all the power and love we need.

Lord, give us faith to trust that your power makes all things possible.
Amen.

Surrender Your Control

Oh, the depth of the riches of the wisdom and knowledge of God!
How unsearchable his judgments, and his paths beyond
tracing out! "Who has known the mind of the Lord?
Or who has been his counselor?" ROMANS 11:33-34

Sometimes we think we know exactly how our life should be. We use calendars and lists to stay on track. We browse online to plan our next purchase. We dream and plan ahead for our next vacation or birthday celebration. In our minds, we imagine where we should go, what we should do, and how our plans should turn out.

No matter how clever and organized we might be, we can't control the future. Our minds can't know the true outcome of all of our choices. We might win or lose. Climb to new heights or fall down in failure. Gather friends or find ourselves alone. Our wisdom and knowledge have limits since we're only human.

We serve a God who knows everything. His plans are good and right. His will for you and me is "good, pleasing, and perfect" (Romans 12:2). He knows if our faith needs hard testing or generous blessings to grow from day to day. Instead of holding tightly to our hopes for tomorrow, we can trust God knows best. Let's surrender our lives to his control and worship him for his perfect wisdom.

Lord, your ways are higher than our ways and your thoughts
are higher than our thoughts. Teach us to trust
in the riches of your wisdom. Amen.

Humble Hearts

Live in harmony with one another. Do not be proud,
but be willing to associate with people of low position.
Do not be conceited. ROMANS 12:16

A home should be a place where everyone is welcome. Family members reach out their hands to each other, and never let go. Everyone has a voice to speak and be heard. A family honors each other's feelings and ideas and everyone matters. In a family, every member is equally special and important.

When we hold those values, our home is loving. We get along and live in peace. We treat each other with respect and kindness. It all goes wrong, though, when pride creeps into our hearts.

Pride says, "Me first!" It demands attention and wants its way. Pride is rude, refusing to listen and interrupting what others have to say. Pride argues, insults, and makes others feel small. Pride thinks it's too cool to honor someone else or submit to authority. When pride comes in the door, harmony goes out.

We need humble hearts to have peace in our house. Let's "do nothing out of selfish ambition or vain conceit. Rather, in humility value others above [ourselves], not looking to [our] own interests but each of you to the interests of the others (Philippians 2:3-4). If we love and serve with the humility of Jesus, we'll find joy together.

Lord, guard us from pride that will tear us apart. Amen.

MARCH 24

The Bigger Picture

*Do not fret because of those who are evil or be envious of those
who do wrong; for like the grass they will soon wither,
like green plants they will soon die away.* PSALM 37:1-2

Sometimes it seems like the bad guys win. Bullies get away with picking on you. The cheaters get ahead without getting caught. People lie and steal to get what they want. We can feel like honesty and hard work are getting us nowhere. Jealous and angry, we wonder if justice will ever come.

God encourages us to take a different view. He says, "With the Lord a day is like a thousand years, and a thousand years are like a day" (2 Peter 3:8). A cheat or a thief might get ahead for now. Evil people may hold power for a season. Yet God's children have the hope of eternity. God holds an inheritance for each of us that can never perish, spoil, or fade (1 Peter 1:4). God's heavenly blessings are better than anything this world can offer.

Let's remember this world is in God's hands. He has a perfect plan to make all things right. Let's fix our eyes on Jesus and his promises. His love is better than life, so we can live in joy both now and always.

Lord, we struggle with the sin and evil in this world.
Help us to trust you to love us, keep us,
and make all things new in your perfect time. Amen.

Stop, Think, Pray

Like one who grabs a stray dog by the ears is someone who rushes into a quarrel not their own. PROVERBS 26:17

A fight steals peace and joy from the room. There can be yelling. Insults and accusations. Blaming and shaming. Each wants to be heard but nobody wants to listen. In a quarrel, each one is determined to get their own way and have the last word.

It's hard to stand by when friends or family are fighting. You want to make peace. You'd like to speak words that are true and reasonable. You want to bring people together who have pushed each other apart.

We have to think twice before stepping into someone else's fight. Ugly words could be aimed our way. We might be pressured to pick sides. As we try to make our voice heard, the fight can grow bigger and louder. Instead of making peace, we might make new enemies.

Before we enter into a quarrel, we should stop, think, and pray. Is the issue really our business? Can they work it out on their own? Will we add to the gossip, anger, or hurt feelings? Do we have selfish motives to win friends by fighting their enemy? Do I want their quarrel to become my battle, too? Let's follow God's Word that tells us, "If it is possible, as far as it depends on you, live at peace with everyone" (Romans 12:18).

Lord, give us wisdom to stay out of other people's quarrels.
Help us to live in peace. Amen.

From Tent to Palace

*For we know that if the earthly tent we live in is destroyed, we have
a building from God, an eternal house in heaven, not built by
human hands. For while we are in this tent, we groan and
are burdened, because we do not wish to be unclothed
but to be clothed instead with our heavenly dwelling,
so that what is mortal may be swallowed
up by life.* 2 CORINTHIANS 5:1, 4

A tent can feel crowded and stuffy. It won't hold all we need, such as clothes, the bathtub, or the refrigerator. It would be no fun to live in a tent all the time.

It's hard to live in these bodies, too. We get hurt and struggle with sickness. We lose energy and muscle as we grow old. Hard times bring fear and grief. Our spirits battle between sin and obeying the Word. We can feel used up and worn down. It's hard to wait for Jesus to take us to heaven.

We know when Jesus comes, we'll be healed from pain. The weak will be strong. The hungry will be filled, and those who cry will be comforted. We'll be set free from sin, once and for all. Instead of the "tent" of this world, we'll be home forever in the glorious place Jesus made for you and me.

Knowing the future, we don't have to be afraid. Each day brings us closer to Jesus. Nothing we lose compares to what we gain in heaven. We have joy and hope because we know what's to come.

Lord, you give us beautiful life forever. Amen.

God's Special Treasure

"Or suppose a woman has ten silver coins and loses one.
Doesn't she light a lamp, sweep the house and search
carefully until she finds it? And when she finds it,
she calls her friends and neighbors together and says,
'Rejoice with me; I have found my lost coin.' In the
same way, I tell you, there is rejoicing in the presence of
the angels of God over one sinner who repents." Luke 15:8-10

Imagine the coin in your wallet is solid gold, like you'd find in a treasure chest. If it were lost, you'd feel sad and upset. You would search everywhere until you found it. Then, you would call your friends to celebrate!

Did you know God sees you like that coin? You're chosen to be his treasure (Deuteronomy 7:6). Just like a coin can be lost, people are "lost" when they separate themselves from God. We're lost if we ignore him, disobey him, or refuse to belong to him.

God loves you too much to let you stay lost. He sent Jesus to make a way to him. He invites you to become part of his family. Jesus is praying for you in heaven, asking God to find you and give you to him as his treasure.

Do you want to be "found" by God today? When you love him and believe in Jesus, there's a huge party in heaven! He'll never stop loving you and searching for your heart.

Lord, we're worth so much more than the coins in our hands.
Thank you for calling us your treasure and sending Jesus
to find us. We want to belong to you forever. Amen.

Seeing with Your Heart

Then he said to Thomas, "Put your finger here; see my hands.
Reach out your hand and put it into my side. Stop doubting and believe."
Thomas said to him, "My Lord and my God!" Then Jesus told him,
"Because you have seen me, you have believed; blessed are those
who have not seen and yet have believed." JOHN 20:27-29

Until Jesus comes, we can't see God with our eyes. Yet we can know him and recognize him in our lives. We see the way he answers prayer. Bible verses encourage us right when we need them. The love of our brothers and sisters in Christ show God's love in tangible ways. Even the beauty and forces of nature point to a real and powerful God. We don't need him to stand in front of our eyes before we believe.

God knows we struggle with doubt sometimes. We can ask him to open the eyes of our heart to see him working all around us. Great blessings come when we believe without seeing.

Lord, we want to see you! Help us to recognize the signs all around us of your love and power. Give us faith to believe in you always. Amen.

Choose to Listen

*But my people would not listen to me; Israel would not submit
to me. So I gave them over to their stubborn hearts to follow
their own devices. If my people would only listen to me, if Israel
would only follow my ways, how quickly I would subdue their
enemies and turn my hand against their foes!* PSALM 81:13-14

Have you ever pulled your pillow over your head to block out the alarm? Do you fake deaf ears when you're called to work? Have you been so caught up in a movie or book, you didn't notice your friend trying to get your attention? We have ears to hear, but we don't always listen!

God has lots to say to you and me. He's knows if we listen, we're blessed. His Word teaches what's right. If we obey his voice, it leads to safety. Happy homes and friendships. Trustworthy habits that earn respect and rewards. Listening to God gives the peace of a clean conscience. We find courage to face scary, tough situations. Listening to God is the way to joy and life.

Do we plug our ears and tune out God's words? We might trust the others' opinions over God's wisdom. We run after our wishes and wants instead of following Jesus. Today, let's choose to listen. If we're hearers and doers of the Word, we'll find freedom and be blessed in what we do (James 1:25).

Lord, open our ears so we listen to your voice. Amen.

Choosing a Good Example

Dear friend, do not imitate what is evil but what is good.
Anyone who does what is good is from God.
Anyone who does what is evil has not seen God. 3 JOHN 11

You can't choose the color of your eyes or your height. You have both natural talents and challenges. You didn't get to choose the language you speak or when you'd be born on this planet. Yet although you can't choose every part of who you are, you can choose what you do.

The people around us—even in our own house—choose to do what's right or wrong. They're honest or deceitful. Gentle or violent. Grateful or grumbling. Respectful or rude. Hard-working or lazy. Generous or selfish. Caring or cruel. As you look around, you can see if others are living God's way or their own way.

Who are we imitating today? Do we choose friends who do what's right? Are we too impressed by celebrities, athletes, or social media stars? Do we act like the world to fit in or get ahead? As children of God, let's copy those who know him, love him, and obey him in every way. If we follow the example of God's faithful people, we'll be imitating Jesus too.

Lord, we want to be like Jesus. Put examples of godliness
in front of us so we can imitate what they do. Amen.

Because of the Cross

"He himself bore our sins" in his body on the cross, so that
we might die to sins and live for righteousness;
"by his wounds you have been healed." 1 Peter 2:24

Two thousand years ago, Jesus was born into this world. At that time in history, the cross was the most terrible form of punishment for a criminal. It was painful, bloody, and violent. It was a slow and tortured way to die. The suffering of a crucifixion is hard for us to understand or imagine.

Why would Jesus die on a cross? He was innocent of any crime. He committed no sin. Jesus healed the sick and fed the hungry. He set people free from evil, and he raised the dead to life. Every minute of every day, he showed God's compassion and love.

We're not innocent like Jesus. We sin. We're selfish and unloving. Born into sin, we were doomed to die. In God's great love, he gave us his Son Jesus. He was willing to take the full punishment for our sin on the cross. As he was hurt and killed, we received healing and life.

Do you believe Jesus died on the cross for you and me? Do you know that just as he was raised to life, we can be alive with him forever? Because of the cross, we "shall not perish but have eternal life" (John 3:16).

Lord, we believe Jesus died on the cross so we could live. Amen.

April

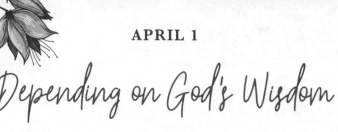

Depending on God's Wisdom

The fear of the LORD is the beginning of knowledge, but fools despise wisdom and instruction. Those who trust in themselves are fools, but those who walk in wisdom are kept safe. PROVERBS 1:7, 28:26

We struggle with pride in our heart that says, *I can do it on my own. I don't need any help. I should stand on my own two feet.* We avoid asking questions, pretending we have all the answers. In our decisions we fail to "look before we leap." We keep our mistakes and failures a secret. Ignoring advice, we're determined to figure life out on our own.

That kind of pride is foolish. It separates us from God's wisdom. It keeps us from learning from teachers, coaches, colleagues and those who care about us. We set ourselves up for trouble and danger. We feel stressed and confused. Instead of growing, we stay stuck in our bad choices and attitudes.

God is holding out his gifts of truth, help, and love for us today. Let's humble our hearts and depend on him. As we remember we're small and he's great and mighty, we'll receive more and more of his blessings.

Lord, it's foolish to depend on ourselves. Make us humble
and wise as we put our trust in you. Amen.

Like Little Children

He said to them, "Let the little children come to me, and do not hinder them, for the kingdom of God belongs to such as these. Truly I tell you, anyone who will not receive the kingdom of God like a little child will never enter it." And he took the children in his arms, placed his hands on them and blessed them. MARK 10:14-16

God gives a serious instruction to parents to help their kids get closer to Jesus. But sometimes obstacles stand in the way of moms and dads leading them toward God. Busy schedules can keep us from church or having faith conversations at home. Screens and devices can distract us from prayer or Bible study. Time with friends can take priority over friendship with Jesus.

You need to teach your children that Jesus loves them and wants to be close to them all the time. It gives him joy when your children pray, sing, attend church, and read their Bible. Jesus wants them to ask questions about him and hear how he loves them. They need to know that he's so excited to spend eternity with them, he's preparing a place for them right now.

We must make sure not to let our priorities or plans get out of balance because it will keep our kids from the love and blessings God wants to share with them.

Lord, you love our kids and our family. Show us how
we can move closer to you every day. We want to know
your love and your blessings. Amen.

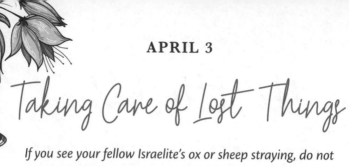

Taking Care of Lost Things

If you see your fellow Israelite's ox or sheep straying, do not ignore it but be sure to take it back to its owner. Do the same if you find their donkey or cloak or anything else they have lost. Do not ignore it. DEUTERONOMY 22:1, 3

You know the frustration of losing something important to you. A misplaced library book brings a fee to pay. Lost keys or wallets interrupt our plans. A mislaid jacket makes you cold on a chilly day. A lost pet leaves you heartbroken. Losing our things can be stressful, costly, and sad.

Others feel the same when they lose their belongings. We show the love of Jesus by restoring lost items to their owners. Caring for a friend's book says, "I care about you." Returning lost money says, "Here is God's provision for you." Handing in a lost phone says, "I want you to know blessing instead of trouble." When we value people's property, we value them too.

Jesus is the ultimate example of finding what's lost. Because we are "God's special possession," he came to this world "to seek and to save the lost" (1 Peter 2:9, Luke 19:10). God knew we were lost in sin and separated from him. Jesus found us, saved us, and restored us to the Father.

Lord, let us love others by caring for what's been lost.
Thank you for finding us and bringing us home. Amen.

APRIL 4

The Blessing of Rain

*Yet he has not left himself without testimony: He has shown kindness
by giving you rain from heaven and crops in their seasons; he provides
you with plenty of food and fills your hearts with joy.* ACTS 14:17

We don't always see rain as a blessing. Raindrops can spoil a picnic, a hike, or a trip to the beach. Muddy puddles dirty our shoes, our car, and our floors. Thunderstorms can feel a little scary, and flooding can do great damage. As rain interrupts our life, we can feel upset or disappointed.

Yet without rain, we would have no fresh fruit, vegetables, or grains for our picnic. No green grass would cover our yard and the fields. Rivers and seas would lose their fresh, cool water. Rain is a gift of God to provide the water and food we need for life.

When we see clouds in the sky, let's grab our umbrellas and celebrate. Each raindrop is proof of our Father's love. The rain falls, the crops grow, and we're given strength. The trees and flowers God created give us shade and beauty. Rain freshens the air we breathe and sustains the animals and creatures of the earth. Rain is a sign of God's love for the world. Because of his love, we can be filled with joy.

Lord, you show your kindness by giving us rain.
Make us joyful in your love. Amen.

APRIL 5

The Golden Rule

For the entire law is fulfilled in keeping this one command:
"Love your neighbor as yourself." If you bite and devour each other,
watch out or you will be destroyed by each other. GALATIANS 5:14-15

If someone tosses you a ball, you'll most likely toss it back and start a game of catch. When you say, "I love you," to a loved one, you'll get an "I love you" in return. If you smile at a colleague, they will probably smile back at you. The way we speak and treat others is often how they will speak and treat us in return.

This is especially true if we're rude, selfish, or hurtful toward other people. It's hard for someone to respond to mean words with kindness. If we refuse to be generous and share, others won't want to give to us, either. Harshness or criticism won't make anyone feel respectful or friendly in return. Fighting leads to more fighting until a happy, caring relationship is impossible.

Today we can move our friendships in the right direction. We can choose to love like Jesus—treating others with kindness and respect like we want to be treated. Every time you are considerate, honoring, and loving, you invite others to get closer and treat you well. How can we choose the way of love every day?

Lord, keep us from "biting" others with harsh words
and hurtful choices. Show us how to love our neighbors
as ourselves every day. Amen.

Acknowledge Mentors

Now we ask you, brothers and sisters, to acknowledge those
who work hard among you, who care for you in the Lord
and who admonish you. Hold them in the highest regard
in love because of their work. 1 THESSALONIANS 5:12-13

Caring teachers and coaches spend years practicing, studying, and training to be their best. They find great joy in helping kids grow their talents and skills. Think back to when you were in school, when you succeeded, teachers celebrated with you. If you struggled, they helped you to overcome. God put them in your life to help accomplish his plans for you.

In the same way, godly leaders and teachers are a gift to help us grow in faith. They are God's gifts in our lives, and they should never be taken for granted. To "acknowledge" means to say, "I see you. You count. You're important and you're making a difference." Today we can bless our pastors, teachers, and mentors by letting them know we appreciate all they do.

God knows we learn from others with experience and know-how. Our leaders at church have studied the Bible and seen God keep his promises in so many ways. They want to help us know God's love just like they do.

God gave us a great challenge to honor our leaders. As we give thanks for all they do, let's "acknowledge" God for giving us each one as a blessing.

Lord, thank you for those who teach us to love
and obey Jesus. Give us grateful hearts so we show
respect and love all the time. Amen.

It's Okay to Cry

When Mary reached the place where Jesus was and saw him,
she fell at his feet and said, "Lord, if you had been here,
my brother would not have died." When Jesus saw her
weeping ... he was deeply moved in spirit and troubled.
Jesus wept. Then the Jews said, "See how he loved him!"
JOHN 11:32-33, 35-36

When you love someone you hurt when they hurt. You see their tears of frustration, anger and grief. The sadness in their heart touches your spirit, too. And the same happens in their heart when they see you upset and grieving, because they love you.

Jesus loves you most of all. He knows every detail about why you hurt. Psalm 56:8 says God counts the nights you lay awake, and he writes down every tear you cry. Each time you feel sad, Jesus cares.

Do you feel like it's okay to cry? Do you try to put on a brave face for other people? Maybe you hold in your tears and push away your feelings inside. With Jesus, you don't have to pretend. You can pray and share your heart. Tell him you're disappointed. Tired. Lonely. Scared. Ask him for help and comfort. He will hear you, encourage you, and listen to your cry (Psalm 10:17).

Lord, we need your love in our sadness. Amen.

Walking in Light and Love

Anyone who loves their brother and sister lives in the light,
and there is nothing in them to make them stumble.
But anyone who hates a brother or sister is in
the darkness and walks around in
the darkness. 1 JOHN 2:10-11

It's hard to separate love for God from love for others. If we know him, love him, and walk by his Spirit, he fills us with love for others. We're patient instead of hot-tempered. We're helpful and generous instead of selfish. We use kind, encouraging words that build each other up. Our relationships are blessed and loving, and filled with his light.

Is your life bright with the love of God? Or, are you stumbling over sin in the darkness? Maybe you're sarcastic or bend the truth. Instead of praising others, do you point out every little mistake you see? When we lose our temper we hurt each other's hearts. In sin, we love ourselves more than each other.

God wants to shine his light in our lives. If we confess how we've stumbled, he forgives. He'll help us to forgive each other, too. His love will fill us up so we can walk in love and light together.

Lord, fill us with your love for each other. Amen.

Life's Last Stop

*As they entered the tomb, they saw a young man dressed
in a white robe sitting on the right side, and they
were alarmed. "Don't be alarmed," he said. "You are
looking for Jesus the Nazarene, who was crucified.
He has risen! He is not here." MARK 16:5-6*

A tomb is a finish line. It's the last stop in the journey of living. A grave is a steppingstone from this world to the eternal afterlife. Once a person dies, they don't wake up with breath and a heartbeat to exit the tomb.

When Jesus' friends came to his tomb, they panicked. The stone was rolled away and Jesus' body was nowhere in sight. Where had he gone? Had his body been stolen? How could he leave the tomb on his own two feet?

Amazed, Jesus' friends discovered he had risen from the dead. Just as he told them in Matthew 17:22-23, "The Son of Man is going to be delivered into the hands of men. They will kill him, and on the third day he will be raised to life."

Jesus conquered death by his resurrection. We can walk out of our own "tombs" of sin and death to be alive, always. "For God so loved the world that he gave his one and only Son, that whoever believes in him shall not perish but have eternal life" (John 3:16).

Lord, in your life, we find life forever. Amen.

An Epic Battle

For though we live in the world, we do not wage war as the world does.
The weapons we fight with are not the weapons of the world.
On the contrary, they have divine power to demolish strongholds.
We demolish arguments and every pretension that sets itself up
against the knowledge of God, and we take captive every thought
to make it obedient to Christ. 2 CORINTHIANS 10:3-5

Boxers strap on gloves to fight in the ring. Politicians write clever speeches to beat their opponents and win the vote. Soldiers battle enemy forces with tanks and missiles. The world uses money, weapons, and skill to win its battles.

God's children face the most epic battle of all. We fight sin. Satan. Enemies of God's truth. Doubts and fears. We fight temptation to disobey God's Word. Our struggle is against an enemy we can't see with our eyes—"the spiritual forces of evil in the heavenly realms" (Ephesians 6:12).

We don't have to be afraid or give up the fight. God gives powerful weapons for victory. We have the truth of the Bible, and the Spirit to write it in our hearts. We have salvation that guarantees eternal life. We have faith as a shield against enemy attack. And, we have prayer to call on our God to save. By believing and obeying God, we demolish "the powers of this dark world" (Ephesians 6:12).

Lord, teach us to use your weapons against the darkness. Amen.

APRIL 11

A Letter from Christ

*You yourselves are our letter, written on our hearts, known
and read by everyone. You show that you are a letter
from Christ, the result of our ministry, written not with
ink but with the Spirit of the living God, not on tablets
of stone but on tablets of human hearts.*

2 CORINTHIANS 3:2-3

If I wanted a new job, I would send a letter. I would tell my name, my skills, and my goals. If you had an acquaintance far, far away, you would write about your home and family. You'd share your favorite foods and hobbies. Our letters would help others to know who we are.

God wants everyone to know him, too. Yet he doesn't send an envelope to every mailbox in the world. Instead, he makes you and me "a letter from Christ" to tell who he is. As his children, we have God's Spirit and his Word in our hearts wherever we go.

When you give your friend a second chance, it shows God is forgiving. If I treat people fairly, it shows "the Lord loves righteousness and justice" (Psalm 33:5). If we help our elderly neighbor or a single mom, it says, "The Lord watches over … the fatherless and the widow" (Psalm 146:9). Each time we show integrity, it says all God's words are true (Psalm 119:160). Our kindness and love show God to the world.

Are we ready to be "mailed" today? Let's say, "Here am I. Send me!" (Isaiah 6:8).

Lord, send us as your letters of hope and love. Amen.

Safe Under His Wings

Whoever dwells in the shelter of the Most High will rest in the shadow of the Almighty. He will cover you with his feathers, and under his wings you will find refuge; his faithfulness will be your shield and rampart. PSALM 91:1, 4

A baby bird is tiny and fragile. Without full-grown feathers, it's unable to fly. It can't escape from dangerous predators. When it's hungry, it can't explore to find food. A little bird won't stay warm by itself on a wet or chilly day. It needs the strong wings of its mother to keep it safe.

We can do all we can to keep ourselves and our loved ones safe and secure. We can buy healthy food, clothes for each season and secure locks for our doors. But we can't shelter ourselves or our loved ones from all harm no matter how hard we try.

Our hope comes from our mighty, loving God. He is our safe place. He draws us close to cover us with his wings. Under God's care, we don't have to be afraid. We find comfort and rest when we're tired. He's faithful to hear our prayers and give us what we need. When we are weak, he is strong.

Lord, keep us under your wing so we're safe. Amen.

The Real Winners

*"Instead, whoever wants to become great among you must be
your servant, and whoever wants to be first must be slave of all.
For even the Son of Man did not come to be served, but to serve,
and to give his life as a ransom for many."* MARK 10:43-45

Who is a winner? Is he the one who comes in first? The one with the most trophies on the shelf? The student with top grades and perfect attendance? Is a winner the one with the most money? Is she the one in charge who's making the rules? The world would say a winner is the best and the brightest. If you're not a winner, you're nobody.

If we look at Jesus, he seems like that kind of winner. He's the King of kings. He's the most powerful and perfect, and he knows everything. Yet Jesus chose to give up the glory and fame he deserves. He gave his life to serve and rescue ordinary people like you and me.

Do we want to be winners in this world? Or, do we want true greatness like our Lord Jesus? He calls us to serve, give, and help. We put others first. We make God's name great instead of our own. As we lay down our pride to lift others up, we become great in heaven's eyes.

Lord, you sent your Son to give us life forever.
Teach us to serve and love like Jesus. Amen.

Snared by Fear

*Fear of man will prove to be a snare, but whoever
trusts in the LORD is kept safe.* PROVERBS 29:25

If you have an enemy, you're always looking over your shoulder to make sure you're safe. Stage fright will keep even the best performer from singing or playing their part. Some spend hours in front of the mirror to look perfect on the outside so they feel good enough inside. Others might spend too many hours at work to keep their boss happy. You or I might lie to cover up a mistake. Fear is a snare that stops us in our tracks.

Fear can keep us from standing up to bullies and using our voice. It can make us pretend to be someone else. Worst of all, we might listen to people instead of our conscience. We can be more afraid of what others think than what God has to say.

Is fear trapping you or me today? Do we choose our clothes, our words, and our friends to stay popular? Do we tell the truth, even if means a consequence? Do we say "yes" to God when everybody else says "no"?

God says we can trust him. He loves us no matter what. He stays by our side and helps fight our battles. We can put our reputation, our struggles, and our lives in his hands. His love never fails.

Lord, may we live to please you alone. Amen.

The End of Worries

"Therefore I tell you, do not worry about your life, what you will eat or drink; or about your body, what you will wear ... Look at the birds of the air; they do not sow or reap or store away in barns, and yet your heavenly Father feeds them. Are you not much more valuable than they?" MATTHEW 6:25-26

Stress. Anxiety. Fear. Concern. Panic. We have many words for worry because we worry about many things! Will we have groceries and clean clothes for the week? Does my bank account hold enough to pay the bills? Will I be healthy and strong? Will I make friends or be alone? What if I try my best, but it's not enough? How can I protect myself from trouble? Worries swirl in our minds and we fear what tomorrow will bring.

We forget we have a loving Father. We see him care for the littlest creatures he's made. He makes the sun shine every morning. "The earth is the Lord's, and everything in it, the world, and all who live in it" (Psalm 24:1). Will the God who holds everything refuse to give us what we need?

If we trust in God's love, our worries fade away. We know he'll fill our plates with food and cover us with clothing. He'll answer prayers for help and strength. If we don't know what to do, his offer of wisdom is there for the asking. You and I are God's delight and treasure. He'll never leave us on our own.

Lord, turn our fear to faith in you. Amen.

A Reason for Obedience

*Children, obey your parents in the Lord, for this is right. "Honor your father
and mother"—which is the first commandment with a promise—
"so that it may go well with you and that you may
enjoy long life on the earth."* EPHESIANS 6:1-3

"Take out the trash." "Stop playing and get ready for bed." "No, you can't eat more sugar." "Mind your manners." "Sit still and do your work." "Listen and obey." Parents have to take charge and set limits to care for their kids. Their rules and requests keep children safe, well, and learning what's right.

Even so, God knows it's tough for kids to submit. After all, no mom or dad is perfect. Rules don't always make sense. The word "no" is hard to hear when it interferes with their good time. Kids wonder if their parent really knows what's best for them. God's direction to honor and obey can feel hard or unfair.

If your kids are resisting instruction maybe it is time to remind them that God loves them. He wrote every commandment for their good. He promises to bless them greatly when they honor and obey you. Remind them of times when your limits kept them from getting hurt. God will use your obedience to move you and your children toward the abundant life he has planned for all of you.

Lord, help my child to obey by trusting in your love.
Help me to obey you by disciplining them as I should. Amen.

A Healing Touch

While Jesus was in one of the towns, a man came along who was covered with leprosy. When he saw Jesus, he fell with his face to the ground and begged him, "Lord, if you are willing, you can make me clean." Jesus reached out his hand and touched the man. "I am willing," he said. "Be clean!" And immediately the leprosy left him. LUKE 5:12-13

In a game of tag or jump rope, you avoid touch to win the game. In ancient times, you would avoid touch to stay safe and well. An infectious disease like leprosy was a threat to the community. Close contact with a sick person could endanger your life. Strict rules separated those with leprosy from their family, friends, and neighbors.

How would you feel if sickness banished you from home or the office? What if you couldn't attend church or go shopping? It would be scary, sad, and lonely to suffer a disease with no cure.

Jesus had compassion for those with leprosy. He ignored the rules so he could show God's love. Reaching out to touch the sick, he performed wonderful miracles of healing. God's power was shown to everyone as he brought health and life.

Do you ever feel alone or turned away? Are you afraid of rejection for your sins and failures? You can trust Jesus' promise that nothing in all creation can separate you from God's love (Romans 8:38-39). He will seek you, restore you, and love you always.

Lord, we thank you for your healing touch. Amen.

God Is Always Awake

Awake, Lord! Why do you sleep? Rouse yourself! Do not reject us forever. Why do you hide your face and forget our misery and oppression? PSALM 44:23-24

In the morning it usually only takes one alarm or "good morning" to wake us from sleep. We don't always feel motivated. Sometimes we hit "snooze" too many times. But we almost always listen to the alarm and get out of bed. If we ignored our alarm and pulled the covers over our head, we'd have a rough start to the day.

We trust in a God who doesn't just get up on time—he doesn't sleep at all! He never feels bored, drowsy, or lazy. When we're stressed, we never have to worry he's closing his eyes and ignoring our problems. He sees when we feel hurt and scared. He knows what we need before we ask him. He's wide awake and keeping his eyes on us every moment.

Sometimes our problems don't have a quick fix. We face the same issue day after day, with no relief in sight. We can wonder if God is really awake and paying attention. Our faith is tested while we're waiting for him to help us.

Don't worry. God is never late. He knows what we need. His rescue will come right on time. Our faith is growing while we wait.

Lord, we've been struggling for a long time. Help us to believe
you're awake and working while we're waiting.
We want to trust in your love. Amen.

Pointing Fingers

*Do not accuse anyone for no reason—when they
have done you no harm.* PROVERBS 3:30

We have all been wrongly blamed for something, and perhaps even falsely accused others at some stage in life. It's not fair to take the punishment for someone else's mistake. It hurts when others question our honesty and integrity. Trust is broken when our friends let us take the fall for their bad choices.

If you're falsely accused, there's hope. Doing the right thing day after day will protect your reputation. Responding to finger-pointing with quiet patience can ease the stress and drama that's been stirred up.

Let's be careful with others' reputations, too. If we're frustrated, let's not "sin in our anger" by making somebody look bad (Ephesians 4:26). We make sure we've listened to all the facts before laying blame on anyone. We should avoid gossip and keep what we hear to ourselves. Let's be loyal and stand up for our friends and family if they're falsely accused.

Jesus went to the cross after suffering lies and false accusations against him. When we struggle against injustice and blame, he stands by our side. Take your worry and hurt to him in prayer.

Lord, keep us kind and honest with our words so we love others
like you. Protect us from accusations so we can live in peace. Amen.

More Than You Can Imagine

*Now to him who is able to do immeasurably more than all we ask
or imagine, according to his power that is at work within us,
to him be glory in the church and in Christ Jesus throughout
all generations, for ever and ever! Amen.* EPHESIANS 3:20-21

Your imagination is awesome! There is no limit to what we are able to think about, create with our hands and share with each other. Whether it is writing or painting, gardening or baking, decorating or building, we are able to create so much beauty and inspiration.

Your imagination proves the Bible true. It says, "So God created mankind in his own image, in the image of God he created them." (Genesis 1:27) Your creativity is a mirror of the limitless imagination of the God who made you.

Do you believe God holds great things for you? Is there any hope or request that's impossible for him to handle? Put your trust in our mighty God, commit your way to him, and watch his glorious imagination unfold in your life.

Lord, we're amazed by your creativity and love. Your power
in our lives will do more than we can imagine. Amen.

APRIL 21

Taking on Daunting Challenges

But the men who had gone up with him said, "We can't attack those people; they are stronger than we are. All the people we saw there are of great size. We seemed like grasshoppers in our own eyes, and we looked the same to them." NUMBERS 13:31-33

Is a gigantic problem making you feel as small as a bug? You can feel outnumbered, with nobody to stick up for you. You're afraid you'll be crushed before you find a way out. The impossible is staring you in the face. Maybe all you can do is cut and run.

When our struggles loom that large, we're tempted to quit before we try. Yet God says to stop measuring the enemy's strength and our own weakness. Instead, we can fix our eyes on his almighty power. No one can stop him, and nothing can keep us from his love.

With God, we can attack every challenging obstacle in front of us. We can press on through hard times. When the enemy tries to stir up fear and doubt in our hearts, we can stand firm. We hold up our heads when others put us down. Instead of "I can't," we will say, "Everything is possible for one who believes" (Mark 9:23).

Lord, we're in over our heads. Show us your mighty power as you fight for us. Move us forward into all you have planned. Amen.

Bearing Fruit

But the fruit of the Spirit is love, joy, peace, forbearance,
kindness, goodness, faithfulness, gentleness and self-control.
Against such things there is no law. GALATIANS 5:22-23

What's on the inside shows on the outside. If we've put our trust in Jesus as our Savior, we have the Spirit in us. As he changes our hearts and minds, it shows in what we say and do.

The Spirit takes our stress and worry away and gives his peace. We're brave when we face problems and enemies. We pray instead of panic. The Spirit's peace helps us to stay calm and keep our heads when we're surprised by trouble.

The Spirit makes us strong. We're able to take on a challenge without backing down or giving up. We stand firm when we're tempted. Our faith hangs tough through whatever comes our way. We follow Jesus without looking back. The Spirit gives us patience to wait for the blessings God has in store.

The Spirit teaches the way of love. We're gentle and kind instead of harsh and angry. He gives us joy to give, serve, and help other people. We offer the same mercy and forgiveness we've found in Jesus. We love others as we love ourselves.

How do we know we have the Spirit? We look at our fruit. The Spirit transforms us from the inside out.

Lord, you make us new in every way. Thank you for your Spirit,
who bears fruit in each of us. Amen.

Knowing and Believing

And this is the testimony: God has given us eternal life, and this life is in his Son. Whoever has the Son has life; whoever does not have the Son of God does not have life. I write these things to you who believe in the name of the Son of God so that you may know that you have eternal life. 1 JOHN 5:11-13

You are smart and competent in your job. You know a lot about a variety of things and you have life sort of figured out.

Yet for all you know and understand, you can have doubts about God. You might wonder, am I a Christian? Is the Bible really true? What if God changes his mind about me? Does he really see me and know me? Am I going to heaven? Doubts and fears make God feel far away.

God doesn't want you to be afraid. If you and I believe in Jesus and trust him for salvation, we can be confident we have eternal life. You can be sure that "neither death nor life, neither angels nor demons, neither the present nor the future, nor any powers, neither height nor depth, nor anything else in all creation, will be able to separate us from the love of God that is in Christ Jesus our Lord." (Romans 8:38-39)

Lord, we believe in Jesus. Through him, we're yours forever. Amen.

Our Map Through Life

How can a young person stay on the path of purity?
By living according to your word. I have hidden your word in
my heart that I might not sin against you. PSALM 119:9, 11

Would you give a little child the keys to a truck? No, he couldn't see over the steering wheel. He wouldn't know which was the brake or the gas. He couldn't operate the lights or windshield wipers. If he managed to put it in gear and pull out on the road, he couldn't steer. He'd become lost, scared, and probably crash. A child needs to grow up and train to drive before he can travel safely.

When we first believe in Jesus, we're like little children. We're learning what it means to obey God. Our trust is small as we learn to pray and depend on him. We struggle with old habits and temptations. Our friends might question why we believe. We want to follow Jesus, but we need help to stay on the path.

God gave his Word to keep us from driving off the road of faith. It grows us up in our salvation (1 Peter 2:2). It teaches us "to say 'No' to ungodliness and worldly passions, and to live self-controlled, upright and godly lives" in the world (Titus 2:12). The Bible is our map through life. As we hide it in our hearts, we follow God each step of the way.

Lord, write your Word on our hearts. Amen.

Resist the Enemy

*Be alert and of sober mind. Your enemy the devil prowls
around like a roaring lion looking for someone to devour.
Resist him, standing firm in the faith, because you know
that the family of believers throughout the world
is undergoing the same kind of sufferings.* 1 PETER 5:8-9

From the time you were a kid, you learned the dangers of a hot stove or playing with matches. A fire can do a lot of damage to our bodies and our property if we're not careful. By paying close attention, we can stay safe and happy.

God tells us of another kind of danger. Our enemy, Satan, brings pain and destruction wherever he goes. He wants to wreck our lives by tempting us to sin. He twists God's truth to make us think good is bad, and bad is good. His lies deny God's love and make us question if the Bible is true. Satan wants to steal our joy, our hope, and our peace any way he can.

Yet Satan has no power if we stay alert! We can hold on to the truth when we hear his lies. We can run away from temptation and do what's right. We can stick close to other believers who encourage our spirits. If we say "yes" to God and "no" to the devil, he will flee from us (James 4:7).

Lord, help us to resist the enemy. Keep us alert
and ready so we can stand our ground. Amen.

Praying for Others

Dear friend, I pray that you may enjoy good health
and that all may go well with you, even as your soul
is getting along well. 3 JOHN 2

When we love somebody, we care about every part of their life. We feel their pain if they're sick or hurt. Their stress feels like our own when they're in trouble. We feel grieved if they're far from God. Since we care, we want them to be well in body, mind, and spirit.

Even so, we're unable to fix all of people's problems. We can't heal them from sickness. We can't control if they succeed at school or work. It's impossible to keep them safe or protect them from heartache. We see the lonely, but we can't make others be their friend. No matter how much we love and tell of Jesus, we can't get inside others' hearts to make them believe. What can we do when we care so much but can't make a difference?

When we have no power, we go to the One who holds it all. God is eager for you and me to pray for all the people in our lives. We can ask him to heal, help, and save the ones we love. Every time we pray, God says, "This is good, and pleases God our Savior, who wants all people to be saved and to come to a knowledge of the truth" (1 Timothy 2:3-4).

Lord, keep our loved ones well and close to you. Amen.

APRIL 27

Stuck in the Dark

As he went along, he saw a man blind from birth. His disciples
asked him, "Rabbi, who sinned, this man or his parents,
that he was born blind?" "Neither this man nor his parents
sinned," said Jesus, "but this happened so that the works
of God might be displayed in him." JOHN 9:1-3

When bad things happen to us, we're tempted to believe God is punishing us for something we did wrong. We think, If I was better, nicer, or stronger, everything would be okay. But God is only kind to his children—he allows us to struggle or suffer so he can come to our rescue. It's in our troubles that we discover his powerful love and the ways he keeps his promises. He shines light into our dark days so we see how wonderful he is.

We can feel like a lamp with no light bulb. We can't accomplish what we were created to do. We're helpless to overcome the darkness of our situation. After trying everything we know to do, we can't fix that friendship. We can't reach our goals. We can't kick that bad habit. Sickness and worry go on. But God wants to bring hope, help, and healing so everybody can see his power. His love will shine like a light in our lives.

Lord, display your light in our family. As you care for us and help us,
open the eyes of those who need to see you. Amen.

Blind Faith

*Now faith is confidence in what we hope for and assurance
about what we do not see.* HEBREWS 11:1

*"No one has seen the Father except the one who is from God;
only he has seen the Father. Very truly I tell you,
the one who believes has eternal life."* JOHN 6:46-47

We would be silly to believe the only reality is what we can see and touch. We know we love one another. Our hopes, dreams, and ideas are important. The universe holds wonders from the depths of the sea to the outer reaches of space. It's the unseen that captures our hearts and imaginations.

Faith is believing in God, even though we haven't yet seen him with our eyes. The signs of his life and power are everywhere. We experience hope and joy in tough times. His wisdom guides our choices. The Spirit teaches us right from wrong and makes us more like Jesus. Answered prayers show he's listening and cares. Every time we seek him with all our hearts, we find him (Jeremiah 29:13).

Do you feel confident in God's love? Do you believe Jesus came from heaven to save us and belong to him forever? If your faith feels small or you struggle with doubt, you can pray. God will give you what you need to put your hope and trust in him.

Lord, we want faith that can believe without seeing. May we trust
in Jesus with all our hearts and be with you forever. Amen.

A Love That Sticks with Us

For I am convinced that neither death nor life, neither angels
nor demons, neither the present nor the future, nor
any powers, neither height nor depth, nor anything else
in all creation, will be able to separate us from the love
of God that is in Christ Jesus our Lord. ROMANS 8:38-39

Separation hurts. It's hard to say goodbye when a loved one moves away. It cuts deep when friends turn their back and leave you alone. When you and your friend are apart for too long, your hearts can't wait to be together again.

Separation is scary, too. You feel lost. You wonder who will protect you and help you find your way? We never want to disconnect from the ones who care and love us most.

Jesus knows the pain of separation. When he went to the cross, he took the sins of the world on himself. In that moment, sin separated him from his holy, heavenly Father. He cried out, "My God, my God, why have you forsaken me?" (Mark 15:34). Jesus bore the torture of separation so we could be united with God forever. We're adopted as his children when we believe and trust in his love.

God's love follows you wherever you go. Nothing you do can make him love you less. God's love is in you and always will be.

Lord, may we trust in your love that holds us forever. Amen.

Try and Try Again

Therefore, since we are surrounded by such a great cloud of witnesses,
let us throw off everything that hinders and the sin that
so easily entangles. And let us run with perseverance the race
marked out for us, fixing our eyes on Jesus, the pioneer
and perfecter of faith. HEBREWS 12:1-2

When learning to tie your shoes, you tangle the laces before you get it right. While learning to cook, you might burn some meals before you're confident in the kitchen. A baby falls down over and over before she crosses the room on her own little feet. To read, we move from ABC's to simple words to chapter books over time. To get where we want to go, we have to try and try again.

We want to follow Jesus and obey his Word. Yet we struggle with sin no matter how hard we try. "For I do not do the good I want to do, but the evil I do not want to do—this I keep on doing" (Romans 7:19). It's a battle between our sin and our love for God inside.

When we're tired and discouraged, hope is found in Jesus. He put faith, life, and love in our hearts. He'll give strength to keep going. The Spirit gives wisdom to steer clear of temptations that trip us up. God's people will cheer us on and help along the way. In this race, let's stick together and never stop running until we see Jesus.

Lord, let us run to you without giving up. Amen.

May

Lost and Found

"What do you think? If a man owns a hundred sheep, and one
of them wanders away, will he not leave the ninety-nine
on the hills and go to look for the one that wandered off?
And if he finds it, truly I tell you, he is happier about that
one sheep than about the ninety-nine that did
not wander off." MATTHEW 18:12-13

A bank locks up its cash in a vault so every dollar is accounted for. Animals have a leash, a crate, or a fence so they won't wander away. A mother holds her little child's hand so he won't run into the street. We keep what's precious and valuable as close and safe as we can.

Even so, money gets lost or stolen. Sheep escape their fields and fences. Children test the limits by going too far, too soon. Everyone, young and old, is tempted to move far from God and go their own way.

In our sin, we wander. We want to try the world's kind of fun and excitement. We run from rules and authority to do our own thing. After running from God, we find ourselves lost. Guilty, tired, and disappointed, we don't know how to find our way home.

God searches for the lost. His love means kindness and mercy. Forgiveness and a second chance. When he finds you and brings you to himself, all of heaven celebrates.

Lord, keep us from wandering from your love. Amen.

Living Like God's Children

*Do not be yoked together with unbelievers. For what do righteousness
and wickedness have in common? Or what fellowship can light have
with darkness? Therefore, "Come out from them and be separate,
says the Lord. Touch no unclean thing, and I will receive you."
And, "I will be a Father to you, and you will be my sons and
daughters, says the Lord Almighty." 2 CORINTHIANS 6:14, 17-18*

When we put our faith in Jesus, we're changed. We become completely "new creations" (2 Corinthians 5:17). God calls us his friends, sons, and daughters. It's no longer we who live, but Christ living in us! (Galatians 2:20). We're given a whole new identity and future.

As God's people, we don't fit in with the world around us like before. The Bible sets our standard for right and wrong. We love people who nobody likes or who don't love us back. We hope for treasure in heaven that's better than money, popularity, or the world's kind of pleasure.

God asks us to live like we're his. We partner with close friends who encourage us to follow him. We think about what's "pure, right, and excellent" instead of ugly, wrong, and useless (Philippians 4:8). We separate from our old life and move closer to Jesus every day.

> Lord, set us apart as your children. Give us courage
> to follow you. Keep us from trying to mix in with
> the world around us since we love you. Amen.

Shining Lights

*"Neither do people light a lamp and put it under a bowl.
Instead they put it on its stand, and it gives light
to everyone in the house. In the same way, let your
light shine before others, that they may see your good
deeds and glorify your Father in heaven."* MATTHEW 5:15-16

The world is a dark place. People suffer from war and sickness, loneliness and poverty. Everyone is searching for truth, hope, and peace but they don't know where to look. We are blessed to know the love of God that rescued us from darkness. He calls us to shine his light so others can see Jesus, too.

Are we hiding God's light or shining brightly for him today? We can feel shy or nervous to talk about the Bible. Maybe we think only smart, perfect people can speak up about their faith. We're afraid we'll say the wrong thing or make a mistake. We keep Jesus' love a secret instead of sharing it with others.

Yet, all we have to do to shine our light is to love people. When we are generous, kind, and compassionate, Jesus shines in us. As we obey God and do what's right, we sparkle in the darkness. Let's bring glory to God by letting our light shine in front of everybody.

Lord, show yourself to the world through our us.
Let our love shine brightly to everyone. Amen.

Limitless Love

How precious to me are your thoughts, God! How vast is the sum of them!
Were I to count them, they would outnumber the grains of sand—
when I awake, I am still with you. PSALM 139:17-18

Our brains can't hold all the ideas, plans, and questions we face each day. In the rush to pack your bags before a trip, you leave your toothbrush behind. A pet might go without dinner while we're busy preparing our own. We forget the name of the person we met just last week. We're easily distracted and forgetful in the busyness of our days.

Aren't you glad that God's mind has no limits? He knows every detail about each person he made. He counts every strand of hair on your head (Luke 12:7). He knows when you wake and sleep, go out or stay home. Your words and thoughts are an open book to the Lord (Psalm 139:2-4). God has enough love and attention to care for everybody, including you!

God doesn't just know all about you, he thinks about you every moment. He has more thoughts of you than the sand at the beach or the stars in the sky. His thoughts cover you day and night, so when you wake up God is right there with you. Why does he pay such close attention? He loves you with an everlasting love (Jeremiah 31:3).

Lord, you never forget the ones you love,
and you're with us always. Amen.

Sharing the Lord's Table

*Is not the cup of thanksgiving for which we give thanks
a participation in the blood of Christ? And is not the bread
that we break a participation in the body of Christ?
For whenever you eat this bread and drink this
cup, you proclaim the Lord's death until
he comes.* 1 CORINTHIANS 10:16, 11:26

We share meals every day. If we're hungry, we pick up a fork and spoon and eat. Our thirst is easily satisfied. Eating and drinking is so ordinary, we rarely remember what's on the table from week to week.

What makes the bread and cup of communion so different? Why do we interrupt our regular worship to share the Lord's table? It is Jesus who taught us to participate in communion. Before he went to the cross, he set the example for his disciples:

The Lord Jesus, on the night he was betrayed, took bread, and when he had given thanks, he broke it and said, "This is my body, which is for you; do this in remembrance of me." In the same way, after supper he took the cup, saying, "This cup is the new covenant in my blood; do this, whenever you drink it, in remembrance of me. (1 Corinthians 11:23-25)

God knows we're distracted and forgetful. He sees our battle with sin. We struggle to trust his mercy when we're guilty and ashamed. In his love, he invites us to his table. There, we remember Jesus' death on the cross. We celebrate our new life. Our faith is made strong and we're filled with new hope.

Lord, may we always remember Jesus at your table. Amen.

MAY 6

Love vs Revenge

"Do not seek revenge or bear a grudge against anyone among your people, but love your neighbor as yourself. I am the Lord." LEVITICUS 19:18

You know how it feels to be insulted and put down. Your things have been taken, broken, and lost. You've been friendly and kind, only to be ignored or pushed away. Friends you trusted have broken promises or hurt your feelings. Mean words and unfair treatment are hard to forget.

Yet when we refuse to let go of anger and pain, it adds to the damage. Holding a grudge will harden our hearts and silence our prayers. Our spirits will grow bitter and negative. It keeps us from fixing what's broken between us. A grudge will keep us from loving each other like Jesus.

If we refuse to forgive those who hurt us, we deny how we've been forgiven by God. His Word says to "forgive as the Lord forgave you" (Colossians 3:13). If it's hard to let go of a grudge, pray for a humble heart. Remember all the ways God has been patient and forgiving. Ask his Spirit to fill you with compassion. He'll give you all you need to love others as yourself.

Lord, you set us free from the power of sin, so we can choose
love instead of anger and revenge. Help us to forgive
as we've been forgiven. Amen.

The Joy of Worship

*Praise the LORD. Sing to the LORD a new song, his praise
in the assembly of his faithful people. Let them praise
his name with dancing and make music to him with
timbrel and harp.* PSALM 149:1, 3

God is happy when you go to a quiet, private place to pray. You can share your needs, confess your sins, and tell God how much you love him. Yet he also wants us to meet with him all together. Every time we gather as a group to praise his name, he is blessed.

God also knows how we become tired and discouraged. When we meet with our brothers and sisters in Christ, we're built up. Hearing about others' answered prayers reminds us of God's power. Our friends' and family's gratitude reminds us of all the ways God shows his love. Putting our praises to music stirs our excitement to know the one true God who calls us his own.

Let's celebrate God through music and praise every chance we get. Our family—and our church family—can "shout for joy to the Lord" and "worship the Lord with gladness" (Psalm 100:1-2). When we do, we'll have an even greater joy in Christ than we've known before.

> Lord, put a song of praise in our mouths and our hearts.
> You are wonderful in every way and we love you! Amen.

The Wonderful Story of God

*Jesus did many other things as well. If every one of them
were written down, I suppose that even the whole world
would not have room for the books that
would be written.* JOHN 21:25

The Bible is made up of many books, but it tells one huge and wonderful story: God's plan to save his people through Jesus. It spans all of history from the creation of life in the beginning until we reach our eternal home with God in heaven. In the gospels of Matthew, Mark, Luke, and John, we're told of the few short years Jesus spent in the world as a man. His words, miracles, and signs were too great to fit into all the books in the world!

We can be confident, though, that the Bible gives us all we need to know. When we read of Jesus' healing the sick, we realize he's our healer too. As we see him reach out in friendship to all kinds of people, we see his kind, compassionate heart. The accounts of his victory over demons, the weather, and death itself give us confidence in his mighty power. Every story in scripture was hand-picked to help us know and believe in our Savior.

The Bible proves Jesus' love is invincible. He's the Son of God who overcomes the world! We'll hear stories of his life and love for all time.

Lord, thank you for filling your Word with stories of your love.
Keep teaching us the awesome works of Jesus. Amen.

Overcoming "I Can't"

Therefore encourage one another and build each other up,
just as in fact you are doing. And we urge you, brothers
and sisters, ... encourage the disheartened, help the weak,
be patient with everyone. 1 THESSALONIANS 5:11, 14

Two little words do a lot of damage—I can't. We think, I can't finish this project on time. I can't make new friends. I can't get along with my family. I can't fix my problem. I can't do the right thing. I can't accomplish my goal. I can't grow or change for the better. The more we say, "I can't," the more we believe it. We feel sad and stuck right where we are.

God knows how hard it is to overcome the power of "I can't." He wants us to help our brothers and sisters in Jesus find hope and strength. Our words can fill others' hearts with courage to do hard things. We can remind our friends and family that God is with us. No matter how tired or weak we might feel, "Everything is possible for one who believes" (Mark 9:23).

Do you struggle with "I can't" today? Let's stick together and pray all the time. Let's help each other remember our good God who loves us. He'll teach us how to hold each other up so we can face whatever comes our way.

Lord, you're "our refuge and strength, an ever-present help
in trouble" (Psalm 46:1). Show us how to encourage
each other with that truth. Amen.

Overflowing with Joy

*Our mouths were filled with laughter, our tongues with songs
of joy. Then it was said among the nations, "The LORD
has done great things for them." PSALM 126:2*

God created a beautiful world for us to enjoy. He surrounds us with the love of friends and family. The sun comes up every morning with a fresh new day full of possibilities. Because God loves us so much, he wants us to fill us with joy that spills out into smiles and laughter.

Have you noticed how laughter is contagious? The joy in you and me gets the attention of everyone around us. When we're thankful and amazed at God's goodness, people notice. The peace we feel inside and the happiness we show outside stand out in a sad and hopeless world. Every time we let our joy shine brightly, we're putting God's love on display.

God offers joy in the good days and bad. We know that in every struggle, he's loving and helping us get to the other side. Our peace and joy through it all give hope to others who are hurting. They, too, can discover the good news of God's love. Let's keep smiling!

Lord, thank you for the joy we can have every day. Let our laughter
show the world how much you love us. Amen.

MAY 11

Let Down Your Nets

[Jesus] said to Simon, "Put out into deep water, and let down the nets for a catch." Simon answered, "Master, we've worked hard all night and haven't caught anything. But because you say so, I will let down the nets." When they had done so, they caught such a large number of fish that their nets began to break. LUKE 5:4-6

Have you worked really hard to accomplish something, but you failed to achieve what you wanted? You stepped up for months to earn a promotion, but it was given to someone else? You've practiced a song over and over, but your fingers still stumble on the piano keys? You offer kindness and friendship without fail, but you're still shut out of the group? We might throw out our best effort until we're exhausted, only to feel empty-handed.

When you've done all you can, Jesus is waiting. He wants to give you strength to keep going. He offers wisdom and direction so you know what to do. Instead of bearing the heavy weight of stress and worry, he invites you to "cast your cares on the Lord" (Psalm 55:22). Instead of giving up, put your goals, hopes, and struggles in his hands. Trust him and he will do more than you can ask or imagine (Ephesians 3:20).

Lord, our nets have been coming up empty.
Fill us with faith as we wait for your blessing. Amen.

You're Free!

Therefore, there is now no condemnation for those who are in Christ Jesus, because through Christ Jesus the law of the Spirit who gives life has set you free from the law of sin and death. ROMANS 8:1-2

What happens if you break the law? If you break the speed limit, you get a ticket. If you steal or hurt someone, you could be arrested and charged with a crime. Imagine standing in court before a judge and hearing, "Guilty!" You'd feel ashamed and terrified of the punishment that was coming.

As much as we try to follow the rules, we're not perfect. We know we break the "law" in the Bible, too. As much as we want to keep the ten commandments and obey God, we fail every day. But instead of hearing "Guilty!" we can hear God say, "You're free!"

Jesus died on the cross for our sins, taking the punishment that we deserve. If we put our faith in him and ask God to forgive our sins, he says we're clean. We're innocent. We're adopted as his own children forever. His love washes away all our fear and shame. Do you want to be free forever? Receive the gift of salvation in Jesus.

Lord, thank you for giving us Jesus so we can be free from
condemnation. Your love is better than life. Amen.

A New Life

Jesus replied, "Very truly I tell you, no one can see the kingdom of God unless they are born again." "How can someone be born when they are old?" Nicodemus asked. "Surely they cannot enter a second time into their mother's womb to be born!" JOHN 3:3-4

Nicodemus thought Jesus was asking something impossible when he said that Nicodemus would need to be born again. He knew every person is born from a mother. Once born, our bodies are made to eat, sleep, and grow in this physical world for the years we're given to live. But to be part of God's spiritual, kingdom family, we need a new kind of birth.

In John 3, Jesus explained, "No one can enter the kingdom of God unless they are born of water and the Spirit. Flesh gives birth to flesh, but the Spirit gives birth to spirit. You should not be surprised at my saying, 'You must be born again.'"

To be born into this new life, we put our trust in Jesus. We believe he is God's Son who died on the cross to take the punishment for our sins. He was raised to life again so we can live with him forever. When we believe in him, we receive his Spirit and are "born again" as God's children. We have the hope of eternal life with him and all God's people.

Lord, thank you for giving us new life so we can belong
to you forever. We love you. Amen.

MAY 14

Part of God's Family

*For those who are led by the Spirit of God are the children
of God. The Spirit you received does not make you slaves,
so that you live in fear again; rather, the Spirit you received
brought about your adoption to sonship. And by him
we cry, "Abba, Father." The Spirit himself testifies with
our spirit that we are God's children.* ROMANS 8:14-16

When we believe in Jesus, we receive proof that we're part of God's family. God gives the Holy Spirit to claim us as his adopted sons and daughters. We're not just servants, friends, or his royal subjects—we're his own children forever.

When God is our Father it changes everything. We have an inheritance waiting for us in heaven. We're free to call him "Daddy" and run to him with all our joys and troubles. We'll live with him together, forever. Just like I'll always love you, God will be your Father for eternity.

Remember whose you are—a child of the Father God who created you and loves you always. You are never alone. You always belong. You're a priceless gift to your family, and a delight to God's heart forever.

Lord, thank you for adopting us as your children. May your Spirit
give us confidence that we belong to you forever. Amen.

MAY 15

All Glory to God

Not to us, LORD, not to us but to your name be the glory,
because of your love and faithfulness. PSALM 115:1

We woke up this morning with breath in our lungs because God gave the gift of life. He gives strength to move us through our day—learning, working, and growing. Every victory, whether showing kindness to a difficult person or finishing a tough job, is made possible by God. He equips us with talent and skill. Wisdom, compassion, and love are gifts from his Spirit. Every good thing we have and do is from our God.

Even so, we're tempted to crave attention and applause. We like to hear, "Excellent work! Good job! You're the best!" We soak in the praise for ourselves without praising the Source. We get in the way of the light of God's glory shining for all to see.

Let's use our achievements to make God's name great. We can tell everyone how faithful he is to give what we need. In prayer, we can thank him for helping us succeed. Let's give him the credit whenever we're generous and kind. As we obey him and do the great things he's planned for us to do, we can give him the glory for it all.

Lord, you are faithful to do wonderful work in our lives.
May we give you all the glory, always. Amen.

Shining Like Stars

Do everything without grumbling or arguing, so that you may become blameless and pure, "children of God without fault in a warped and crooked generation." Then you will shine among them like stars in the sky as you hold firmly to the word of life. PHILIPPIANS 2:14-16

Does it seem like people are angry everywhere you go? You see drivers honking their car's horn and shouting in traffic. Parents yell at the referee during their kid's soccer game. Customers scold the cashier for making mistakes at the register. Neighbors argue loudly in their front yard, and kids fight to be first in line on the playground. Little problems lead to big blowups, with everybody complaining and arguing. It makes the world feel dark and cold.

When we believed in Jesus, God turned our "wailing into dancing" and dressed us up in joy (Psalm 30:11). Instead of complaining, we're thankful. Instead of arguing and fighting, we become "peace-loving, considerate, submissive, full of mercy and good fruit" (James 3:17). Instead of taking revenge or holding a grudge, we forgive. Jesus fills us with his love so we will love our neighbor as ourselves. We shine his light in the darkness around us.

In God's eyes, you're a star. Your light shines when you trust him and obey his Word. It shines when you're patient. When you're kind to your enemies. When you do hard things with a willing spirit. You shine when you love like Jesus.

*Lord, we want to shine like stars by loving you
and holding on to your Word. Amen.*

Reasons for the Wait

But do not forget this one thing, dear friends: With the Lord a day is like a thousand years, and a thousand years are like a day. The Lord is not slow in keeping his promise, as some understand slowness. Instead he is patient with you, not wanting anyone to perish, but everyone to come to repentance. 2 PETER 3:8-9

We worry and complain if we're stuck in a traffic jam. We check the mailbox every day if a special package is on its way. When you're starved, you can hardly wait to sit at the table. If the calendar shows a birthday or holiday is coming, it's too exciting to think about anything else. It's a struggle to wait for troubles to end and blessings to arrive.

Right now, we're waiting for what's best of all. Jesus promised he'd come to bring us home. "For the Lord himself will come down from heaven … ," and we "will be caught up … in the clouds to meet the Lord in the air. And so we will be with the Lord forever" (1 Thessalonians 4:16-17). From that day on, "There will be no more death or mourning or crying or pain" (Revelation 21:4). Does it feel like it's taking too long for Jesus to come again?

There's a reason for Jesus' delay. He wants the lost to be found. He's waiting for the gospel to go around the world so they can hear and believe. As we wait for Jesus, let's tell everyone about his love.

Lord, give us patience as we wait for you. Amen.

Worth the Trust

"Whoever can be trusted with very little can also be trusted with much, and whoever is dishonest with very little will also be dishonest with much. So if you have not been trustworthy in handling worldly wealth, who will trust you with true riches? And if you have not been trustworthy with someone else's property, who will give you property of your own?" LUKE 16:10-12

As we grow and mature, people count on us more and more. Teachers will ask kids to finish their homework and turn it in on time. In a young person's first job, the boss expects them to help customers or keep the workplace clean and safe. With your first driver's license in your wallet, the police expect you to drive carefully so no one gets hurt. Over time you might grow a career and a family, with colleagues and loved ones who depend on you every day.

Have you grown and proved you're trustworthy today? Do you keep your promises? Can you remember what you're asked to do? Do others experience peace with you, knowing you're reliable?

God is ready to give us what we need to be faithful. Today, he'll help you follow the rules and tell the truth. He'll give you strength to do hard things and honor your commitments. When you do those things, you'll earn people's trust and be rewarded.

Lord, teach us to be trustworthy. We want to be faithful
just as you're faithful to us in every way. Amen.

Paying Your Debts

Give to everyone what you owe them: If you owe taxes, pay taxes;
if revenue, then revenue; if respect, then respect; if honor,
then honor. Let no debt remain outstanding, except
the continuing debt to love one another, for whoever
loves others has fulfilled the law. ROMANS 13:7-8

We work hard to earn money so we can pay for what we need. We exchange money from our bank account for our home, food and clothes, and extras like vacations. The government takes a portion of taxes from our earnings to pay for things like roads and schools in our community. We show integrity by paying our bills and covering the cost of what we need and use.

There's one debt that we can't pay—Jesus' love and payment for our sins on the cross. Nothing we offer could match the priceless worth of his salvation. He asks us to pay back his love for us by loving each other all the time. We love one another because he first loved us (1 John 4:19).

How can we love our family, friends, and others? God says, "Love does no harm to a neighbor," and to "love your neighbor as yourself" (Romans 13:9-10). We can be thoughtful. Generous. Forgiving. Helpful. Kind. We can build each other up with our words. We can encourage and pray for each other every day. Our love shows the love of Jesus to everyone.

Lord, make us faithful to pay what we owe.
Show us how to love you by loving others. Amen.

A Time of Preparing

*"My Father's house has many rooms; if that were not so, would I have
told you that I am going there to prepare a place for you?
And if I go and prepare a place for you, I will come back
and take you to be with me that you also may
be where I am."* JOHN 14:2-3

I wouldn't spend all day preparing a delicious meal, only to leave it on the stove and go to bed hungry. We wouldn't bake a cake, wrap gifts, and send invitations, only to lock the door and cancel the party. It would be foolish to get a driver's license and buy a new car, only to leave it parked in the garage. We expect our preparations to accomplish goals and bless our lives.

Jesus is making plans and preparations, too. He promised to come back for us and take us home. Right now, he is preparing a place where we can be together forever. We're not just wishing and hoping he'll come again—we can be confident he'll keep his word.

As Jesus prepares for us, are we preparing for him? Each day we can know and love him more. We can invite the Spirit to work in us and make us new. We can use our spiritual gifts to serve God's people. We can "encourage one another daily" to be faithful and turn from sin (Hebrews 3:13). While we wait for Jesus, we can love and obey him in every way.

Lord, we want to be where you are. Make us ready! Amen.

God to the Rescue

"Because he loves me," says the LORD, "I will rescue him; I will protect him, for he acknowledges my name. He will call on me, and I will answer him; I will be with him in trouble, I will deliver him and honor him." PSALM 91:14-15

In a fairy tale, a princess cries from her tower for rescue from the dragon. Movies show heroes battling villains to save the day. Emergency vehicles answer 9-1-1, racing across town to put out fires and help those in trouble. At home, we're ready with a hug and a bandage if our family is hurt. When we cry for help, we want to know someone is listening.

God hears us every time we call on him. He's ready to battle our enemies. If we feel left out and unwanted, God's arms are open wide. When we're sick, he can heal. If we need money, he can provide. No problem is too great for God to handle. No burden is too heavy for him to carry. All we have to do is call and he will answer.

When you pray, God hears your voice. He's always ready and watching—he "will neither slumber nor sleep" (Psalm 121:4). God is faithful to help his children when they call. Do you need rescue today? Are you afraid of disaster? Do you feel too tired to go on? Pray and trust the God who loves you today.

Lord, we believe in your power and love. Amen.

An Example to Others

*Don't let anyone look down on you because you are young,
but set an example for the believers in speech, in conduct,
in love, in faith and in purity.* 1 TIMOTHY 4:12

You are a unique person. There is no one like you! God created you in every detail, from the color of your eyes to the wonderful sound of your laugh. He saw you before you were born, and he planned your days before the beginning of time (Psalm 139:16). You are not a mistake, an accident, or an afterthought. You are loved.

You might still be a young woman as you read this and think that you are not as of much value as the older women in your church. But remember God treasures you. When you believed in Jesus he gave you his Spirit. The Spirit gives you power to do what's right. He gives wisdom to understand Scripture and tell the gospel. He fills your heart with his love. As God's child, he "has blessed [you] in the heavenly realms with every spiritual blessing in Christ" (Ephesians 1:3). Your faith is real, and you can serve the Lord.

God wants to use you as an example to others. They'll imitate your kindness and honesty. You'll show how to be patient and forgiving. Through your gentle spirit, you'll be a peacemaker. Your words, your choices, and your trust in God will teach what it means to follow Christ.

Lord, thank you for raising up young women to serve you. Amen.

Peace in the Worst of Times

"I have told you these things, so that in me you may
have peace. In this world you will have trouble.
But take heart! I have overcome the world." JOHN 16:33

You might go out for a walk on a sunny day, and then run for cover as a sudden storm pours down rain. You may feel well at bedtime but wake up sick and sore. We obey Jesus and do the right thing, only to be criticized and rejected. Trials come when we least expect them.

God says in this world we'll have trouble. Instead of feeling scared and surprised, we can expect hard days to come. We suffer disappointment, emergencies, and stress. No matter how we try to play it safe, we can't avoid the hurt of a broken world.

God doesn't leave us in our fear. We don't have to be gloomy, expecting the worst to happen at any moment. We hold on to hope because God's promises give us peace:

- "With God all things are possible" (Matthew 19:26).
- "The Lord your God is with you, the Mighty Warrior who saves" (Zephaniah 3:17).
- "He is my loving God and my fortress, my stronghold and my deliverer … " (Psalm 144:2).
- "If God is for us, who can be against us? No, in all these things we are more than conquerors through him who loved us" (Romans 8:31, 37).

Our troubles are no match for the power, glory, and love of our God.

Lord, give us your perfect peace. Amen.

Dressed in Salvation

So in Christ Jesus you are all children of God through faith,
for all of you who were baptized into Christ have clothed
yourselves with Christ. GALATIANS 3:26-27

I delight greatly in the LORD; my soul rejoices in my God.
For he has clothed me with garments of salvation and arrayed
me in a robe of his righteousness, as a bridegroom adorns his head
like a priest, and as a bride adorns herself with her jewels. ISAIAH 61:10

How do we recognize a bride? By her beautiful white dress and veil. A graduate proudly wears a cap and gown to take his diploma. A queen's crown declares her royal status. An officer takes authority by gearing up in uniform. An athlete puts on a jersey and cleats. Clothing is a powerful symbol of honor, leadership, and purpose.

When we put our trust in Jesus, we are "dressed" in our salvation. As God transforms us on the inside by his Spirit, it shows on the outside by our love and good deeds. It's as if we're putting on kindness and compassion. Generosity and patience. Compassion and grace. Wisdom and purity. Faith, hope, and love are displayed in our lives for all to see.

As we are "clothed with Christ," we look more and more like Jesus. Our old ugly habits and sins are taken off and we're dressed in righteousness forever.

Lord, thank you for salvation that changes how we look on the inside
and out. We love you and praise you for covering us with Christ. Amen.

MAY 25

Yes, You Can Change!

But one thing I do: Forgetting what is behind and straining toward what is ahead, I press on toward the goal to win the prize for which God has called me heavenward in Christ Jesus. PHILIPPIANS 3:13-14

Have you heard the expression, "You can't teach an old dog new tricks."? "People never change."? "A leopard never changes its spots."? The world seems to think we're doomed to stay just as we are.

Yet with God, we have hope. He says, "If anyone is in Christ, the new creation has come: The old has gone, the new is here!" (2 Corinthians 5:17). "We all … are being transformed into his image with ever-increasing glory" (2 Corinthians 3:18). You and I no longer live, but Christ lives in us (Galatians 2:20). Once we believe, we're changed from the inside out.

Still, it's hard to forget the sins of our past. We carry shame for our mean words. Our lies and broken promises. Our cravings and temptations. We remember the ways we disobeyed God—and still do—and wonder if our faith is real. We can be so discouraged about yesterday, we lose hope for tomorrow.

Hope isn't found in our willpower to do what's right. We hope in God's promise "that he who began a good work in you will carry it on to completion until the day of Christ Jesus" (Philippians 1:6). Let's trust him to keep his promise so we keep running for the prize. Our reward is Jesus, and he's waiting!

Lord, we want to win the prize that your love has in store. Amen.

Feeling Sorry

Yet now I am happy, not because you were made sorry, but because
your sorrow led you to repentance ... Godly sorrow brings
repentance that leads to salvation and leaves no regret,
but worldly sorrow brings death. 2 CORINTHIANS 7:9-10

We know how it feels to be sorry. We make bad choices and mistakes every day. We might lose our temper or lose our jacket. We cut people off in traffic or cut them off when they're trying to talk. We go when we should stay, or hold back when we're supposed to move forward. Sometimes we're forgetful and careless, rude and unkind, or stubborn and angry. We feel sorry when we fail to do what's right.

If we hurt others or let them down, it's good to say, "I'm sorry." Yet true sorrow is more than words—it changes our hearts, minds, and actions. If we're truly sorry for breaking a promise, we learn to be faithful. If we regret spreading gossip and rumors, we start watching our words. If we're selfish, we become giving and generous. God can use our sorry hearts to turn us to him. He'll help us grow to be more like Jesus.

Are you feeling sorry today? Take your guilt to God in prayer. He'll forgive and use your godly sorrow and mine to make us new.

Lord, we're sorry for the times we fail to love and obey.
Give us clean hearts that love you. Amen.

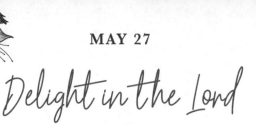

Delight in the Lord

*Take delight in the LORD, and he will give you
the desires of your heart.* PSALM 37:4

When we delight in the Lord, we look to him all the time. We read stories in the Bible to see how he conquered armies, helped the sick and suffering, and performed miracles. In prayer we share our thoughts and invite him to speak to our hearts and minds. We sing and worship and meet with God's people. All through the day, we focus our minds on the One we love.

As we delight in the Lord, something big changes inside of us. We start to want what God wants. What's important to him becomes important to us. Our dreams and hopes for tomorrow start to agree with his will and plans for our lives. Our wants and wishes begin to mirror what he holds in store. He transforms our hearts to enjoy Jesus more than anything in the world.

As we delight in God, we can know he delights in us too. He loves to bless us. His desires for us are better than anything we could imagine on our own. As we love and follow him, he'll satisfy our hearts in every way.

Lord, you created us and you "rejoice over us with singing" (Zeph. 3:17).
May we delight in you and receive all the blessings
you have in store. Amen.

Taking Blessings for Granted

"When I fed them, they were satisfied; when they were satisfied, they became proud; then they forgot me." HOSEA 13:6

Have you seen a kid so excited to play with a gift that she forgot to say thank you? Have you sat down to a holiday feast, but moments later were too full to enjoy dessert? Have you been pleased with a high score, a bonus, or a promotion because you thought it was just what you deserved? When we feel satisfied, we often take our blessings for granted. We can be proud and take the credit for what we've got.

If we look around, we see God's kindness everywhere. We're warm, safe, and fed. Our shelves hold books and fun things to do. We run out of room in drawers and closets to hold all we've been given. Nothing keeps us from learning, working, and growing. God is a faithful provider who satisfies our needs. He does more than we ask or imagine. He is worthy of all our praise and thanks.

In God's love, we're never forgotten. He knows what we need before we ask him (Matthew 6:8). He's our helper, protector, and provider every day. Do we remember all he's done to take care of us? We can pray for humble hearts that remember his love. He'll help us understand that "every good and perfect gift is from above, coming down from the Father of the heavenly lights" (James 1:17). In him, we'll be satisfied forever.

Lord, may we never forget that every good thing is from your hand.
Let us thank you always. Amen.

Truly Trusting in God

*"Ignorant are those who carry about idols of wood, who pray
to gods that cannot save. Turn to me and be saved, all you
ends of the earth; for I am God, and there is no other.
They will say of me, 'In the Lord alone are deliverance
and strength.'"* Isaiah 45:20, 22, 24

Who can give us eternal life? Who holds victory over sin and Satan? Who gives strength when we're tired? Who promises to rescue us when we're in trouble? We can depend on many things for help—money, other people, our own talent and success—but God holds more power than anyone or anything.

At the heart of our sin is pride that says we can take care of ourselves. We trust in what we can see and touch instead of God in heaven. When trouble comes, we try to fight our own battles. It's tempting to think we're strong and smart enough to handle what comes our way.

The Bible says that's foolish thinking. God announced to the whole world that he is where help comes from. He is the deliverer from sin, death, and darkness. He leads us to live in his glorious light. He comforts our pain and rescues us from our enemies. We can call on him and know he'll answer.

Lord, we're ignorant to think idols of our own making can save us.
Teach our hearts to trust you as our true Savior. Amen.

God Knows Our Limits

*The Lord is my shepherd, I lack nothing. He makes me lie down
in green pastures, he leads me beside quiet waters,
he refreshes my soul. He guides me along the right
paths for his name's sake.* Psalm 23:1-3

In this world, people try to be independent and tough. If you struggle, you're told what to do: "Pull it together!" "Stand on your own two feet." "Get back up and try again." "Quitters never win and winners never quit." You can't show feelings or admit your weakness.

Yet God knows our limits. We can pretend to be strong, but he knows when we're afraid. Nobody knows all the answers. Everybody feels hurt, disappointed, and alone at times. Life is too hard to handle on our own.

God is a shepherd who loves his sheep. He cares for us and leads where we should go. If we follow him, he gives all we need. He takes away the pressure to work and win so we can rest. When we feel we're not good enough, he tells us we're loved. If we're confused or lost, he takes us by the hand to guide our way.

Our Shepherd says, "Peace I leave with you; my peace I give you. I do not give to you as the world gives. Do not let your hearts be troubled and do not be afraid" (John 14:27). Let's follow him today.

Lord, lead us to your peace and rest. Amen.

Transforming Hearts

"But they refused to pay attention; stubbornly they turned
their backs and covered their ears. They made their hearts
as hard as flint and would not listen to the law or to
the words that the LORD Almighty had sent by his
Spirit through the earlier prophets." ZECHARIAH 7:11-12

While dough is soft, we can shape it into any form we like. It can be flattened, rolled, or decorated any way we please. Our hearts are like that, too. When they're soft, God can shape us to look like Jesus. He molds our attitudes so we're kind and loving. His Word changes our thoughts and moves us to do what's right. The seal of the Spirit is pressed on our hearts to show we're his.

If we ignore the Lord and his Word, our hearts grow hard. We forget the sound of God's voice. We become stubborn and refuse to obey. We have no interest in prayer. Pride takes hold so we lose patience and compassion for others. The love in us grows cold.

Do we have soft hearts today? We can ask God to make his Word true in us: "I will give them an undivided heart and put a new spirit in them; I will remove from them their heart of stone and give them a heart of flesh … They will be my people, and I will be their God" (Ezekiel 11:19-20).

Lord, give us soft hearts so we will listen,
obey, and love you always. Amen.

June

Loyalty to God and Each Other

*They set up Baal-Berith as their god and did not remember
the LORD their God, who had rescued them from the hands
of all their enemies on every side. They also failed to show
any loyalty to the family of Jerub-Baal (that is, Gideon) in spite
of all the good things he had done for them.* JUDGES 8:33-35

Loyalty says, "I'm with you, and you're with me." You open your wallet to help cover his bill. He cries for your pain and you celebrate his success. We stick up for each other if we feel harassed or insulted.

When the load is heavy and the work is too hard, we tackle it together. We remember who has our back.

That kind of loyalty makes us better together. We don't have to face hard times on our own. We help each other remember God's love.

In the face of temptation or life's battles, we fight side by side. The greater our loyalty, the harder it is to break us apart.

Lord, keep us loyal to you and faithful to each other. Amen.

JUNE 2

You Have God's Full Attention

Hear my prayer, LORD; let my cry for help come to you.
Do not hide your face from me when I am in distress.
Turn your ear to me; when I call, answer me quickly. PSALM 102:1-2

When you need to talk to God, he's never too busy to listen. You don't have to wait for him to set aside his work or devices. He doesn't ask you to be quiet while he finishes something more important. God will never ignore you, plug his ears, or turn his face away. You're his child and you hold his attention the moment you pray.

Do you have a worry on your mind today? Is there a problem or struggle that won't go away? Are you scared, upset, or confused? Call on God and tell him all about it. Ask him for help. Trust him to listen and answer. He cares how you feel and wants to show how much he loves you.

Lord, you never hide your face from your children. Teach us to trust
your love and cry out to you whenever we need your help. Amen.

By Way of the Heart

*If you declare with your mouth, "Jesus is Lord," and believe
in your heart that God raised him from the dead, you will
be saved. For it is with your heart that you believe and
are justified, and it is with your mouth that you
profess your faith and are saved.* ROMANS 10:9-10

Everybody is born with a sin problem. We're blind to God's truth and determined to go our own way. Separated from God, we have no hope of heaven. We need rescue from the power of sin and darkness. How can we be saved?

We're not saved by our hands and feet—by what we do and where we go. We're not saved by our brains, through intelligence and clever thinking. Salvation isn't found in our stomach, by what we eat or drink. We're not saved by our eyes as we read and look for answers. Salvation comes by way of the heart as we believe in Jesus, and with our mouths we tell what he's done.

Have you put your faith in God to be saved? Jesus is God's only Son, sent to "seek and save the lost" (Luke 19:10). He took the punishment for our sins on the cross, so we may be called innocent. He'll give courage to tell everyone that we believe. He wants to save you and make you his child forever.

Lord, we thank you for "so great a salvation" (Hebrews 2:3).
Your love is life. Amen.

JUNE 4

A Picture of God's Love

*Husbands, love your wives, just as Christ loved the church and
gave himself up for her ... In this same way, husbands ought
to love their wives as their own bodies. He who loves his wife
loves himself. After all, no one ever hated their own body,
but they feed and care for their body, just as Christ does
the church—for we are members of his body.*
EPHESIANS 5:25, 28-30

God uses the family as a picture of his love for us. He calls himself our Father to show he takes care of us like a good dad. He calls Jesus our brother to show he's always right by our side. And, he compares his love for his people—the church—to the love a husband has for his wife.

When a husband loves like Jesus, he puts his wife first. He does all he can to meet her needs and protect her from harm. If she lets him down, he is patient and forgiving. A loving husband takes care of his wife's heart by showing respect, patience, and understanding. If she's sad, he comforts her. When she's hurt or tired, he offers his help and strength. He earns her trust by telling the truth and keeping his promises. A godly husband is faithful in every way.

Jesus' love is perfect and never fails. He wants us to know how kind, caring, and generous he truly is. Every time we see a husband who loves his wife, we see the love of God.

Lord, reveal the love of Jesus through our family.
Teach us how to love each other like you. Amen.

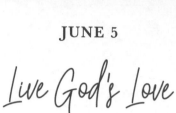

JUNE 5

Live God's Love

Even small children are known by their actions, so is their conduct really pure and upright? PROVERBS 20:11

It's important to remind our children that just because they're young, it doesn't mean people aren't watching their actions! Their actions and choices are giving them a reputation. Their words and habits get noticed and have the power to influence others for good.

Every time they talk to teachers and coaches with respect, they set a standard for their friends to follow. Friendships grow every time they avoid gossip and teasing and use their words to build people up. Their honesty gives people faith in their word. Their generosity is contagious, and their hard work pays off. Every time they do what's right, they become the kind of person others can count on.

Remind your kids that they are never too young for God to use. Jesus is ready to love people through the love and kindness they share. They can talk about his Word and share God's truth. God has made each one of us an important part of his family. You don't have to wait until you're older to serve God and make a difference.

Lord, everybody counts in your family.
Reward my kids' love and obedience to you. Amen.

JUNE 6

Wondering About Heaven

And he carried me away in the Spirit to a mountain great and high,
and showed me the Holy City, Jerusalem, coming down
out of heaven from God. REVELATION 21:10

Everybody wonders about heaven. Revelation 21 describes the city where we'll live with God forever:

It shone with the glory of God, and its brilliance was like that of a very precious jewel, like a jasper, clear as crystal. It had a great, high wall with twelve gates, and with twelve angels at the gates. There were three gates on the east, three on the north, three on the south and three on the west.

[The angel] measured the city with the rod and found it to be [1400 miles] in length, and as wide and high as it is long. The wall was made of jasper, and the city of pure gold, as pure as glass. The foundations of the city walls were decorated with every kind of precious stone. The twelve gates were twelve pearls, each gate made of a single pearl. The great street of the city was of gold, as pure as transparent glass.

The city does not need the sun or the moon to shine on it, for the glory of God gives it light, and the Lamb is its lamp. On no day will its gates ever be shut, for there will be no night there (vv. 11-13, 16, 18-19, 21, 23, 25).

God is preparing this beautiful place for us even now. We have a future of perfect joy together with him.

Lord, we're excited to see you and our glorious home.
Give us patience and joy as we wait for you. Amen.

The Race of Faith

Do you not know that in a race all the runners run, but only one gets the prize? Run in such a way as to get the prize. Everyone who competes in the games goes into strict training. They do it to get a crown that will not last, but we do it to get a crown that will last forever. 1 CORINTHIANS 9:24-25

It takes months of training to run the 26 miles of a marathon. Day after day, mile after mile, runners build up endurance and strength. They can run the race without giving up. At the finish line, they celebrate and receive their reward.

We're running a tough race of faith. We stumble over temptation to sin. We "become weary in doing good" and helping others (Galatians 6:9). False teachers confuse our minds, pulling us off course. Doubt and fear stop us in our tracks. How do we keep running with so much against us?

To run the race, we keep our eyes on Jesus. We pray to know his love. We listen to the Word and do what it says (James 1:22). We commit to the church that will encourage us as we run side by side. And, we trust God to get us to the finish line. "He will also keep you firm to the end, so that you will be blameless on the day of our Lord Jesus Christ" (1 Corinthians 1:8).

Lord, give us strength to run the race of faith to the end. Amen.

Thirsting for God

*As the deer pants for streams of water, so my soul pants
for you, my God. My soul thirsts for God, for the living God.
When can I go and meet with God?* PSALM 42:1-2

Remember the excitement you felt right before the final school bell rang before vacation? You've watched the clock, waiting for someone special to arrive for a visit. After a long, exhausting day, all you've wanted to do is fall into bed and sleep. And when you're sick or hurt, you can feel desperate for medicine to take the pain away. In our waiting, it's hard to think about anything else!

Imagine a thirst for God that feels like your life depends on it. You can't wait to hear what he has to say. You're desperate for his help in the middle of your problems. When you feel bullied or alone, you want your best friend Jesus by your side. As he loves you in every way, you're excited to worship and give thanks.

Yet instead of "thirsting" for God, we can take him for granted. We grow used to his gifts. We forget to call on him when we're hurting. Our busy days distract us from prayer or reading the Bible. We can ask God to change our hearts. By his Spirit, we can love him and depend on him more and more.

Lord, we want to want you! Make our hearts thirsty
for more and more of your love. Amen.

Take a Look in the Mirror

"Why do you look at the speck of sawdust in your brother's eye and pay no attention to the plank in your own eye? How can you say to your brother, 'Brother, let me take the speck out of your eye,' when you yourself fail to see the plank in your own eye?" LUKE 6:41-42

We've all got a problem with sin. We struggle to be honest and admit our mistakes. We lose our patience and our tempers. We forget our promises and let people down. Even with the best of intentions, we fail to love and we disobey God's Word.

We'd like to wear a blindfold so we don't have to look at the ways we miss the mark. It's hard to face the guilt, embarrassment, and consequences of our sins. Yet, we're quick to notice how others have failed to do what's right. It's tempting to focus on others' failures instead of our own.

Before we point fingers and try to fix everybody around us, let's take a close look at ourselves. If we disobeyed God, let's pray and confess what we've done. If we hurt someone, let's make it right. If we have a bad habit or a secret sin we're holding on to, let's repent and turn back to God. He is ready and waiting to forgive and make us new.

Lord, forgive us for hypocrisy that judges others for what we do ourselves. Create a pure heart in us, and help us to love like you. Amen.

Open Your Eyes

*For in him all things were created ... all things have been created
through him and for him. For since the creation of the world
God's invisible qualities—his eternal power and divine nature—
have been clearly seen, being understood from what has been made,
so that people are without excuse.* COLOSSIANS 1:16, ROMANS 1:20

Even though we can't see God with our eyes, he's not hiding. He wants everyone to discover he's real, he's close, and he's full of love. He shows himself to each person through the natural world he created.

God's mighty strength is shown through the winds of a storm and the waves in the ocean. The cycle of seasons and the movement of planets across the galaxy prove his precise control of the universe. The sun's warmth and the moon's light remind us he shines light in the darkness of our hearts. Tiny seeds grow into towering trees, revealing his power to "do immeasurably more than all we ask or imagine" (Ephesians 3:20). The earth is a living testimony of the beauty and glory of our God.

If you're feeling like God is far away or hard to recognize, look outside. Let his creation refresh your heart and mind. The earth is intricate, awesome, and very good—just like the One who made it.

Lord, open our eyes to see your qualities in the world you made.
Inspire us to worship you as we enjoy your creation. Amen.

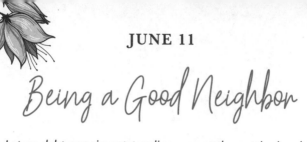

JUNE 11

Being a Good Neighbor

*Let no debt remain outstanding, except the continuing debt
to love one another, for whoever loves others has fulfilled
the law. ... whatever other command there may be,
are summed up in this one command:
"Love your neighbor as yourself."* ROMANS 13:8-9

Who do we call our neighbors? Are they the people who live on our street? Who work at our company, shop at our local stores, and visit our library? Are neighbors the ones who look like us and speak our language? Do they share our views on politics, religion, and education? What makes someone our neighbor?

When a religious person in the Bible asked Jesus that same question, Jesus told a story. A wounded man was ignored until a stranger showed mercy and helped him. Jesus called the helper a "neighbor" to show us what it means (Luke 10:29-37). We're neighbors when we're kind and generous. Neighbors love their enemies and forgive. They're gentle and respectful, honest and trust-worthy. Neighbors pray and build each other up. When times are tough, they stay by your side.

Who is God calling us to love as a neighbor? Who needs care in their sickness or struggle? Who needs forgiveness for offending and hurting our feelings? Who is lonely and waiting to be included? Who needs patience and prayer to overcome their sins and weaknesses? Which neighbor needs mercy today? Let's choose to love others like Jesus loves you and me.

Lord, may we love our neighbor as ourselves for your name's sake.
Amen.

What Do You Think?

*Finally, brothers and sisters, whatever is true, whatever is noble,
whatever is right, whatever is pure, whatever is lovely, whatever
is admirable—if anything is excellent or praiseworthy—
think about such things.* PHILIPPIANS 4:8

We can control our fists when we're angry. If we're trying to eat healthy foods, we can keep sugary treats off our plate. We can leave money at home to keep from overspending at the store. If our friends begin to gossip, we can turn and walk away. We grow in strength to stand firm and do what's right.

Yet even as we choose to do good on the outside, it's difficult to control what's inside our hearts and minds. We imagine the ugly words we'd say when we're mad. Browsing online stores and catalogs, we covet what we can't afford to buy. In our thoughts, we criticize others' looks and habits. Unwholesome shows we've seen replay in our heads. If we let our thoughts go where they like, they can take us where we don't want to go.

With God's help, we can control our thoughts just like our words and our bodies. The Spirit is renewing our minds to make us more like Jesus (Romans 12:2). We've been set free from the power of sin. We have all we need to "take captive every thought to make it obedient to Christ" (2 Corinthians 10:5).

Lord, make our thoughts true, loving, and worthy of praise. Amen.

JUNE 13

Finding True Life

"Whoever does not take up their cross and follow me is not worthy of me. Whoever finds their life will lose it, and whoever loses their life for my sake will find it." MATTHEW 10:38-39

We want our life to count. Even as kids, we imagine the life we want. We might aim for college scholarships to build a career and a bank account. A young athlete might train for years so he can be recruited and go pro. A girl could strive for an image that wins fame on social media. We dream of the life we're looking for.

Can we find life in money and success? Fame and popularity? Friends and family? Adventure and fun? God says if we look for life in this world, we'll be disappointed.

Nothing here can satisfy our souls. In the end, all we've gained will pass away. God offers life that's better than anything the world can offer. He sent Jesus who said, "I have come that they may have life, and have it to the full" (John 10:10). Through his death on the cross, we can be reborn into eternal life. By serving him with all our heart, we earn "treasure in heaven that will never fail, where no thief comes near and no moth destroys" (Luke 12:33).

Jesus leads to the life of peace and joy we're searching for. "The world and its desires pass away, but whoever does the will of God lives forever" (1 John 2:17).

Lord, life is found in you alone. May we take up our cross
and follow you. Amen.

What Is Money For?

*Command those who are rich in this present world not to be
arrogant nor to put their hope in wealth, which is so uncertain,
but to put their hope in God, who richly provides us
with everything for our enjoyment.* 1 TIMOTHY 6:17

We use money to pay for groceries, clothes, and home supplies. We pay the bills for our phone, electricity, and water. Money pays for books to read, trips to exciting places, and tickets to the movies. Our money allows us to eat, stay clean and comfortable, and have fun together.

But for many, money is not just for shopping and bills. Money is a security blanket that makes them feel safe. They think, "If I have enough money, nothing bad will happen to me. I'll always have what I need."

For others, money makes them feel important. They drive new cars that turn heads on the road. Expensive clothes stand out in the crowd. They use their money to say, "I'm a success. I can buy whatever I want. Don't you wish you were rich like me?"

As God's children, we know money is a gift from God. We're thankful for all he provides. Instead of looking for peace at the bank, we find it in our Father. Let's trust him with humble hearts and make his name great.

Lord, you are the source of all we need. Amen.

JUNE 15

A Fragrant Offering

... a woman came with an alabaster jar of very expensive
perfume, made of pure nard. She broke the jar and poured
the perfume on his head. Some of those present were saying
indignantly to one another, "Why this waste of perfume?"
And they rebuked her harshly. "Leave her alone,"
said Jesus. " ... She has done a beautiful
thing to me." MARK 14:3-6

Sometimes it's as wonderful to give a gift as to receive one yourself. You know the excitement of watching your friend or family unwrap what you've prepared just for them. As they receive your special gift, joy fills your heart, too.

Wouldn't you like to give a gift to Jesus? Imagine spending all your money, creativity, and time on a gift that says, "I love you" to the Savior. Yet without him here in the flesh, wrapping a lavish gift is impossible.

What can we give to Jesus? What he wants most is our love. To Jesus, love means feeding the hungry and opening our door to the stranger. Love is caring for the sick and visiting those in prison. Love remembers the thirsty and those in need. Jesus tells us, "Whatever you did for one of the least of these brothers and sisters of mine, you did for me" (Matthew 25:37-40).

Let's care for others to show we love Jesus. Our gifts will be "a fragrant offering, an acceptable sacrifice, pleasing to God (Philippians 4:18).

Lord, may our love be a fragrant offering to you. Amen.

JUNE 16

Saying 'No' to Forbidden Fruit

*Now the serpent was more crafty than any of the
wild animals the L𝐨𝐫𝐝 God had made. He said to
the woman, "Did God really say, 'You must not eat
from any tree in the garden'?"* G𝐄𝐍𝐄𝐒𝐈𝐒 3:1

The garden was a perfect home for Adam and Eve. They had water, the animals, and time with God face-to-face. Delicious fruit was ripe for the picking. God gave just one rule: "You are free to eat from any tree in the garden; but you must not eat from the tree of the knowledge of good and evil, for when you eat from it you will certainly die" (Genesis 2:16-17).

The snake, or Satan, tempted them to disobey that rule. Even though they could eat from any other tree they liked, he made them crave more. His question, "Did God really say?" made them doubt God's goodness and love.

Sometimes we crave forbidden fruit, too. We're greedy or jealous of others. We want to go our own way. We feel we're missing out. The enemy whispers, "Did God really say?" We doubt God and choose to sin.

God will help us answer the question. His Spirit "will teach you all things and will remind you of everything [Jesus] said to you" in the Bible (John 14:26). We can pray for strength to stand firm and know the Word. We have all we need to love and obey.

Lord, give us faith to obey your Word. Amen.

JUNE 17

A Fantastic Show of Strength

When [God] thunders, the waters in the heavens roar; he makes
clouds rise from the ends of the earth. He sends lightning with
the rain and brings out the wind from his storehouses. JEREMIAH 10:13

We've heard the expression, "Where there's smoke, there's fire." The scent of cinnamon and apples is a good sign a delicious pie is in the oven. Music, balloons, and a cake show it's time to celebrate a birthday.

God gives signs to the world to show he's real and powerful. A storm is a fantastic show of his strength. What other voice can boom like thunder in the clouds? Who else shines as brightly as a flash of lightning? Whose breath can blow like the wind, toppling trees and tossing waves in the sea? What other hand can water the earth with fresh rain?

A storm can be frightening. We cover our ears and flinch when thunder and lightning cross the skies. Yet our fear turns to courage when we see God's power in the storm. It's his mighty strength that keeps us safe. He conquered death, sin, and the evil one. He not only brings the clouds, he quiets the winds and waves with one word. He holds the heavens and the earth in his hands.

Lord, let us praise your mighty name in every storm. Amen.

What Money Can't Buy

The decrees of the LORD are firm, and all of them are righteous.
They are more precious than gold, than much pure gold;
they are sweeter than honey, than honey from the
honeycomb. By them your servant is warned; in
keeping them there is great reward. PSALM 19:9-11

Imagine if we discovered a buried treasure chest full of gold coins. With those riches, we could move into a mansion. We could buy shiny new cars, shop at pricey boutiques, and take exotic vacations around the globe. Everybody would say we had the world at our feet.

Yet no matter what money can buy, God offers something much better. His Word is a priceless treasure. Money can buy a house, but the Bible tells how to build a strong family. Wealth can pay for an education, but God's truth transforms your mind with wisdom. A rich person might be popular, but the Bible tells how to be friends with the King of kings. God's Word offers true joy, hope, and eternal life.

Earthly treasure is easily stolen, lost, or wasted. Let's turn our hearts toward something sweeter and more precious—the knowledge and wisdom of God in his Word. "Jesus said, 'If you hold to my teaching, you are really my disciples. Then you will know the truth, and the truth will set you free'" (John 8:31-32).

Lord, teach us to hold the Bible as our greatest treasure.
Your Word is our life. Amen.

JUNE 19

No Place Like Home

"Suppose one of you has a hundred sheep and loses one of them. Doesn't he leave the ninety-nine in the open country and go after the lost sheep until he finds it? And when he finds it, he joyfully puts it on his shoulders and goes home." LUKE 15:4-5

There is no place like home. It's so familiar, you can make your way through its rooms in the dark. Your own bed feels wonderful after returning from a trip. You can help yourself to what's in the refrigerator. It offers privacy and a spot just for you.

Home is where you can be yourself. It's where you rest when you're sick and tired. Home surrounds you with those who know you best and love you no matter what. At home, you belong.

As God's child, you belong to him too. He's creating an eternal home for us right now. We can lose our way home by falling into sin and doubt. We may turn away from church and the Bible. We can grow stubborn and determined to go our own way. No matter how far we wander, God will go and find us. He'll do whatever it takes to bring us home to himself.

Today, are you living close to God or have you traveled far from him? Call on your Father and he'll bring you home to stay.

Lord, we thank you for Jesus who came to seek and save the lost.
We want to be home with you forever. Amen.

Waiting for Joy

... weeping may stay for the night, but rejoicing comes in the morning.
You turned my wailing into dancing; you removed my sackcloth
and clothed me with joy, that my heart may sing your praises and
not be silent. LORD my God, I will praise you forever. PSALM 30:5, 11-12

When your friends have left your side, you think you'll be lonely forever. After losing a dear loved one, it seems the tears of grief will never stop. When the money runs out, you see trouble in front of you with no end in sight. Are we truly doomed to suffer stress and sadness forever? Is the darkness a night with no end?

God offers hope in our struggles. Just as the sun brightens the sky each morning, God will bring joy once more. We can trust in his promise in Lamentations 3: Because of the Lord's great love we are not consumed, for his compassions never fail. They are new every morning; great is your faithfulness. I say to myself, "The LORD is my portion; therefore I will wait for him" (vv. 22-24).

What breaks your heart today? Which burdens weigh you down? Don't give up ... God will put a smile of joy on your face. You'll celebrate his healing and help. The darkness of today will give way to his joyful light.

Lord, help us to trust that morning is coming because of your love.
Amen.

JUNE 21

The Right Direction

*Trust in the LORD with all your heart and lean not
on your own understanding; in all your ways submit to him,
and he will make your paths straight.* PROVERBS 3:5-6

Even kids face tough decisions. Should they play soccer or join the cross-country team? What might they do for a career when they grow up? Will they save their money or spend it on something new? Should they go away to camp or stay home for the summer? Choices are difficult for anyone. We're afraid we'll make a mistake or regret what we've done.

It's especially hard when we run into trouble. We look at all the options to solve our problem. We ask for advice and for answers to our questions. As we worry, we search for a safe and simple road to safety.

God knows every detail of our lives. Our struggles come as no surprise, since he holds our days in his hand. When we panic, he's strong and faithful. When we're confused, he's wise and knows what to do. If we feel trapped with no way out, he can open the door and set us free.

Are you standing at a crossroads today? Do you feel afraid? If we ask God, he'll give wisdom and point you in the right direction. He'll give you courage to move forward. Let's trust him, listen to his voice, and obey him in everything.

Lord, may we trust you to guide our steps. Amen.

Put God in Charge

*"For my thoughts are not your thoughts, neither are your ways
my ways," declares the LORD. "As the heavens are higher
than the earth, so are my ways higher than your ways
and my thoughts than your thoughts."* ISAIAH 55:8-9

If you climbed a tree, stood on a mountain, or flew in the sky on a plane, you could see much farther all around you. When we're low to the ground, we're only able to see what's close by. God is above all things so he understands the big picture of how our lives fit together. We can trust him completely because he can see and understand all that's happening.

God is ready and able to help when we feel confused or discouraged. He knows which way we should go. He's fully in control of our situation. As our Father, he knows what's best and will use even hard times for our good in the end.

Since God knows everything and only does what's right, let's put him in charge. Let's obey him and follow wherever he leads. He is worthy of our faith and our worship all the time.

Lord, you hold all knowledge, wisdom, and understanding.
Help us to trust you completely. Amen.

JUNE 23

The Right Attitude

*"Be careful not to practice your righteousness in front of others
to be seen by them. If you do, you will have no reward
from your Father in heaven. … But when you give to the needy,
do not let your left hand know what your right hand is doing,
so that your giving may be in secret."* MATTHEW 6:1, 3-4

As followers of Jesus, we're called to be givers and helpers. If a neighbor's refrigerator is empty, we can drop off a bag of groceries. If the homeless are cold and hungry, we can serve or donate to a shelter. If a coworker loses their transportation, we can offer a ride in the morning. Whether it's clothes, food, money, or a helping hand, our gifts can make a difference.

Yet as we give, we have to examine our hearts. Are we giving for others or for ourselves? Do we expect gratitude and attention for our giving? Do good deeds make us feel proud or superior? Are we trying to show off our blessings? God says true giving comes from love. Not love for ourselves and our own reputation, but love for God and the ones he sent Jesus to save.

Let's be cheerful givers who make God's name great instead of our own. We can give quietly, respectfully, and prayerfully so God gets all the glory.

Lord, make us humble as we serve the ones you love. Amen.

Stay Attached to the Vine

*"I am the vine; you are the branches. If you remain in me and
I in you, you will bear much fruit; apart from me you can
do nothing. This is to my Father's glory, that you bear much
fruit, showing yourselves to be my disciples."* JOHN 15:5, 8

God holds the greatest blessings if we stay attached to him. Just like a branch is joined to a vine, we stay close to God. This means praying every day about your troubles, joys, and questions. You learn to hear his voice as you pray.

Remaining in God means listening to his words. In the Bible, we discover the love, power, and wisdom of our Father. It teaches how we can love him, too, by obeying God and loving people around us. His living Word changes us from the inside out.

Prayer, the Bible, the Spirit, and the church keep us connected to God. We then bear fruit like love, joy, and goodness in our lives. If we remain in Jesus, we become like Jesus.

Lord, keep us close to you all the time. Amen.

Fertile Ground

*For as the soil makes the sprout come up and a garden
causes seeds to grow, so the Sovereign LORD
will make righteousness and praise spring up
before all nations.* ISAIAH 61:11

*"But the seed falling on good soil refers to someone who hears
the word and understands it. This is the one who produces
a crop, yielding a hundred, sixty or thirty times what
was sown."* MATTHEW 13:23

What kind of fruits, vegetables, or grains did you eat today? Can you imagine where your food came from? Carrots and tomatoes, berries and beans, oats and wheat begin as one little seed. If a seed falls on hard, dry ground it may never sprout at all. Rocks, weeds, and thorns keep a seed from becoming a fruitful plant. Just like a farmer plants in good, rich soil to grow an abundant crop, God puts seeds of faith in you and me.

The "soil" of our heart and mind can be like hard ground. The Bible warns, "Today, if you hear his voice, do not harden your hearts … See to it, brothers and sisters, that none of you has a sinful, unbelieving heart that turns away from the living God" (Hebrews 3:7-8, 12). A hard heart will not trust, obey, or love Jesus.

With good soil, we're eager to hear God's Word. We love the Lord with all our heart, soul, mind, and strength (Mark 12:30). He'll grow us so we know him and share his love with the world.

Lord, grow righteousness and praise in the soil of our hearts. Amen.

Choose Your Friends Wisely

The righteous choose their friends carefully,
but the way of the wicked leads
them astray. PROVERBS 12:26

We make choices every day. Some decisions are simple, such as which socks to put on our feet or what to eat for lunch. A sandwich isn't going to change our life, so we don't spend too much time worrying about it.

Other decisions, however, make a huge impact. Today's spending affects tomorrow's savings. Using a helmet or seatbelt keeps us from serious injuries. The places we live, work, learn, and worship affect us every day. One of the most important choices we make is our friendships.

When we decide who to share our lives with, we must choose carefully. Will they build us up or tear us down? Will they encourage us to do what's right or tempt us to sin? Can we trust them with our hurts, fears, and secrets? Have they put their trust in Jesus? Will they pray for us and praise God with us in the ups and downs of life? Are they generous and kind? Honest and respectful? Our friends shape our thoughts and attitudes. True friends give joy that lasts.

A friend is a gift from God. He'll help us to choose wisely. And, he'll show us how to be the kind of friends who love like Jesus.

Lord, help us to choose our friends carefully. Keep us
from those who will lead us away from you. Amen.

Hope and Joy in Every Season

*There is a time for everything, and a season for every activity
under the heavens: a time to be born and a time to die, a time
to plant and a time to uproot ... a time to weep and a time
to laugh, a time to mourn and a time to dance ... a time
to search and a time to give up, a time to keep and a time
to throw away, a time to tear and a time to mend, a time
to be silent and a time to speak ...* ECCLESIASTES 3:1-2, 4, 6-7

The variety of seasons is fun. During the year we can enjoy popsicles and pools, apples and pumpkins, cocoa and snowmen, and eggs and flowers. Each season brings its own weather, holidays, and sports to enjoy.

Life has seasons, too. The school year is a season for learning. A new baby brings days of cuddles and joy. Sickness forces a time of rest. Do you notice how in the middle of one season, we grow impatient for the next one to come? It's hard to be content right where we are.

God offers help and hope every day of the year. We can say, "But I trust in you, LORD; I say, 'You are my God.' My times are in your hands" (Psalm 31:14-15). What are the hard and happy parts of this season? What are you looking forward to? What is God teaching us today?

Lord, you planned all our days and you're in control.
No matter the season, you're working for our good
because you love us. Amen.

JUNE 28

Talk to God

And pray in the Spirit on all occasions with all kinds of prayers
and requests. With this in mind, be alert and always
keep on praying for all the Lord's people. EPHESIANS 6:18

With technology, we can stay up to date with everyone we know. We find out who is sick, going on a trip, or celebrating a special occasion. People share their feelings about everything from politics to the weather outside. We're able to communicate at any moment about anything!

Yet even as we view others' situations, we can't do much to change them. With God it's different. He's available to us every second of the day through prayer. Whenever we're worried, excited, or concerned for others, we can ask him for help. He wants to hear everything on our minds, and he's ready to make a difference in every detail of our lives.

Nothing is too big or small to talk about with God. He's always listening and promises to answer when we call on him. Let's pray about our fears and worries. Our joys and praises. Our plans and dreams. We can pray all the time about everything, both for our family and those around us.

Lord, thank you for inviting us to pray to you about all things.
Teach us to go to you with our problems. Take care
of the people in our lives. Your love and power
give us hope every day. Amen.

JUNE 29

Spreading the Good News

"Everyone who calls on the name of the Lord will be saved."
How, then, can they call on the one they have not believed in?
And how can they believe in the one of whom they have
not heard? And how can they hear without someone
preaching to them? ROMANS 10:13-14

Who first told you about the Lord? Did you learn from a parent or relative, a teacher, a pastor, or a friend? Before you heard his name, you didn't know about our God. You didn't know he created you, loves you, and sent his Son into the world to save you. You had not heard about the hope of eternal life in heaven. Once someone preached or told you about Jesus, you could understand and believe.

Now that you know the Lord, you can tell others about him. It's more than being nice and kind. It goes beyond good deeds and helping the poor. While our actions show our faith in God, we need to use our voices too. We tell the truth about Jesus so others can know him.

What can we tell about Jesus today? We can share how he's answered our prayers. We can share verses from the Bible about God's love. We can tell how he took away our guilt, fear, and shame and gave us freedom and joy. Wherever we go, we speak about the One who gave us life.

Lord, thank you for those who told us about Jesus.
Give us courage to tell the good news! Amen.

Living for the Next Life

*Jesus said to her, "I am the resurrection and the life. The one
who believes in me will live, even though they die;
and whoever lives by believing in me will never die.
Do you believe this?"* JOHN 11:25-26

Have you heard of people who make a "bucket list"? They imagine all the exciting things to do and places to travel before they die. Others chase success and money, trying to gain as many rewards and riches as possible in their lifetime. They say, "You can't take it with you." "You only live once." "It's now or never." "If this is the only life there is, we have to make the most of it."

Those people are right—our life in this world will end. Yet they ignore God's Word that says we pass on to eternal life. If we believe in Jesus, he will raise us to life with him forever. He'll take us home to the place he's preparing even now. There, we'll live in glory with his people. We'll have no pain. No crying. No sin or fear. We'll be with our heavenly Father, always.

Our eternal life with Jesus is better than anything this world can offer. If we suffer a little while here, we know that joy is coming that will never end. Do you believe this? If we trust in Jesus, we have hope for all time.

Lord, in you we're alive for eternity. Amen.

July

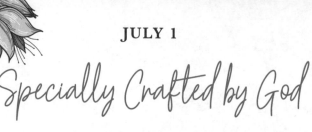

JULY 1

Specially Crafted by God

For you created my inmost being; you knit me together
in my mother's womb. I praise you because I am fearfully
and wonderfully made; your works are wonderful,
I know that full well. PSALM 139:13-14

When we craft something with our own hands, we cherish it. It's satisfying to see an idea in our minds take shape in our hands. We feel a sense of pride as we put our work on display or share it for others to enjoy. As people made in the image of God, our creativity is a little expression of Jesus' imagination as he created all things.

God's most precious creation is you, me, and all the people made. He says we are wonderful (v. 14). We are known. Seen. Planned. Precious and honored. Chosen. Loved. As the work of God's hands, he knows every detail about you. He knows your ideas, hopes and dreams, and fears. He knows your thoughts and the words you say. He's counted every hair on your head and numbered each day of your life. As "God's handiwork," he holds you as his "special possession" (Ephesians 2:10, 1 Peter 2:9).

Is it hard to believe you're truly a "wonderful work" in the eyes of God? When you look in the mirror, do you only see flaws or mistakes? Take another look and see the person God loves through and through.

Lord, we praise you as our Maker. Let us trust in your love
as your treasured children. Amen.

Put Others First

"Do you understand what I have done for you?" he asked them. "Now that I, your Lord and Teacher, have washed your feet, you also should wash one another's feet. I have set you an example that you should do as I have done for you." JOHN 13:12, 14-15

Who is Jesus? He's the Son of the Most High. He's the King of kings. Prince of Peace. Mighty one. The way, the truth, and the life. The Word. The name that is above every name. He is worthy of our praise forever and ever.

Yet this Jesus, whom we worship and obey, chose to serve his servants! He bent his own knee to wash his disciples' feet. Since Jesus shows his love by helping and giving with a humble heart, we know how we should love others, too.

How can we follow Jesus' example? We put others first. We care for their needs. We take every opportunity to respect and honor our family, colleagues, and neighbors. Instead of working to feel important in this world, we do all we can to please our God. "For even the Son of Man did not come to be served, but to serve, and to give his life as a ransom for many" (Mark 10:45).

Lord, humble our hearts so we serve like Jesus.
Help us to follow his example of love. Amen.

Stirring Up Our Nest

[God] shielded him and cared for him; he guarded him as the apple of his eye, like an eagle that stirs up its nest and hovers over its young, that spreads its wings to catch them and carries them aloft. DEUTERONOMY 32:10-11

A mother eagle is a bit like a parachute. As her baby is launched from the nest, she will fly to catch it before it falls to the ground. On its mother's back, the baby can experience the feeling of flying without danger or fear.

Do you feel like you're being launched into new situations that feel a little scary? Are you trying to learn a new skill, but you struggle no matter how hard you try? Does it feel like certain people or problems are set against you? No matter what kind of trouble you face, you have a loving God watching over you. You're the "apple of his eye" and he cares for you like a Father.

God is going to "stir up our nest" to keep us from getting too comfortable. He knows if our lives were perfect and easy, we'd never learn to trust him. He couldn't teach us to hang in there and overcome with his help. He wants us to experience the excitement of answered prayers, generous blessings, and greater love than we've known before. When we do, we'll feel like we're soaring closer to heaven.

Lord, we want to fly with you! Shield us from trouble,
catch us when we're falling, and lift us up today. Amen.

Let Jesus Set You Free

Jesus said, "If you hold to my teaching, you are really my disciples.
Then you will know the truth, and the truth will set you free ...
Very truly I tell you, everyone who sins is a slave to sin. So if the
Son sets you free, you will be free indeed." JOHN 8:31-32, 34, 36

The world says the Bible is full of boring rules. It says its way is better than God's way. It doesn't know that sin is a trap. It leads to addiction. Fighting. Pain. Confusion. Sin craves more and more but is never satisfied. It leads to death. Sin separates us from God and his love.

God knows we can't break the chains of sin on our own. He sent Jesus to set us free. When he died on the cross, he took our sins away. Instead of sin controlling what we think, say, and do, we're under the power of God. He gives a life of love and joy with him forever.

Do you feel tied up by sin today? Do you struggle with temptation over and over? Are you guilty or scared? God wants to set you free from shame, fear, and regret. "If we confess our sins, he is faithful and just and will forgive us our sins and purify us from all unrighteousness" (1 John 1:9). Let Jesus set you free today.

Lord, you broke the chains of sin. Thank you for the love
and freedom we find in Jesus. Amen.

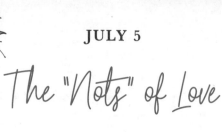

JULY 5

The "Nots" of Love

[Love] does not envy, it does not boast, it is not proud. It does not dishonor others, it is not self-seeking, it is not easily angered, it keeps no record of wrongs. Love does not delight in evil but rejoices with the truth. 1 CORINTHIANS 13:4-6

Your friends and family know you for who you are—your name and age, your real hair color and your quirks. The people close to you know your favorite song and which flavor of ice cream you crave the most. They know what you enjoy doing and who can make you laugh. In the same way, they know who you're not. You're known for what you don't like and will not do.

Love is like that. Just as love is loyal and kind, it does not treat others like they're worthless or unimportant. Love is generous and cares for others, while it's not selfish and all about you. It's not proud, but humble. Not cruel and harsh, but gentle. Not sneaky and deceitful, but honest and true. Every time we are jealous of our friends, use rude words to our family, lose our temper, or hold a grudge, we're not choosing to love.

As children of God, we're called to love like him. Let's pay attention to the "nots" of love so we can shine like Jesus in this world.

Lord, may we not fail to love as you love us so greatly. Amen.

More Mercy, Less Judgment

"Do not judge, and you will not be judged. Do not condemn, and you will not be condemned. Forgive, and you will be forgiven. Give, and it will be given to you. A good measure, pressed down, shaken together and running over, will be poured into your lap. For with the measure you use, it will be measured to you." Luke 6:37-38

What we see on the outside doesn't always match what's inside. A shirt may look soft but feel scratchy to our skin. The weather can be chilly even when the sun is shining. An appealing book cover may hold a boring story inside. We can't judge what something is like simply by its appearance.

The same is true for people. We're tempted to judge what's inside by what they look like, say, or do. But, "The Lord does not look at the things people look at. People look at the outward appearance, but the Lord looks at the heart" (1 Samuel 16:7). God alone is the judge of salvation.

Do we care more about others' sin than our own? Are we quick to point out when someone breaks the rules? Do we look down on those who struggle to do what's right? Instead, we're called to show mercy. God has forgiven us for all our sins. Our salvation is a free gift we could not earn. Let's give the same grace and forgiveness we've received to everyone we know.

Lord, give us humble hearts that forgive without judging others. Amen.

The Significance of Baptism

Philip went down to a city in Samaria and proclaimed the Messiah there. But when they believed Philip as he proclaimed the good news of the kingdom of God and the name of Jesus Christ, they were baptized, both men and women. ACTS 8:5, 12

When we put our trust in Jesus, we take on the identity of Christians. We believe Jesus is God's Son who was killed on the cross, buried, and raised from the dead. Putting our faith in Jesus, our flesh is "crucified" with him and we die to our sins. We are raised to new life in him, and we look forward to eternal life in heaven.

Just as a ring shows we're married or an ID card names our citizenship, baptism shows on the outside who we are on the inside. Going under water symbolizes death and burial as we die with Christ. Rising out of the water is a sign of raising to new life with him.

The Bible shows how baptism is a powerful event for every believer. It is God's plan for all his people to be baptized. It shows we've received Jesus as our Savior and taken our place in the family of God.

Is anything keeping you from baptism today? If Jesus is your Lord and Savior, pray about obeying God through baptism.

Lord, thank you for paying for our sins through Jesus' death on the cross. We praise you for new life in him. Give us courage to declare our faith and obey you in baptism. Amen.

JULY 8

Crying on God's Lap

*A good person produces good things from the treasury of
a good heart, and an evil person produces evil things
from the treasury of an evil heart. What you say flows
from what is in your heart.* PSALM 34:17-18

God is so close, you can whisper your worries and know he hears them loud and clear. With just one little cry, he's listening. He notices every worried look, shiver of fear, and nervous tap of your fingers on the table. He knows every time you have to say goodbye or feel disappointed. The Bible says he writes down the story of our sorrows and tears because he's on our side (Psalm 56:8-9).

You might feel embarrassed to show your feelings to others, but God knows your heart all the time. No problem you face is too small to be important to our Father. He's waiting for you to cry out to him in prayer with whatever is troubling you today.

Can you name the reasons you're stressed right now? What is creating sadness in your heart? Does anxiety or grief keep you awake at night? Today is the day to tell God all about it. He's right here, waiting to bring help and comfort. In his love, he'll mend your broken heart and make a way through your problems. He's listening.

Lord, thank you for staying close by our side. We're hurting
and need your help. Put your joy in our hearts again. Amen.

The Lid of Our Heart

"A good person produces good things from the treasury of a good heart, and an evil person produces evil things from the treasury of an evil heart. What you say flows from what is in your heart." LUKE 6:45

Our mouth is like the lid of our heart. Once we open the lid and speak, we find out what's inside. If our hearts hold fear, we're going to worry and fret. Our heart's pride will brag and boast out loud. A selfish heart will whine, complain, and beg for more. Rude, ugly, angry speech spills out of a hateful heart.

When we put our faith in Jesus, God says, "I will give you a new heart and put a new spirit in you" (Ezekiel 36:26). A new heart holds grace and compassion. It's humble and forgiving. Our new heart is peaceful, even in hard times. It's brave and trusts in God's power. Our hearts overflow with God's love.

The words we speak reveal our new heart. We build others up. We tell the truth, and we admit when we're wrong. Our mouths say "thank you" for our blessings. We speak in prayer and sing praises to God. Our words are gentle and care for others' feelings. God's wisdom guides our conversations with everyone.

Let's listen closely to how we speak to one another. Our words will help us know the condition of our hearts. We can depend on God to fill us up with love that speaks in all we say.

Lord, you give us new hearts that are good. Fill our mouths
with wise and loving words. Amen.

JULY 10

The Best Bread of All

"For the bread of God is the bread that comes down from heaven and gives life to the world." "Sir," they said, "always give us this bread." Then Jesus declared, "I am the bread of life. Whoever comes to me will never go hungry, and whoever believes in me will never be thirsty." JOHN 6:33-35

No matter where people live in the world, they eat some type of bread. From pita bread in Greece to Brazilian corn bread, Navajo fry bread to Irish soda bread, every culture is nourished by grain. In God's goodness, he provides sunlight and rain so we can grow food for us to live.

In the book of John, Jesus knew the people he was talking to. He understood the hard work of plowing fields, planting seeds, harvesting grain, and then grinding it for flour to make bread. The people depended on a good crop at the risk of starving and losing their lives. When Jesus offered a free gift of bread coming down from heaven, they were excited!

But Jesus was offering more than a quick meal. He was offering himself. Bread might keep us alive for a few days, but Jesus gives life that lasts forever. Our stomachs can be satisfied for a few hours, but Jesus satisfies our deepest hopes and needs with himself. When we have Jesus, we have the best "bread" of all.

Lord, you are a better gift than all the bread in the world.
Teach us to come to you to meet all our needs.
Let us find life in you that lasts forever. Amen.

Learning God's Ways

*... from infancy you have known the Holy Scriptures,
which are able to make you wise for salvation through
faith in Christ Jesus. All Scripture is God-breathed
and is useful for teaching, rebuking, correcting and
training in righteousness, so that the servant of God
may be thoroughly equipped for every
good work.* 2 Timothy 3:15-17

Does the Bible sometimes seem difficult to read? It's long, with over a thousand chapters in 66 books. Is it just a boring history book or a list of dos and don'ts? Is it just for Bible scholars to study?

The Bible is a gift from God to everyone, no matter their age. Its pages tell every baby, young person, and adult how much he loves them. It shares God's plan for salvation from the beginning of time. Scripture teaches his ways so we can obey and be blessed. It offers wisdom for loving, serving, and telling the good news of salvation.

God says, "Fix these words of mine in your hearts and minds" (Deuteronomy 11:18). We do that by listening to teachings at church. Our family can read scriptures and talk about them together. We can memorize verses and sing biblical worship music. Practice the powerful daily habit of reading the Bible, praying for the Spirit to help you understand it. It will become your greatest treasure.

Lord, teach us your Word so we can know you more and more. Amen.

A Taste of Heaven

All the believers were one in heart and mind. No one claimed
that any of their possessions was their own, but they
shared everything they had. And God's grace was so
powerfully at work in them all that there were no
needy persons among them. ACTS 4:32-34

Can you imagine our home in heaven? It will be beautiful, safe and secure, and close to our brothers and sisters in Jesus. No one will feel lonely or afraid. Hungry or sick. Sad or angry. In heaven, all we'll know is love and joy every moment.

When the church first began, the people had a little taste of heaven on earth. They were filled with God's Spirit and love. As their hearts overflowed with God's grace, it spilled over onto everyone they knew. If you were hungry, your brother in Jesus gave you food. If you were alone, you shared your sister's table. If you needed money, it was given to you. No believer was left cold, hungry, or in need.

To have that same taste of heaven today, we change our perspective. We look at our house like it belongs to Jesus. Then, we open the door wide to welcome God's people. Our money and possessions belong to anyone in need. We take all of God's gifts to our family and offer them back. We share as the Spirit leads. By loving like that, the joy of heaven is ours.

Lord, make us willing to share all we have. Amen.

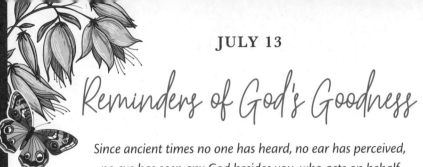

Reminders of God's Goodness

Since ancient times no one has heard, no ear has perceived,
no eye has seen any God besides you, who acts on behalf
of those who wait for him. ISAIAH 64:3-4

Do you have eyes but fail to see, and ears but fail to hear?
And don't you remember? MARK 8:18

The Bible is full of amazing stories of God's miracles and wonders. He parted the Red Sea, fed thousands with just a basket of lunch, and raised the dead to life. He conquered armies and knocked down Jericho's walls. As we listen to the Bible, God reveals his awesome power and love for his people.

Today, we both hear and tell stories of answered prayers. God brings help from unexpected places. He gives wisdom for tough decisions. His Word speaks just when encouragement or insight is needed. We have a God who still does wonderful things for those who call on him.

Even so, we're quick to forget all he's done. We fail to listen to his Word and clearly see his hand in our lives. Let's remind each other of his goodness when we're struggling. Just as he was faithful to help us in the past, he holds our future in his hands. He's always good and his love never fails.

Lord, we want to hear your words of love and hope.
Never let us forget your love and goodness to us. Amen.

JULY 14

Focusing on the "Less Than"

When [a man who was lame] saw Peter and John about to enter,
he asked them for money. Then Peter said, "Silver or gold
I do not have, but what I do have I give you. In the name
of Jesus Christ of Nazareth, walk." Taking him by the
right hand, he helped him up, and instantly the man's
feet and ankles became strong. ACTS 3:3, 6-7

It's a challenge for kids to earn money before they're grown up. A lemonade stand, an allowance, or walking the neighbor's dog won't make you rich. It's fun to have a little spending money, but it won't buy all you dream of.

We can have a "less than" point of view. Our bank account might hold less than is comfortable. We might be less talented, less healthy, or less successful than others. As we focus on our limits, our hopes become less than, too.

In today's verse, the man was as poor as could be. He'd been disabled from birth. His request was small—he only asked for a few small coins. God wanted to give him much more than he asked for. Through his healing power, the man started "walking and jumping, and praising God" (Acts 3:8). He asked for little but received more than he could imagine.

Jesus says to pray in faith that he'll provide. We can ask for just a little, or we can ask him to give what we need most of all.

Lord, teach us to trust in your power and love when we pray. Amen.

A Godly Helper and Teacher

*"If you love me, keep my commands. And I will ask the Father,
and he will give you another advocate to help you and be
with you forever—the Spirit of truth. But the Advocate,
the Holy Spirit, whom the Father will send in my name,
will teach you all things and will remind you of everything
I have said to you."* JOHN 14:15-17, 26

God is talking all the time. He shows himself through the world he created, whether in the power of a hurricane or the faithful rising and setting of the sun. His Word describes his perfect plan of salvation through Jesus. Godly teachers and leaders set an example of living by the truth. Yet unless we can hear and understand what God has to say, we're lost on the journey of faith.

Is it hard to recognize God in creation? Does the Bible seem confusing and hard to understand? Do sermons and lessons go right over your head? Does the trust and wisdom you see in others seem impossible to find for yourself? In God's kindness, he sent us a helper—the Holy Spirit—to help us know God and learn his Word and his ways.

Headphones allow us to hear and enjoy music. The Spirit opens our spiritual "ears" to hear and comprehend God's voice. He hides the Word in our hearts, teaches us what it means, and helps us to remember it always.

Lord, we want to hear you and know your Word.
Thank you for your Spirit, who helps us every day. Amen.

*Get rid of all bitterness, rage and anger, brawling
and slander, along with every form of malice.* EPHESIANS 4:31

Sometimes you and I lose our temper. You stub your toe and in pain, you blurt out ugly words. If someone jumps out to startle you as a prank, you might call names in your fear and surprise. A little argument over household chores can escalate into a shouting match before you know it. Your emotions can rise quickly and without warning. When tempers settle down, you feel sorry and work to make it right.

Malice is more than acting out of a hot temper. It calls names, makes fun, and uses ugly, hurtful words. Using deceit, gossip, or tricks, malice plans and schemes to bring harm to another person. Rather than mean words slipping out in the heat of the moment, malice sets out to hurt others on purpose.

The opposite of malice is kindness. As children of God, we "turn from evil and do good; [we] must seek peace and pursue it" (1 Peter 3:11). Instead of revenge, we forgive. Rather than bullying, we help and protect those around us. Our words build up others' self-respect and reputation. We honor people's property, personal space, and feelings. As the Spirit grows the fruit of kindness in our hearts, malice gives way to love.

Lord, make us kind to everyone. Protect us
from the malice of our enemies. Amen.

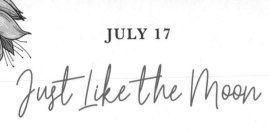

JULY 17

Just Like the Moon

*When I consider your heavens, the work of your fingers,
the moon and the stars, which you have set in place,
what is mankind that you are mindful of them,
human beings that you care for them?* PSALM 8:3-4

The moon is a ball of rock circling our planet. Dry and dusty, rough and barren, it's empty of the comforts we enjoy on earth. Yet by God's awesome, creative power, it reflects the brightness of the sun. It gives light in the darkness. The moon stands as a shining display of the glory of God.

Do you ever feel a little like the moon? Maybe you don't feel you're much to look at. In and of yourself, you don't stand out and shine. You've been beaten and bashed by "asteroids" of hurt and trouble. You feel small and insignificant against the expanse of the night sky.

Like the moon, God "knows how we are formed, he remembers that we are dust" (Psalm 103:14). He has compassion for our weakness as human beings. In his great love, he created us to reflect his light just as the moon reflects the sun. Jesus says, "You are the light of the world … let your light shine before others, that they may see your good deeds and glorify your Father in heaven" (Matthew 5:14, 16). Let's shine in his love.

Lord, let us shine your light as we love others in your name. Amen.

A Humble Heart

Let someone else praise you, and not your own mouth;
an outsider, and not your own lips. Pride brings
a person low, but the lowly in spirit
gain honor. PROVERBS 27:2, 29:23

Everybody wants to feel like a winner. Whether it's a strong performance review, a standing ovation, or a well-earned prize, success feels amazing. It boosts our confidence as we stand out in the crowd.

There are two ways to stand on the pedestal of success: pride or praise. Pride steps on others to get to the top. It exaggerates our talent. It says, "Look at me! I'm the best!" to get attention. If we climb up on a pedestal by our own pride, we're going to fall.

True honor comes through the praise of others. Instead of boasting, we can be still. People will notice if we work hard and get results. Integrity and kindness build a strong reputation. A humble heart wins friends and builds trust. Quietly doing the right thing brings rewards that last.

Do you dream of standing on a pedestal today? We can boast our way to the top, or we can let others reach down and pull us up by their praise. A humble spirit will earn God's favor too. "For the LORD takes delight in his people; he crowns the humble with victory" (Psalm 149:4).

Lord, keep us from pride that will bring us down.
We want to be humble and loving like Jesus. Amen.

Learning God's Instructions

These commandments that I give you today are to be on your hearts. Impress them on your children. Talk about them when you sit at home and when you walk along the road, when you lie down and when you get up. Tie them as symbols on your hands and bind them on your foreheads. Write them on the doorframes of your houses and on your gates. DEUTERONOMY 6:6-9

All of God's commands are designed to help us love him and love each other like Jesus. They protect us from trusting in money, success, or people instead of God. We're taught to respect God's name and honor him in every way. His commandments teach us how to treat others like we want to be treated— with integrity and kindness all the time. His instructions keep us from harm and allow his blessings to grow in our lives.

How do we remember what God wants us to do? We keep talking about his Word. We can read the Bible every day and talk about what it means. In the car we can listen to worship music that puts our focus on Jesus. We pray for each other as we're coming and going. In our everyday conversations we share our questions and thoughts about God. His truth should be woven through all we do.

Lord, we want to think and talk about you all the time.
Fill us with your Word. Amen.

In the Midst of the Storm

Suddenly a furious storm came up on the lake, so that the waves swept over the boat. But Jesus was sleeping. The disciples went and woke him, saying, "Lord, save us! We're going to drown!" He replied, "You of little faith, why are you so afraid?" Then he got up and rebuked the winds and the waves, and it was completely calm. MATTHEW 8:24-26

What kind of "storm" are you in right now? Are you drowning in work or have too much to do? Is a loved one sick or in trouble? Did a friend take offense and pull away? Do you feel upset because your situation feels impossible to overcome? In the middle of our storms we can feel like Jesus is sleeping and clueless about our problems.

Yet the God who calmed the wind and waves is the same God who loves us today. We can trust that he's with us and will bring us to the other side. We can pray, "Lord, save us! Rescue us from danger. Heal our hurts. Bring us through the storm. Help us to believe you're good, you're here, and your power is enough."

Lord, our faith can be so small when storms and troubles
come our way. Be our peace and our help through it all. Amen.

Help in Temptation

*Because [Jesus] himself suffered when he was tempted, he is able
to help those who are being tempted. For we do not have
a high priest who is unable to empathize with our weaknesses,
but we have one who has been tempted in every way,
just as we are—yet he did not sin.* HEBREWS 2:18, 4:15

It's hard to listen and follow all the rules. We'd rather keep our blessings instead of sharing them. Rude teasing spikes our temper. We put off our work to relax and do our own thing. All through the day, we're tempted to sin. We want to please ourselves instead of God.

Jesus knows what it's like to be tempted. He was hungry, tired, and hurt just like you and me. His closest friends argued and doubted his words. Insulted and abused, he was killed by the ones he came to save. Yet no matter how he suffered, he trusted God. He served with a humble heart. He forgave his enemies. Jesus was faithful and obedient to God through it all.

Jesus has compassion when we're tempted. He knows our fear and anger. The battle with sin is real and we need his help. When you want your own way, ask him for an obedient heart. Pray to be filled with love for everyone. With Jesus, you can stand firm and do what's right.

Lord, you know how we're tempted.
Help us to obey you like Jesus. Amen.

Sharing the Good News

*"The Spirit of the Lord is on me, because he has anointed me
to proclaim good news to the poor. He has sent me to
proclaim freedom for the prisoners and recovery of sight
for the blind, to set the oppressed free, to proclaim
the year of the Lord's favor."* LUKE 4:18-19

Poor. Captive. Blind. Oppressed. Those words describe every person lost without Jesus. They're poor in spirit, with no hope of the "treasures in heaven" promised to God's children (Matthew 6:20).

Unbelievers are slaves to sin, with no power to obey God's Word (Romans 6:20). The enemy has "blinded the minds of unbelievers, so that they cannot see the light of the gospel that displays the glory of Christ" (2 Corinthians 4:4). They are oppressed by "the dominion of darkness" as the enemy comes to steal, kill, and destroy (Colossians 1:13, John 10:10).

It sounds sad and hopeless, doesn't it? Yet God looks at the world he made with compassion. Out of his great love, he sent Jesus "to seek and to save the lost" (Luke 19:10). He came to proclaim God's love. His power over sin and Satan. The way to the Father in heaven. He wants everyone to hear the good news of salvation.

What about you and me? Are we ready to share the hope found in Jesus? Let's pray for courage to proclaim the good news we've found in him.

Lord, you told us of your love and salvation.
Let us tell everyone the good news! Amen.

A Religion of Hope and Rest

"Come to me, all you who are weary and burdened, and I will give you rest. Take my yoke upon you and learn from me, for I am gentle and humble in heart, and you will find rest for your souls. For my yoke is easy and my burden is light." MATTHEW 11:28-30

Some people turn religion into a lot of work. The list of rules is long and feels impossible to keep. You must look or dress a certain way. You have to behave and act just right. You're not allowed to ask questions or change the system. That kind of religion says you must work hard to earn God's love. If you're not good enough, God will be angry. You'll be punished and alone.

Wouldn't that kind of religion wear you out? God would seem cold and distant. You would either try and try to be perfect, or you'd give up and walk away. God loves you and me too much to burden us with empty religion. He sent Jesus to give mercy and forgiveness. Hope and rest. Love that never ends.

We don't have to work for our salvation. "For it is by grace you have been saved, through faith—and this is not from yourselves, it is the gift of God—not by works, so that no one can boast" (Ephesians 2:8-9). You're loved and accepted because of Jesus.

Lord, teach us how to rest in your love and mercy. Amen.

JULY 24

The Sharpest Sword

For the word of God is alive and active. Sharper than any double-edged sword, it penetrates even to dividing soul and spirit, joints and marrow; it judges the thoughts and attitudes of the heart. HEBREWS 4:12

A chain saw can cut the bark and branches from a tree. Knives can peel an apple or slice the crust from a loaf of bread. Scissors cut paper into any shape we choose. A razor can shave the whiskers from a dad's chin. But it's much harder to separate good from bad or right from wrong inside our hearts and minds.

Are we believing truth or lies? Do we have good intentions or bad motives? Are we forgiving or bitter toward others? Who do we love the most—Jesus or ourselves? When we read the Bible, it's like a sharp sword that cuts through to our true thoughts and feelings.

God gave his Word so he can repair our damaged emotions. He can battle the lies of the enemy. We find wisdom so we can make good decisions. And, he can open our hearts and minds to his love. Let's pick up the "sword" of the Bible every day so its power can change our lives.

Lord, thank you for your Word. We pray it will penetrate
our hearts with your love and truth. Amen.

Love That Never Runs Out

*Surely your goodness and love will follow me all the days
of my life, and I will dwell in the house
of the Lord forever.* PSALM 23:6

God's love for his children never runs out. It never gets tired. It doesn't give up or walk away. His love never leaves us on our own. It always forgives and lets us start again. God's love says, "You are mine." It can't be stolen, weakened, or destroyed. God's love is found in Jesus, who left the glory of heaven to come down and save us. God's love endures forever!

God is good to you and to me. He knows what we need before we ask him. He turns his face toward us to hear our prayers. God protects us from danger and leads to safety. He gives the desires of our hearts. He gives our lives meaning and purpose, with good works prepared for us to do. God provides every single thing we need to know him, follow him, and enjoy him forever. Wherever we go, God's goodness goes with us.

We need a God like him. He's the only One who can love us like that. His goodness is better than anything this world can offer. If we "dwell in the house of the Lord" by putting our trust in Jesus, his love and goodness are ours. For how long? Forever!

Lord, your love is better than life. You are good to us all the time.
Thank you for the hope of forever with you! Amen.

You Are Seen and Cherished

*"Are not five sparrows sold for two pennies? Yet not one of them
is forgotten by God. Indeed, the very hairs of your head
are all numbered. Don't be afraid; you are worth
more than many sparrows."* LUKE 12:6-7

God rules over the universe, keeping planets in orbit and holding the stars in the sky. He determines when world leaders and nations rise and fall. He marks the borders of every sea and continent. He created every living thing. With his breath, he could blow out a flaming volcano like a match. His power and authority have no equal.

Yes, our God is awesome. We can wonder, "LORD, what are human beings that you care for them, mere mortals that you think of them? They are like a breath; their days are like a fleeting shadow" (Psalm 144:3-4). But no one is too small for his attention. He notices every little bird and every detail about you and me.

God knows when you feel alone. He sees your smiles and hurts. When you're scared in the night, he's right by your side. He's joyful in your victories and counts your tears when you lose what you love. Moment by moment, you're seen, known, and cherished.

Do you feel invisible today? Is it hard to believe you're worth much at all? Remember you're a child of God. You're never forgotten. His love is so high and wide and deep, he gave Jesus to make you his own.

Lord, help us to believe and know how much you love us. Amen.

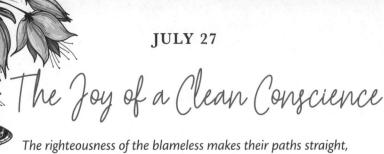

The Joy of a Clean Conscience

The righteousness of the blameless makes their paths straight,
but the wicked are brought down by their own wickedness.
Those who are kind benefit themselves, but the cruel
bring ruin on themselves. PROVERBS 11:5, 17

Can we get something good by doing something bad? If I gossip about one friend, I could be popular with others. If I take credit where it is not due I could get ahead of others at work. If I ignore the speed limit I could arrive at my destination right on time.

It might seem like sin can bring what we're looking for. Yet the Bible says it leaves us worse off than when we started. In gaining that 'A' you'd lose your teacher's trust. Your lie can spare you a consequence, but you'll have trouble when the truth comes out. New friends might like my gossip, but I'll lose the one who really cared. The extra money from the cashier's mistake would pad my wallet, but I'd feel guilty taking what wasn't mine. The sin that tastes sweet at first ends up like gravel in our mouth (Proverbs 20:17).

God is our true source of blessing. He answers our prayers. He rewards obedience both now and in heaven. He forgives and makes us wise. His Spirit gives patience, joy, and hope for tomorrow. We have the peace of a clean conscience. God's gifts are better than anything sin could offer.

Lord, make us blameless and keep us close to you. Amen.

JULY 28

With God, We Always Can

*" ... My grace is sufficient for you, for my power is made perfect
in weakness." Therefore I will boast all the more gladly
about my weaknesses, so that Christ's power may rest
on me. That is why, for Christ's sake, I delight
in weaknesses, in insults, in hardships, in persecutions,
in difficulties. For when I am weak,
then I am strong.* 2 CORINTHIANS 12:9-10

How many times do we say, "I can't"? I can't climb that high. I can't pass my test. I can't stand up for myself. That person is too hard to get along with. I can't get by without a better job. I could never tell people I follow Jesus. I can't find joy until my troubles are over. In our fear and weakness, we quit before we try.

You and I are only human. We'll face battles we can't win. Problems we can't solve. People who are hard to love. Work that takes more than we can give. Busy and tired, we fall on our face. In fear, we'll want to give up or run away.

What do we do when we run out of strength? We call out to God for help. He gives courage and hope. He provides for our needs. In his wisdom, he shows just what to do. He fights our enemies so we can rest. When we are weak, we find strength in our God.

Lord, teach us to depend on your strength instead of our own. Amen.

Wisdom for Tough Decisions

*But when you ask, you must believe and not doubt, because
the one who doubts is like a wave of the sea, blown and tossed
by the wind. That person should not expect to receive
anything from the Lord. Such a person is double-minded
and unstable in all they do.* JAMES 1:6-8

Making decisions is tough. We might have so many choices we feel dizzy trying to pick just one. Perhaps we made a mistake and we're unsure how to make it right. A great opportunity comes along, but we're nervous to make a big change. Decisions can leave us confused and worried, unsure of which way to go.

God made a promise to give us wisdom whenever we ask. Yet if we doubt what he says, we're just as mixed up as when we started. God can't lead us forward if we're slow to follow. If we second-guess his answers to our prayers for wisdom, we keep him from helping us at all.

Are you facing confusing choices today? Do you have a problem you don't know how to solve? Let's ask God for wisdom to know what to do. He'll speak to us through his Word, his Spirit, through good advice, and by shifting our circumstances to steer us in the right direction. As he guides, let's believe and follow him without turning back.

> Lord, thank you for helping us know what to do. Teach us to
> listen to your wisdom so we do whatever you say. Amen.

JULY 30

The Best Way

*When Pharaoh let the people go, God did not lead them
on the road through the Philistine country, though that
was shorter. For God said, "If they face war, they might
change their minds and return to Egypt." Exodus 13:17*

When we're on a road trip, the shortest way might not be the best way. It might be jammed with traffic. It could be icy, damaged, or under construction. Taking a longer route can spare us from danger or delays.

The Bible says, "A person's steps are directed by the Lord" (Proverbs 20:24). All the days he planned for us were written in his book before we were born (Psalm 139:16). As we travel down the road of life, God is leading and guiding. He knows when we should stop, go forward, or turn one way or the other.

Is it hard to trust that God's way is the best way? Do you wonder why it's taking so long to reach your goals? Are you discouraged, thinking you're going nowhere fast? Do you feel like your path is leading in the opposite direction of where you'd like to go?

God says we can trust his leading. He's protecting us from enemies and temptations we can't see. He knows the dangers of the road we would choose on our own. If we go with God, he'll keep us in "his good, pleasing and perfect will" (Romans 12:2).

Lord, may we trust you on the road you've marked for us. Amen.

JULY 31

Finding True Happiness

But as for me, my feet had almost slipped; I had nearly lost my foothold. For I envied the arrogant when I saw the prosperity of the wicked. When my heart was grieved and my spirit embittered, I was senseless and ignorant; I was a brute beast before you. Psalm 73:2-3, 21-22

When choosing our gifts, we almost always want the biggest and best. We feel jealous of those who seem to get whatever they want. It feels unfair to see others get more and more while we have to do without. We grow bitter and angry inside as we count others' blessings instead of our own. Forgetting the kindness of God, our love for him grows cold.

When we carry envy in our hearts, we grumble and complain. We forget God's promises to love and care for us always. Our eyes see what we're missing instead of all the ways he's provided. Material possessions and entertainment seem more appealing than the treasures waiting for us in heaven. We lose our heads and forget we're beloved children of the Most High God.

Jealousy is the opposite of joy. Today, let's remember God's gifts are better than anything the world can offer. True happiness is found in knowing Jesus. Let's choose to say thanks for our life, our family, and the hope of all he has in store.

Lord, our jealousy shows we're ignorant of your love. Teach us to be content and fill our minds with your wisdom. Amen.

August

AUGUST 1

Sticking Together

And let us consider how we may spur one another on toward love and good deeds, not giving up meeting together, as some are in the habit of doing, but encouraging one another—and all the more as you see the Day approaching. HEBREWS 10:24-25

Our close friends and family have powerful influence over our lives. The more we stick together, the more we have in common. We share traditions during the holidays. We make memories at our favorite places to eat, celebrate with loved ones, and explore. We laugh at the same jokes and sing along to the same music. As we live side by side, we share our fears, our hopes, and our struggles.

Families can bring out the best or worst in each other. If junior hears Dad tell a lie, he may think he can be dishonest. If Mom has a quick temper, it might stir up anger in the kids, too. If we worry and complain, the peace in the home will suffer.

God wants us to motivate each other to love. You can challenge your spouse to be kind to the neighbors. You can encourage your kids to be caring, loyal friends. You can set an example of giving and sharing for others to follow. Dad can forgive the people who hurt him, so the family see what grace looks like. Our family and church will help us love and serve like Jesus.

Lord, make us strong in faith and love as we follow you together.
Amen.

No Strength

*"No razor has ever been used on my head," he said, "because
I have been a Nazirite dedicated to God from my mother's
womb. If my head were shaved, my strength would leave me,
and I would become as weak as any other man."* JUDGES 16:17

The Holy Spirit gave Samson strength to win battles against wild animals and enemies of God's people. The key to his mighty strength was obedience—if he disobeyed and shaved his hair, the power of God would leave him.

We disobey God, too, each time we choose our way over his way. If we're stubborn and refuse to love or listen, we shave away our strength in him. But if we live by the Word, we keep "in step with the Spirit" who will "strengthen [us] with power … in [our] inner being" (Galatians 5:25, Ephesians 3:16).

How can we be strong in the Lord? We trust God and wait for his help (Isaiah 40:31). We pray about all our troubles, joys, and praises (James 5:13). In life's battles, we choose to "be on [our] guard; stand firm in the faith; be courageous; be strong. Do everything in love" (1 Corinthians 16:13-14).

Is your strength shaved down to nothing? Are you losing your battle to do what's right? Do you feel scared, stressed, or sad? Trust God, obey what he says, and he will fill you with his power.

Lord, give us strength to love and obey you always. Amen.

The Good Feeling of Giving

*Remember this: Whoever sows sparingly will also reap sparingly,
and whoever sows generously will also reap generously.
Each of you should give what you have decided in your
heart to give, not reluctantly or under compulsion,
for God loves a cheerful giver.* 2 CORINTHIANS 9:6-7

Presents are a delight! We love to see a stack of boxes and bags beside our birthday cake. It's exciting to open the mailbox and find a package with our name on it. It feels good when our friends share what they have and our family gives us what we need. Generosity makes us feel important and cared for.

We can help others have that same good feeling. A gift of money might bring relief from stress and worry. It can put food on the table of a hungry family or bring medical care to the sick. Sharing meals with others around our table says, "You're welcome here." The gift of time and attention can relieve the hurt of loneliness. Giving says, "I love you," without speaking a word.

Sometimes we hold back because we're afraid giving means losing. Yet God made a beautiful promise that the more we give, the more he provides so we can give even more. When we share what we have with a cheerful heart, his name is praised. We bless the One who has blessed us with every good thing.

Lord, we want to give with glad and willing hearts.
Use our generosity to show your love to everyone. Amen.

Honey for the Soul

*Eat honey, my son, for it is good; honey from the comb is sweet
to your taste. Know also that wisdom is like honey for you:
If you find it, there is a future hope for you, and your
hope will not be cut off.* PROVERBS 24:13-14

Honey is more than just a delicious treat. It has been used for centuries as medicine for healing. Honey doesn't spoil, so a sealed jar can last for generations. Honey is a symbol of blessing. God promised his people a land "flowing with milk and honey" (Exodus 3:17). The Bible tells how honey could give energy to the weary (1 Samuel 14:27). God created honey for our good.

Just as honey can help our bodies, wisdom is good for the soul. Wisdom is knowing God's Word and his will. It teaches us how to get along. It shows how to work and learn. Wisdom warns us of danger. When we face tough choices, wisdom steers us in the right direction.

With wisdom, we can receive God's salvation. When we're tempted, we recognize the enemy's tricks and run away. We can tell right from wrong. Wisdom reveals our spiritual gifts and the good works "which God prepared in advance for us to do" (Ephesians 2:10). We can know Jesus, follow him where he leads, and celebrate life with him forever.

Lord, the sweetness of honey can't compare with your gift of wisdom.
Thank you for the hope we find in you. Amen.

Brothers and Sisters behind Bars

*But Saul began to destroy the church. Going from house
to house, he dragged off both men and women
and put them in prison.* ACTS 8:3

*"I needed clothes and you clothed me, I was sick
and you looked after me, I was in prison and
you came to visit me."* MATTHEW 25:36

Since the church began, believers have been persecuted around the world. God's enemies put our brothers and sisters in Jesus into prison. Many have lost their jobs, their homes, their health, and their freedom for following Christ. They've been separated from their loved ones. They "participate in the sufferings of Christ" (1 Peter 4:13).

Those in prison are never forgotten by Jesus. He promises that nothing in all creation can separate believers—or you and me—from God's love (Romans 8:39). He knows their pain is an echo of his suffering on the cross. For us, we must remember and care for the persecuted to show our love and thanks for Jesus. He says whatever we do for suffering believers, we do for him (Matthew 25:40).

How can we remember those in prison? We can pray and support ministries who help. We can petition government leaders to bring justice. We can spread the word that persecution is happening around the world. Let's ask God to show us how to love in his name.

Lord, teach us to love you by loving your people. Amen.

AUGUST 6

A Christian "Accent"

*Nor should there be obscenity, foolish talk or coarse joking, which are
out of place, but rather thanksgiving. For you were once darkness,
but now you are light in the Lord.* EPHESIANS 5:4, 8

We can often tell where a person comes from by the way they speak. Their accent and spoken language are clues to their culture and nationality. For us as God's children, our citizenship is in heaven. We will talk like Jesus since our forever home is with him.

As believers, God says he will fill our mouths with laughter and our tongues with songs of joy (Psalm 126:2). There is a time to laugh and dance (Ecclesiastes 3:4). God promises over and over to make us happy and full of rejoicing (Psalm 68:3).

One way we experience that joy is through joking and laughing together. God's kind of humor lifts people up instead of tearing them down. We don't make fun of how others look. Instead of laughing at someone's mistakes, we show compassion. Since people are created in God's image, we don't make inappropriate jokes about our bodies. We avoid gossip, lies, and profanity.

Instead, we use our words to shine the light of Jesus. We praise God for how good he is every day. Knowing God loves everyone, we speak words of kindness, respect, and encouragement wherever we go. Laughter will overflow from our joy and delight in the world God made.

Lord, laughter is a gift from you. Your love fills us with joy.
Let our words shine your light to everyone. Amen.

Saying "I Will"

"There was a man who had two sons. He went to the first and
said, 'Son, go and work today in the vineyard.' 'I will not,'
he answered, but later he changed his mind and went.
Then the father went to the other son and said the same thing.
He answered, 'I will, sir,' but he did not go. Which of
the two did what his father wanted?" MATTHEW 21:28-31

If you say you'll help a friend with a task, she expects you to go around and help. If we invite friends for dinner, they arrive ready to enjoy a meal. If you keep postponing helping your friend, she will be frustrated. If we have nothing for our friends, they feel forgotten. Words don't mean much without action.

What do we say to God? We say we believe the Bible, but do we obey it? Prayer makes a difference, but do we talk to God every day? The lost need the gospel, but do we share it? We're meant to give and serve, but do we ignore the needs around us? At times, we have to admit we're distracted. Fearful. "Weary of doing good" (Galatians 6:9).

Today, let's say "I will" to God. Let's work in his vineyard—trusting him and showing the world his love.

Lord, let our faith show in all we do. Amen.

The Courage for Something New

*"Have I not commanded you? Be strong and courageous.
Do not be afraid; do not be discouraged, for the LORD your God
will be with you wherever you go." JOSHUA 1:9*

Sometimes the path of our life feels confusing. The future can seem scary, uncertain, and dark. We wonder if we'll have to leave our favorite people or places behind. We're afraid to face problems or lose our way. It's tempting to stay put instead of moving ahead into all God has planned.

If we're afraid to step forward, it can help to look behind us. The God who helped yesterday will help us tomorrow. Just as he gave wisdom in the past, he'll guide us in the future. His Word and all its promises stay true and sure. "Jesus Christ is the same yesterday and today and forever" (Hebrews 13:8). In him, we'll always find love, forgiveness, and strength for whatever comes.

Is God asking you to do a new thing? Have courage because he'll be with you all the way.

Lord, we want to be strong and courageous. Teach us
to trust that you're with us wherever we go. Thank you
for your love that never fails. Amen.

The Ultimate Doctor

When the teachers of the law who were Pharisees saw him eating
with the sinners and tax collectors, they asked his disciples:
"Why does he eat with tax collectors and sinners?"
On hearing this, Jesus said to them, "It is not the healthy
who need a doctor, but the sick. I have not come to call
the righteous, but sinners." MARK 2:16-17

Jesus came because he knew our souls were sick. God says if a person turns against him, "Your whole head is injured, your whole heart afflicted" (Isaiah 1:5). In this world filled with enemies and trouble, we need his help to "strengthen the feeble hands, steady the knees that give way" (Isaiah 35:3). Without God, we're weak and sinful from our head to our toes.

Jesus came to tell everyone about God's love. He gave his body to suffer, die, and be raised to life again so we can live with him in heaven. He washes us clean from our old thoughts and attitudes, sins and habits. Our hearts are healed from bitterness and hurt. He doesn't just put a bandage on our broken places—we are transformed into "members of Christ" and "temples of the Holy Spirit" (1 Corinthians 6:15, 19).

If religious traditions could heal our sin, Jesus would not have come. He knew we needed healing from the inside out. We can go to him as our "doctor" and be made well, forever.

Lord, you give us strength and life. In you, we're made new in every way. Thank you for sending Jesus to make us righteous. Amen.

He Knows Your Name

*He calls his own sheep by name and leads them out. When he
has brought out all his own, he goes on ahead of them,
and his sheep follow him because they know his voice.
"I am the good shepherd; I know my sheep and
my sheep know me."* JOHN 10:3-4, 14

All the snowflakes look identical as they fall from a winter sky. In a forest of trees, none stands out as unique or important. Thousands of stars in the sky shine with the same brightness. Sometimes we feel like we blend in with the crowd. We don't feel special or one-of-a-kind. As much as we want people to know us, we feel ordinary and unseen.

No matter how invisible you feel to those around you, God sees. He knows your name. As your Creator, he knit you together and says you're wonderful! He counts your days, knows your every thought, and never leaves your side (Psalm 139). You are precious and honored in his sight, and he loves you (Isaiah 43:4).

God hears your voice when you pray. He knows your wishes, your feelings, and your fears. Because he's our good Shepherd, we can know his voice too. His Word and his Spirit will guide us every day as he calls us by name to follow him.

Lord, we want to know your voice and follow you always. Amen.

AUGUST 11

Our Hope, Help and Shield

No king is saved by the size of his army; no warrior escapes by his great strength. We wait in hope for the LORD; he is our help and our shield. PSALM 33:16, 20

We try really hard to protect ourselves from problems. We strap helmets on our heads before a bike ride. Money is stashed in savings for future bills and expenses. Locks and gates secure our property. We take vitamins and wash our hands to help our bodies stay healthy. Time, money, and energy are spent to feel safe and avoid every kind of trouble.

Yet no matter how we try, we can't create a perfect, easy life. We don't have an army to surround us at school, at work, or at home. Accidents happen. Things go wrong. The "walls" we build around ourselves come tumbling down. Our problems remind us how little control we really have.

God offers hope when we feel scared or surprised by trouble. He is our helper who's with us all the time. When we pray, he answers. He's bigger, stronger, and more powerful than anyone or anything. He's a mighty warrior, ready to fight to keep us safe. Let's turn our fears into faith as we trust in him to the end.

Lord, thank you for the hope we have in your power. Fill us with peace and courage as we trust you to care for us. Amen.

Without Witness or Reward

Serve wholeheartedly, as if you were serving the Lord, not people, because you know that the Lord will reward each one for whatever good they do, whether they are slave or free. EPHESIANS 6:7-8

You serve your family when you cook for them and work to keep them safe and well. Your child serves her friends by finding their lost toys or sharing her snacks. You can help neighbors by dropping off a meal when they're sick. As we serve, we give others a boost. We pitch in to help when the work is too hard on their own. We give what we've got to share.

Yet sometimes serving is no fun at all. We don't hear a "thank you". We're told our help was too little, too late. Our gifts are tossed aside. We help, but all we receive in return is complaining. Demands for more leave us with less energy, money, and time than when we started. How do we love those who don't love us back?

We remember when we serve others, we serve Jesus. He says, "Whatever you did for one of the least of these brothers and sisters of mine, you did for me" (Matthew 25:40). If we feed the hungry, it's like filling a plate for Jesus. When we offer kind words, we're comforting him. If we lift someone's heavy load, we're taking weight off his shoulders. We love Christ when we love others.

We don't need prizes and thanks for our serving. God knows the good we do, and he's glad. We will be rewarded and blessed as we keep trusting and serving him.

Lord, may we serve you as we serve others. Amen.

Building a Bigger Barn

"Then [a certain rich man] said, 'This is what I'll do. I will tear down my barns and build bigger ones, and there I will store my surplus grain. And I'll say to myself, "You have plenty of grain laid up for many years. Take life easy; eat, drink and be merry."' "But God said to him, 'You fool! This very night your life will be demanded from you. Then who will get what you have prepared for yourself?'" LUKE 12:18-20

It's tempting to think if a little is good, then more is even better. If we have one figurine, we want a whole collection. When we buy a shirt, we want new shoes and a jacket to go with it. If our car still runs but is showing its age, we dream of buying the latest model. We can end up working and pushing for more than we really need.

The Bible reminds us that we can't take our money or possessions to heaven. Storing up money so we can live for ourselves will only end in disappointment. God offers something better—treasure in heaven—as his reward for the generosity, kindness, and love we give away.

What are you working for? Do you want to store up as much "stuff" as you can in this life? Let's give God our hearts and store up treasures in heaven instead (Matthew 6:19-21).

Lord, keep us from selfish hearts that want more and more in this world. We want to love you and find joy in sharing all we have. Amen.

AUGUST 14

The Right Blueprint

"Therefore everyone who hears these words of mine and puts them into practice is like a wise man who built his house on the rock. But everyone who hears these words of mine and does not put them into practice is like a foolish man who built his house on sand. The rain came down, the streams rose, and the winds blew and beat against that house, and it fell with a great crash." MATTHEW 7:24, 26-27

Each of us is building something every day. We're working for success, strong friendships, a close and happy family, and plans for the future. We can build our life like the world, using money, fame, and power to get ahead. Or, we have the blueprint of God's Word. The directions we follow will determine if we succeed or fail, celebrate or lose hope.

The Bible offers perfect instructions for life. It shows how kindness, forgiveness, and love are the building blocks of friendship and family. Generosity and contentment build financial security. Obedience to authority keeps us from getting in trouble and builds a strong reputation. Working "as unto the Lord" allows us to do God's will. When we listen and build our lives on his Word, we don't have to be scared of tomorrow.

Lord, build our home on the rock of your Word.
Help us live for you in every way. Amen.

When You Don't Understand

Show me your ways, Lord, teach me your paths.
Guide me in your truth and teach me, for you
are God my Savior, and my hope
is in you all day long. PSALM 25:4-5

A lot of kids avoid reading the Bible. They think it's too hard to understand. It's full of big words and stories about people and places so different from what we know today. With so many books and chapters and verses, how do you know where to start? Kids might give up and think it's just a book for grown-ups.

Grown-ups don't always understand the Bible, either. Like God says, "As the heavens are higher than the earth, so are my ways higher than your ways and my thoughts than your thoughts" (Isaiah 55:9). His thoughts in Scripture can be too big for our minds to comprehend.

The Bible is God's gift to us, young and old alike. He wants us to know his words of love and the good news of our salvation. In his kindness, we don't have to figure it out on our own. When you and I were saved, we received the Spirit "so that we may understand what God has freely given us" (1 Corinthians 2:12). He opens our minds to understand the truth of God's Word. If we pray, God will make his Word alive in our hearts.

Lord, teach us your truth and love from your Word. Amen.

Hope for Tomorrow

*He has made everything beautiful in its time. He has also set eternity
in the human heart; yet no one can fathom what God
has done from beginning to end.* ECCLESIASTES 3:11

*"Very truly I tell you, whoever hears my word and
believes him who sent me has eternal life ... "* JOHN 5:24

Days, seasons, and years feel like they're flying by. We often say, "Is it time to go already?" "You're growing up so fast!" "Look how many candles are on your birthday cake!" "You'll move on to new things before you know it." Yet even as our lives seem short, we know in our spirits we were created to live forever.

God has a plan for our time here and for our heavenly future, too. He knew the exact point in history he'd place each of us on the planet. In his wisdom, he knows how our lives will affect generations to come. And, the rewards and roles we play in heaven are decided by how we live today. Instead of feeling sad our lives are short, we can celebrate the glorious, unending life we'll have with him.

Eternal life is found by trusting in Jesus. If we believe in who he is and what he accomplished on the cross, we have perfect hope for tomorrow.

Lord, thank you for loving us and calling us your own. Fill us
with hope for the eternal life we can experience with you. Amen.

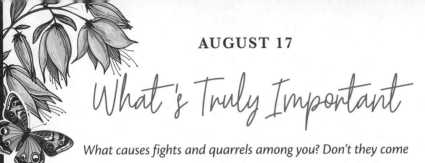

What's Truly Important

What causes fights and quarrels among you? Don't they come
from your desires that battle within you? You desire but
do not have, so you kill. You covet but you cannot get
what you want, so you quarrel and fight. You do not
have because you do not ask God. JAMES 4:1-2

Mine! Me first! It's my turn! Give it to me! No fair! We've all heard and said those words. Anger explodes and we fight to have our way.

Angry feelings are a clue to what's in our heart. Do I love my things more than my family? Are my needs more important than yours? Do I keep score so I get as much as everybody else? If I'm jealous, mad, or complaining, I've forgotten what's truly important.

God offers a better way. He invites us to bring our wants and needs to him in prayer. He is kind and generous. We can trust him to give us the right things at the right time. "Take delight in the LORD, and he will give you the desires of your heart" (Psalm 37:4).

Let's ask God for patience to wait for his blessings. He'll help us to love one another as we love ourselves. His peace will fill our hearts and our home.

Lord, forgive us for the way we argue and fight. Give us new hearts
that trust and love you more. Amen.

AUGUST 18

When You're Sinking

*Then Peter got down out of the boat, walked on the water and
came toward Jesus. But when he saw the wind, he was
afraid and, beginning to sink, cried out, "Lord, save me!"
Immediately Jesus reached out his hand and
caught him. "You of little faith," he said,
"why did you doubt?"* MATTHEW 14:29-31

Can you remember a time you felt terrified? Maybe you were walking into a new school for the first time. Or, you stood at the top of the high dive with the water far below your feet. At the doctor's office, you were told to roll up your sleeve for a shot. Whether we face an accident, an aggressive dog, or a storm in the night, we know the feeling of panic.

In a scary situation that's out of control, it feels like we're drowning in fear. All we can see is danger. Yet as God's children, we don't have to sink. We can cry out for help in prayer. Jesus will reach out with love to catch us. He'll save us from worry and despair. He will "set [our] feet on a rock and [give us] a firm place to stand" (Psalm 40:2). We'll find courage and hope to make it through.

Are you sinking into fear and worry today? Do you wonder if God sees you, hears you, and if he even cares? Trust in his love that will catch you.

Lord, make us brave as we trust in you. Amen.

Always Loved

*"So he got up and went to his father. But while he was
still a long way off, his father saw him and was
filled with compassion for him; he ran to his son,
threw his arms around him and kissed him."* LUKE 15:20

God loves you so much, he gave his own son to make you his own. When you put your trust in Jesus, he made you his own child. He tells his sons and daughters, "I have loved you with an everlasting love; I have drawn you with unfailing kindness" (Jeremiah 31:3). He will be your heavenly Father forever.

God's children fall into sin. At times we question and doubt. Temptation and suffering shake the foundations of our faith. We stubbornly refuse to listen or obey. Yet through it all, God never changes. Nothing can separate you from his love. He waits with open arms for his sons and daughters to turn to him again.

Lord, in your love you made us your sons and daughters.
Keep us close, always. Amen.

AUGUST 20

Words That Build Up

Do not let any unwholesome talk come out of your mouths,
but only what is helpful for building others up according
to their needs, that it may benefit those
who listen. Ephesians 4:29

We know healthy food, exercise, and sleep keep our bodies healthy and strong. If we tried to live on sweets and sat around watching movies all night, we would become sick and exhausted in no time.

Our hearts and minds are the same—we need loving, helpful words to build us up. We can help each other feel confident and happy by the way we speak to each other. If you feel lonely or left out, welcoming words make you feel wanted and included. When you're nervous or scared, you can pray out loud and remember God is with you. If your loved one is working hard to reach a goal or reward, you can cheer them on and celebrate at the end. Wise words that speak the truth and love of God keep each of us strong and full of faith.

On the other hand, mean or critical words can crush our spirits. Every time we open our mouths, we have a choice to make—will we build someone up or tear them down? Let's use our words to care for each other every day.

Lord, you speak truth and love to us all the time.
Teach us how to build each other up with our words. Amen.

Praying Like Jesus

One day Jesus was praying in a certain place. When he finished,
one of his disciples said to him, "Lord, teach us to pray,
just as John taught his disciples." LUKE 11:1

Even though it's easy to recite the alphabet today, it was a challenge when we were very little. We needed a teacher to help us learn the letters and sounds. We would say and sing the alphabet until we had it right. Parents and teachers understand kids need time and practice to learn new things.

Jesus' disciples followed him from town to town, into the wilderness, and across the sea. They heard Jesus pray thanks before meals. He spoke with his Father in the morning and all through the night. Even when busy or tired from teaching and healing the crowds, he spent hours in prayer with God.

The disciples wanted to pray like Jesus. Jesus knew the disciples—and you and I today—need a teacher to show the way. He taught that prayer is worship. It asks for what we need. We confess our sins and ask for grace to forgive others. We admit our struggle with sin and Satan and ask for God's protection. We take our needs and fears, love and praise to the One who hears every word.

Do you want to learn to pray? Follow the teaching of Jesus. God wants to hear your voice.

Lord, teach us to pray like Jesus so we can be close to you. Amen.

Where Are You Planted?

*"But blessed is the one who trusts in the Lᴏʀᴅ, whose confidence
is in him. They will be like a tree planted by the water
that sends out its roots by the stream. It does not fear
when heat comes; its leaves are always green."* Jᴇʀᴇᴍɪᴀʜ 17:7-8

Roots keep plants and trees anchored in the ground. Through wind and rain, they stay right where they can flourish and grow. Roots grow deep to take in the water and nutrients needed to thrive.

Could a tall, leafy maple tree survive in a dry desert? Could we plant roses or daisies in concrete? Planting in good soil and water is the only way for them to stay green and growing.

God says you and I are a lot like trees. If we plant ourselves close to him, we're secure. The storms of life won't blow us over. He protects us from the heat of stress and trouble. The roots of our heart can drink from the "living water" of Jesus (John 4:13-14).

Where are we planted today? Are we trusting God's Word or soaking up the world's point of view? Do we depend on God for everything, or do we count on our own strength? Are we calm and peaceful because we believe his promises? Or, do we feel scared and alone in all we face? Let's put our confidence in God's great love. In him, there's nothing to fear.

Lord, grow deep roots of faith in our hearts. Amen.

Making God Happy

But Samuel replied: "Does the LORD delight in burnt offerings and sacrifices as much as in obeying the LORD? To obey is better than sacrifice, and to heed is better than the fat of rams. 1 SAMUEL 15:22

You and I want to make God happy. But if we're honest, we can try to please God on our own terms. We think, If I go to church on Sunday, I can do what I please on Monday. If I donate a little of my money to charity, I can spend the rest on what I like. If I'm respectful when I talk to my boss, I can gossip behind their back. If I'm honest about big things, little lies don't matter. We give God part of our life but keep the rest for ourselves.

God is wise. He knows our true thoughts and feelings. "He will bring to light what is hidden in darkness and will expose the motives of the heart" (1 Corinthians 4:5). He knows how little or much we love him.

Do we love God halfway or all the way? Since Jesus sacrificed his life for us, we give him our own. We "offer [our] bodies as a living sacrifice, holy and pleasing to God—this is [our] true and proper worship" (Romans 12:1). We give him all we have and go wherever he leads. Our obedience shows how much we love him.

Lord, we want to please you. May we love you in all we do. Amen.

Never Out of Sight

He will not let your foot slip—he who watches over you will not slumber;
indeed, he who watches over Israel will neither slumber nor sleep …
he will watch over your life; the LORD will watch over your coming
and going both now and forevermore. PSALM 121:3-4, 7-8

A goalie can't take his eye off the ball or the other team might score. A doctor can't perform healing surgery with her eyes closed. An artist can't paint a beautiful picture without looking at the canvas. If you fall asleep in the pool, you'll sink! We stay awake and alert to be safe, have fun, and finish what we need to do.

You are worth far more than a soccer game or a painting. Since you are God's treasure, he never takes his eyes off of you. He watches over you at night while you sleep. He knows when you feel scared or sad. Lonely or tired. Joyful and excited. He knows your thoughts, the name of your best friend, the number of hairs on your head. God keeps track of every little detail of your life.

He watches because he loves you. If you put yourself in his hands, you can trust him to take care of you every moment.

Lord, since you watch over us, we're secure in your love. Amen.

Don't Label

Brothers and sisters, do not slander one another. Anyone who speaks against a brother or sister or judges them speaks against the law and judges it. When you judge the law, you are not keeping it, but sitting in judgment on it. JAMES 4:11

We're quick to label the people around us, aren't we? We say they're smart or foolish. Athletic or clumsy. Confident or cowardly. Friendly or stand-offish. Polite or rude. Careful or impulsive. Once we label someone—or have been labelled ourselves—it's hard to be seen as anything else. A label doesn't hold faith we can grow or change.

The worst kind of label is slander that judges the heart. We point fingers at others, calling them bad people who deserve to be punished. The Bible gives a warning: "There is only one Lawgiver and Judge, the one who is able to save and destroy. But you—who are you to judge your neighbor?" (James 4:12). We slander their name as we try to take God's place.

Instead, we're to love our neighbor as ourselves. We stand up for them with love that "always trusts, always hopes, always perseveres" (1 Corinthians 13:7). We use our words to build them up. We trust God to keep his promise to finish the work he started. With the mercy we've been given from God, we show mercy to everyone.

Lord, keep us from slander that hurts. Let us use our words
to show your love. Amen.

A Treasure Chest of Blessings

Praise be to the God and Father of our Lord Jesus Christ,
who has blessed us in the heavenly realms with every
spiritual blessing in Christ. EPHESIANS 1:3

When we put our faith in Jesus, we become children of God. Our Father in heaven opens up his treasure chest of spiritual blessings to give us every single one.

God forgives. He washes away our sins so we have a clean heart. Our lives have purpose as we received the Spirit's gifts and a special plan to use them. We're set free from guilt since he calls us "holy" and "blameless." We join a new kingdom family as God's children. We have hope for the future since we know the glory of heaven will be ours. There are no limits to God's love!

Nothing in this world compares to the spiritual riches we find in Jesus. Do you need courage? It's yours. Armor in the battle with sin and Satan? Put it on! Strength to keep going? God builds you up and moves you forward. Hope or comfort when you're sad? Rest in God's love. Answers to hard questions? Let the Bible tell you all you need to know.

We have so many spiritual blessings, a lifetime isn't enough to discover them all. Let's ask God to help us see them, use them, and celebrate them every day.

Lord, we can't count the ways you love and bless our family.
Thank you for making us your own children. Amen.

Being a True Friend

Wounds from a friend can be trusted, but an enemy multiplies
kisses. Perfume and incense bring joy to the heart,
and the pleasantness of a friend springs from their
heartfelt advice. PROVERBS 27:6, 9

A true friend will tell us what we need to change, even if it's hard to hear. They care too much to let us hurt ourselves through foolish choices. If we struggle with a bad attitude or a harmful habit, they can steer us in a better direction. They encourage us to do what's right, so we avoid trouble and receive rewards and blessings.

We should also have courage to tell the truth to those we care about. If you see a friend or loved one setting themselves up for difficulty, love them enough to give advice. A loving conversation today is better than suffering painful consequences tomorrow.

What kind of advice has protected you from trouble? Who has helped you to make tough decisions, work well, or obey Jesus? A friend's advice is a gift.

Lord, give us humble hearts to listen to good advice.
Let us be friends who speak the truth in love all the time. Amen.

Show Some Love

This is how we know what love is: Jesus Christ laid down his life for us.
And we ought to lay down our lives for our brothers and sisters.
If anyone has material possessions and sees a brother or sister
in need but has no pity on them, how can the love of God be
in that person? Dear children, let us not love with words
or speech but with actions and in truth. 1 JOHN 3:16-18

Love is a verb! It's not just a nice greeting card on our birthday. It's not only a quick goodnight hug or "I love you." Love makes sacrifices, shows compassion, and gives up our own convenience for others. True love backs up words with actions that make a difference.

How can we show love in our home? We listen when someone needs to talk. We offer help when there's work to be done. Sharing, expressing affirmation and gratitude, putting others first are simple ways to keep love active in our family.

We can show love outside our house, too, by giving needed meals, clothes, and acts of service. Our prayer time can remember missionaries or those who are struggling. Think of ways you can put love in action this week.

Lord, you want our love to be more than words. Show us
how we can care for the people around us right now.
Thank you for loving us in every way. Amen.

Mirroring God's Love

*Dear friends, since God so loved us, we also ought to love
one another. No one has ever seen God;
but if we love one another, God lives in us and his
love is made complete in us.* 1 JOHN 4:11-12

It's hard to believe in something you can't see or touch with your hands. People wonder how an invisible God can truly exist. The pain and trouble of this world make many doubt if God's love is real.

God is not hiding or keeping his love a secret. He wants everyone to see him and know his love. Every day, God is revealing himself to the world through his people.

When we put our trust in Jesus, his love becomes a part of us. That love shows in our actions and attitudes. It shines when we forgive those who hurt us. When we give, share, and help. If we offer comfort and kindness. When we're patient with difficult people. If we're grateful instead of demanding and complaining. When we love like Jesus, we show him to everyone. Where love is, God is. If we want to see God, we can start by loving each other.

Lord, make your love complete in us. We want our love
to help others see you. Amen.

God Fights for Us

*... when the priests sounded the trumpet blast, Joshua commanded
the army, "Shout! For the LORD has given you the city!"
When the trumpets sounded, the army shouted, and at
the sound of the trumpet, when the men gave a loud shout,
the wall collapsed; so everyone charged straight
in, and they took the city.* JOSHUA 6:16, 20

What does an army need to conquer the enemy? Weapons? Tanks or fighter jets? Hundreds of soldiers armed for battle?

What might we need to solve a difficult problem? Lots of money? An expert like a doctor, lawyer, or professor? The latest tech and devices? A crowd of friends to cheer us on? In the battles we face, our hurts and struggles can feel impossible to overcome.

For Joshua to defeat Jericho, he didn't need chariots, swords, or an invincible army. He simply listened to God. He obeyed his instructions to march and make some noise. It was God's power—not their own might—that brought them to victory.

We can trust in our own strength to win our battles. We think hard work and smart choices will get us through. Instead, we can listen to God. We can pray he'll tell us what to do. We can be quiet, wait, and watch him fight for us (Exodus 14:14).

What kind of wall is holding you back? Who is against you, making you afraid? Let's trust God to knock that wall down. His love will show the way.

Lord, your power and love are on our side. Amen.

Living in Harmony

*I appeal to you, brothers and sisters, in the name of our
Lord Jesus Christ, that all of you agree with one another
in what you say and that there be no divisions
among you, but that you be perfectly united
in mind and thought.* 1 CORINTHIANS 1:10

Families share their mornings, nights, and everything in between. They eat at the same table. Wash in the same sink. Watch the same screens and sit together on the same furniture. As we live closely side by side, we can find ourselves impatient and annoyed.

Someone might take the last cookie. One might misplace another's library book. Kids play too loudly when Mom needs quiet on the phone. One sibling takes too long to get ready, making another late for practice. They grow grumpy and irritable, and peace is gone.

We don't have to argue and lose our patience. Families can get along. We can act like a team. In our plans and decisions, we can think alike and agree. I can respect your feelings and you can hear my advice. Because of Jesus, we can live in harmony.

"There is one body and one Spirit, just as you were called to one hope when you were called; one Lord, one faith, one baptism; one God and Father of all, who is over all and through all and in all" (Ephesians 4:4-6). If we abide in Jesus, he'll bind us together and make us one.

Lord, unite our family with your love. Amen.

September

Take Time to Encourage

Everyone has heard about your obedience, so I rejoice because of you; but I want you to be wise about what is good, and innocent about what is evil. ROMANS 16:19

Think about a special child or young person in your life. Take the time to encourage that young person in their walk with the Lord. Read them the following and pray for them to remain innocent about what is evil.

You make me feel proud for so many reasons. You deserve the trophies and rewards you worked hard to earn. I like the way you think. Your sense of humor keeps me smiling. You are creative, and your imagination is big and colorful. No one looks exactly like you—God made you wonderful from head to toe.

Yet more than anything else, I'm glad when you look like Jesus. I celebrate each time you tell the truth and show integrity. When you respect others with a humble attitude, I feel joy. As you share what's yours and show kindness, I praise God. You stand out in a crowd each time you stand for what's right and believe God's Word. "I have no greater joy than to hear that my children are walking in the truth" (3 John 1:4).

Every day, you're taking steps toward God or away from him. I'm right beside you, rejoicing in your innocence as you do what's right. When you stumble into sin, I'm praying and believing you'll make your way forward again. As we follow God, we can look forward to sharing life with him together, forever.

Lord, keep us innocent of evil and make us wise about what's good. We want to follow you with joy. Amen.

SEPTEMBER 2

Listening for God's Whisper

After the wind there was an earthquake, but the LORD was not in the earthquake. After the earthquake came a fire, but the LORD was not in the fire. And after the fire came a gentle whisper. When Elijah heard it, he pulled his cloak over his face and went out and stood at the mouth of the cave. 1 KINGS 19:11-13

We pack our days full, don't we? We have meals and cleaning up, school and afternoon activities, errands and appointments. We drive and work and wash. It's go, go, go until something stops us in our tracks. We might wake up sick. The car's tire may go flat. A storm might knock out power so we're in the dark. The interruption gets our attention, showing us how busy we really are.

God wants our attention most of all. Yet we become too busy to listen. We're too tired or distracted to read the Bible. We don't make time to pray. Practices and meetings leave no room for church. We ignore the Spirit speaking God's Word in our hearts.

How can we hear God's whisper? We prepare our hearts to listen. We sit together, just like this, and open his Word. We bring our needs, our confessions, and our praises to him in prayer. We trust his promise that says, "Come near to God and he will come near to you" (James 4:8).

Lord, we want to hear all you have to say. Amen.

What Satisfies Your Heart?

"Come, all you who are thirsty, come to the waters; and you who have no money, come, buy and eat! Why spend money on what is not bread, and your labor on what does not satisfy? Listen, listen to me, and eat what is good, and you will delight in the richest of fare." ISAIAH 55:1-2

A chef will spend hours in the kitchen to prepare a meal that makes your mouth water. Yet within hours, our stomachs are hungry again. It's exciting to drive a new car home from the dealership and park it the driveway. But in time, the car will become damaged, rusty, or boring. New clothes eventually grow worn or out of style. After earning top grades, a student must start over when the new term begins. Not one purchase or achievement can satisfy us forever.

Everyone is laboring or longing for something. Do you want more money? Popularity? Trophies or awards? Fun and excitement? Bigger and better stuff? Are you tired from wishing and working to get what you want?

God alone can satisfy our hearts. He offers freedom from guilt and shame. Peace in hard times. Courage to stand firm. Spiritual gifts to serve and love others. The family of God to walk beside us. He gives life purpose and meaning as he reveals his perfect will. In Christ, we can know true peace and happiness.

Lord, satisfy our hearts with yourself. We want to love you more than anything. Amen.

Every Knee Will Bow

*Therefore God exalted him to the highest place and gave him the name
that is above every name, that at the name of Jesus every knee
should bow, in heaven and on earth and under the earth,
and every tongue acknowledge that Jesus Christ is Lord,
to the glory of God the Father.* PHILIPPIANS 2:9-11

Does it seem like everybody is ignoring Jesus? Angry voices on the radio and TV argue about how to run the world. Science teachers deny the universe has a Creator in heaven. Popular music sings about searching for love that can't be found. Ads spread the lie that money can buy happiness. The world is blind to the power and love of the Lord.

We can feel alone as believers in Jesus. The Bible calls us "foreigners and strangers on earth" as we look toward heaven as our home (Hebrews 11:13). In our hearts we want everybody to know and worship the Lord. We can grow discouraged walking toward God while so many turn away.

Hope is found in God's promise for the future. Jesus is coming back! Every person born on this planet will see and worship the Lord. While we wait, let's pray for family and friends, neighbors and nations to know Jesus. We can ask God "to open their eyes, so that they may turn from darkness to light" and be saved (Acts 26:18).

Lord, you are worthy of all glory and praise.
Make your name great in this world. Amen.

SEPTEMBER 5

Don't Be So Stubborn

I will instruct you and teach you in the way you should go; I will counsel you with my loving eye on you. Do not be like the horse or the mule, which have no understanding but must be controlled by bit and bridle or they will not come to you. PSALM 32:8-9

Have you ever had a slow walk home pushing a bike with a flat tire? Have you sat with a baited fishing line without a single bite? Did you send an urgent message, only to face the silence of no reply? It's frustrating when our efforts to work, play, or connect with others come to nothing.

God feels the same about us. He gave all we need to know him and his Word. He sent Jesus from heaven to seek us, save us, and make us alive. He filled us with his Spirit. The Bible, the Spirit's counsel and help, and godly teachers are available all the time.

Yet just because God speaks, we don't always choose to listen. We ignore the Word and do our own thing. We avoid brothers and sisters in Christ so we can make friends with the world. We tune out the Spirit's voice. Like stubborn mules, we resist God and refuse to follow him.

Today, let's go to God. He'll teach us what's right. He'll guide our steps. We'll become brand-new people who are "transformed by the renewing of our minds" (Romans 12:2). Let's say "yes" to God and allow him to teach us today.

Lord, soften our stubborn hearts so we learn your truth and love.
Amen.

Fishermen of God

*Then Jesus said to Simon, "Don't be afraid; from now on you
will fish for people." So they pulled their boats up on shore,
left everything and followed him.* LUKE 5:10-11

When you believe in Jesus and follow him, he gives you a whole new plan and purpose. He takes you out of the boat of your old life and puts a kind of fishing pole in your hands. Every time you talk to people about Jesus, tell how he answered your prayers, or share what the Bible says, you're helping God "catch" their attention. He's using you to bring lost people into his kingdom family.

Let's pray for our "fish" today—the friends and loved ones who still don't know Jesus. Let's ask God to help them understand who Jesus is. He'll create a moment to talk about him and explain why we follow him. He'll give us courage to speak up and tell the truth of the Bible. God can soften people's hearts and open their minds to understand who he is. The greatest work we'll ever do in the world is telling others how much God loves them.

Lord, our hearts are sad because the people we care about don't
know you. Teach us to be fishermen who take your
good news of salvation to our friends and family. Use our
love and our words to bring them to yourself. Amen.

Seeking God Wholeheartedly

*"Then you will call on me and come and pray to me, and I
will listen to you. You will seek me and find me when you
seek me with all your heart. I will be found by you,"
declares the LORD, "and will bring you
back from captivity."* JEREMIAH 29:12-14

If you lost your keys, you couldn't go where you need to go. Without your wallet, you wouldn't have a way to buy groceries for your family. It would be hard to connect without your phone if you were apart from a loved one. If you lost these important, useful things, you couldn't stop searching until you found them.

Seeking is more than just a glance around the room. It means opening drawers and looking under the furniture. It's digging through your bag and checking all your pockets. If you've turned the house upside-down and still can't find what's lost, you ask for help in the search. You don't rest until it's found.

We lose even more important things in this life. We lose security and the comfort of home. We lose hope of reaching our goals and dreams. We lose courage and confidence. We lose people we love most. Our losses leave us empty inside. When we know God is our only hope, we seek him with all our heart. In his love, he listens and comes to us when we pray.

Seek God when your heart has lost its hope and joy. You will find him and all the love you need.

Lord, may we seek you with all our hearts. Amen.

The Song in Your Heart

Let the message of Christ dwell among you richly as you teach
and admonish one another with all wisdom through psalms,
hymns, and songs from the Spirit, singing to God
with gratitude in your hearts. COLOSSIANS 3:16

How did you learn your alphabet? You sang the letters until you knew them by heart. How do you celebrate another year? We gather around to sing "Happy birthday to you." What makes a road trip more fun? Singing our favorite songs in the car. Music helps to learn new things, celebrate life, and make memories together.

God created music as a gift from him. In the middle of our Bible is a book of psalms to sing to the Lord. Those songs describe life in this world, and they praise the power and love of God through it all. We also sing hymns and worship music to tell God we love him. The lyrics remind us how great, awesome, and loving he is.

Our singing makes God glad. The Bible says we're to "continually offer to God a sacrifice of praise—the fruit of lips that openly profess his name" (Hebrews 13:15). And, God helps us know him better through singing his Word. When we join together to worship, Jesus is with us. "For where two or three gather in my name, there am I with them" (Matthew 18:20). Let's discover God's blessings by singing his praises every day.

Lord, put your song in our mouths and hearts. Amen.

Manna for Every Day

When the dew was gone, thin flakes like frost on the ground
appeared on the desert floor. When the Israelites saw it,
they said to each other, "What is it?" ... Moses said to
them, "It is the bread the LORD has given you to eat.
The people of Israel called the bread manna.
It was white like coriander seed and tasted like
wafers made with honey. EXODUS 16:14-15, 31

God made the people of Israel a tremendous promise—he would rescue them from slavery in Egypt and lead them to a new land of their own. He performed powerful miracles in their sight. He crushed their enemies and created a path through the sea so they could travel to safety. Despite the many signs of God's power, they grumbled when they felt hungry. They accused God of bringing them out to the desert to starve! (Exodus 16:3).

To show his glory once more, God made bread rain from heaven. The people didn't have to buy it, grow it, or search for it—God gave them manna as a generous gift every morning.

God shows his power and love toward us, too. He meets our needs. He protects us from danger. When we're hurt, scared, or sad, he comforts and helps. Even though he proves himself faithful over and over, we still worry and doubt. Today, let's not grumble or complain. We can trust God to care for us every day.

Lord, your mercies are new every morning.
Great is your faithfulness. Amen.

The Best News Ever

*By this gospel you are saved, if you hold firmly to the word I preached
to you … For what I received I passed on to you as of first importance:
that Christ died for our sins according to the Scriptures,
that he was buried, that he was raised on the third day
according to the Scriptures.* 1 CORINTHIANS 15:2-4

Every person is born with a sin problem. Our pride and selfishness, hate and fear separate us from our holy, loving Creator. God's love is so great, he doesn't leave us lost in our sin. He sent Jesus from heaven to earth to rescue us.

Jesus died on the cross to take the punishment we deserve for our sins. He was buried, taking our old life of sin to the grave with him. As God raised him to life, he made it possible for us to be raised to life with him forever. When we believe in Jesus and the gospel, we are saved for all time.

The gospel is the greatest news we'll ever hear, and it's the best news we'll ever tell! We can share it with friends and family, neighbors and classmates, and the whole world. As we receive life through Jesus, we offer hope and eternal life to everyone who hears.

Lord, you saved us through the power of your gospel.
Give us courage to share the gift of Jesus to everyone. Amen.

SEPTEMBER 11

In Your Safe Circle

Be merciful to me, my God, for my enemies are in hot pursuit;
all day long they press their attack. My adversaries pursue
me all day long; in their pride many are attacking me ... .
in God I trust and am not afraid. What can man
do to me? PSALM 56:1-2, 11

Do you feel like you have enemies today? Maybe a boss or colleague is giving you a hard time. Perhaps you're doing your best, but you're told it's not good enough. You've visited every doctor but you're still sick and tired. You can feel under attack with no relief in sight.

People and problems can feel huge, while we feel small and helpless. Yet we have a God whose power and love are greater than anything or anyone we face. He wants to be our "safe circle" that we run to when we're afraid. His words of compassion and kindness are truth—they defend us from whatever mean and hurtful words are thrown our way.

Pray for God to help and protect you today. Ask him to fight for you and keep you from harm. Let him fill you with courage and confidence that no one can take away.

Lord, we feel attacked by people on the outside and our own fears
on the inside. Rescue us from trouble and fight our battles.
Fill us with peace as we trust you to love us all the time. Amen.

Would You Rather ... ?

Walk with the wise and become wise, for a companion of fools suffers harm. Trouble pursues the sinner, but the righteous are rewarded with good things. PROVERBS 13:20-21

Each day, we play a real-life version of "Would You Rather." Would we rather fight or get along? Finish our work or put it off until later? Save our money or spend it? Will we be kind and friendly, or rude and cold? Will we earn people's trust or break our promises? Will we obey the Word or do our own thing? Our choices shape our reputation. They show our character. They reveal our true heart.

We don't answer life's questions by ourselves. Our closest friends play a big part in what we choose to do. We're influenced by the people who share our days. If your friend is dishonest, your integrity will suffer. If another friend is generous, you'll become more willing to share. If your group is disrespectful of those in charge, you'll stop listening and start breaking the rules. When a friend is a gentle peacemaker, you'll learn to control your temper. You and I are changed—for good or for bad—by the people close to us.

How would you describe your friends? Do they bring out the best in you? Do they encourage you to follow Jesus? After you've spent time together, do you feel guilt or regret? Let's choose friends who walk in wisdom. If we do what's right, side by side, we'll be blessed.

Lord, give us friends who help us to love, obey, and follow you. Amen.

SEPTEMBER 13

A Test of Trust

*Search me, God, and know my heart; test me and know
my anxious thoughts. See if there is any offensive way
in me, and lead me in the way everlasting.* PSALM 139:23-24

Our thoughts and emotions let us know when the "heat is on" in our lives. Stress can make us feel grumpy and frustrated. It can be difficult to fall asleep or concentrate. We find ourselves crying more easily or avoiding the ones we love. Worry and fear can take over our minds and feelings in a hurry.

Our troubles are a kind of test to see if our hearts are trusting God or giving in to doubt. A trusting heart says: *This is a challenge, but God is my strength. I'm hurting today, but God's love will comfort my heart. My problem seems impossible, but nothing is too difficult for God to overcome. I don't have what I need today, but God will provide.* Are we going to melt in fear or believe in God's promise to love us all the time?

God loves you and knows all about what you're going through. He listens to every prayer and stays by your side. We can find peace and strength no matter what comes our way.

Lord, we want to trust you all the time. Guard our hearts
from doubt and fear. Amen.

The Proof of Faith

Show me your faith without deeds, and I will show you my faith by my deeds. You believe that there is one God. Good! Even the demons believe that—and shudder. You see that a person is considered righteous by what they do and not by faith alone. James 2:18-19, 24

Our beliefs determine our actions. If we believe an egg is raw, we'll handle it carefully. If we trust a friend is loyal, we'll share our personal thoughts and feelings. If we say we want to succeed, we'll work very hard to do our best. What we think shows in what we do.

Faith in God is more than just believing he exists. Faith trusts him as our Savior and the Lord of our lives. Faith depends on his Spirit for wisdom and comfort. Faith prays and invites God into every situation. Do we believe God is real, or do we also believe he's real for *us*?

The proof is in what we do. Do we look to the Bible for truth? Do we love our neighbors and show kindness to others? Are we humble or proud, thankful or complaining? Our words, choices, and actions show what we truly believe in our hearts.

Lord, we don't just want to know about you,
we want to trust you. Put our faith into action
as we love and obey you in everything. Amen.

The Best Combinations

*Love and faithfulness meet together; righteousness
and peace kiss each other.* PSALM 85:10

Some things are just meant to go together. Peanut butter and jelly. Movies and popcorn. A fuzzy robe and slippers. Paint and paper. A baseball and bat. Parents and kids. As a pair, they're far better than they would each be alone.

God knows what goes together as we follow him. It takes both love and loyalty to make a strong family, friendship, or faith. Love means we keep our promises. We stick close when a loved one is sad or struggling. We keep praying and seeking God every day. Love without faithfulness is just a warm feeling. Faithfulness without love becomes rules without a relationship. God designed love and loyalty to meet together for good.

Righteousness is obeying God in everything. Yet without a peacemaker's heart, our righteousness can be selfish. We can do good things to impress people or get a reward. We compete to prove who's the best. Yet if righteousness and peace "kiss each other," we do good works to bless others. Our hearts are humble so we're ready to forgive and get along. We care and serve like Jesus.

Is our family loving and faithful to each other? Are we peaceful and obedient to God's Word? Let's ask God to show us the way.

Lord, make love and faithfulness, righteousness
and peace kiss each other in our home. Amen.

SEPTEMBER 16

Follow the Leader

Have confidence in your leaders and submit to their authority, because they keep watch over you as those who must give an account. Do this so that their work will be a joy, not a burden, for that would be of no benefit to you. HEBREWS 13:17

You needed your childhood teacher to help you understand your schoolwork. City planners design roads and signs so vehicles can travel safely and get where they need to go. Parents help kids eat right, get to bed on time, and learn right from wrong. Government officials pass laws to limit crime. If we cooperate with those in authority, we stay safe and well. We're able to thrive at home and in our community.

It's the same in the church. God provides his people with leadership to help us follow him. Godly pastors preach the Word so we know God's heart and mind. Teachers and leaders encourage us to trust and obey. They help us discover our spiritual gifts and how to use them. If we become confused or fall into sin, they challenge us with truth so we can turn back to God. Our spiritual leaders help us stay faithful every day.

Will we cooperate with those God has put in authority? Do we have humble hearts to listen and learn? Let's support our church leaders and thank God for them.

Lord, show us how to honor the leaders who help us follow you. Amen.

SEPTEMBER 17

Set Apart for God

May God himself, the God of peace, sanctify you through and through. May your whole spirit, soul and body be kept blameless at the coming of our Lord Jesus Christ. The one who calls you is faithful, and he will do it. 1 THESSALONIANS 5:23-24

Jesus promises that he will sanctify—or set apart—those who believe in him.

We are set apart from the world to be holy. Our minds are set apart to think God's thoughts. Our hands are set apart to touch, use, and work in ways that please him. Our feet are set apart to walk wherever he asks us to go. With our mouths, we speak sanctified words of truth, wisdom and love. We don't think like the world, act like the world, or even feel like the world. We're transformed to be like Jesus.

How do you know you're being sanctified? Think back to the person you used to be. Since then, has Jesus made you more patient? Giving? Gentle and kind? Do you show a little more self-control or bravery? I am "confident of this, that he who began a good work in you will carry it on to completion until the day of Christ Jesus" (Philippians 1:6).

Lord, we're set apart for you. Keep us in your love. Amen.

SEPTEMBER 18

Forgiveness without Limits

*Then Peter came to Jesus and asked, "Lord, how many times shall
I forgive my brother or sister who sins against me? Up to
seven times?" Jesus answered, "I tell you, not seven
times, but seventy-seven times."* MATTHEW 18:21-22

Forgive as the Lord forgave you. COLOSSIANS 3:13

The best of friends still let us down. They break promises and tell our secrets. We love our family, but we sometimes fail to share, help each other out, or show respect. Every day we face the tough choice between frustration or forgiveness.

It's even more challenging when we deal with the same sin over and over. We calm down, pray, and forgive, only to be hurt and offended once more. How do we keep forgiving when our friends and family won't stop sinning against us?

Jesus shows the way. Think of all the times we disobeyed his Word. We've lied and taken what doesn't belong to us. We've argued and complained. When we could have been generous, we grabbed more for ourselves. Every time we sin against one another, we sin against God himself. Yet every time we confess and ask him to forgive, he says yes!

The patience and mercy of Jesus can be ours, too. His Spirit will give us the love we need to forgive those who sin against us. We can give the grace we've found in Jesus to everyone we know.

Lord, we want to forgive like you, without limit.
Fill us with your love. Amen.

SEPTEMBER 19

You Are Wonderfully Made

Shall what is formed say to the one who formed it, "You did not make me"? Can the pot say to the potter, "You know nothing"? Yet you, LORD, are our Father. We are the clay, you are the potter; we are all the work of your hand. ISAIAH 29:16, 64:8

As Christians, we believe this world is created by God. Each leaf on every tree, each water droplet in the ocean, and every cell in our bodies was made by his wisdom and power. When he finished creating the world in the beginning, he said all he made was "very good" (Genesis 1:31).

Yet when we look at ourselves, we can wish we were different. We're jealous of our friends' talent or gorgeous appearance. Quiet personalities want to be outgoing, and lively women work to settle down and blend in. We look at the rich and famous and think, *If only I could be like them, life would be perfect.*

We could spend a lot of time, energy, and money trying to change. We forget we're God's children who he made this way on purpose. Our complaints tell God he did a poor job as our Creator. We lose faith in his wisdom and love.

Today, name the wonderful qualities you see in the mirror. Remember all the ways you're "fearfully and wonderfully made" (Psalm 139:14).

Lord, you are the potter and we are the clay. Help us to be content with the way you made us. We want to trust you've got wonderful plans for us, just the way we are. Amen.

The Cure for Loneliness

A father to the fatherless, a defender of widows, is God in his holy dwelling.
God sets the lonely in families, he leads out the prisoners with singing;
but the rebellious live in a sun-scorched land. Psalm 68:5-6

Family is God's cure for loneliness. In a family, you have a name. You're cared for when you're sick or discouraged. Holidays, birthdays, and victories are celebrated. You're safe since your family has your back and protects you from harm. A family has you for keeps, no matter your struggles and mistakes. You know love, laughter, and life together.

Sometimes a family is made through marriage and babies. It might form through adoption or inviting others to come in and stay. Every child of God is part of his kingdom family—the church—that will last forever. A family is a little taste of heaven and the togetherness God shares with his people.

Love your family well. If you show the kind of love that "always protects, always trusts, always hopes, always perseveres," you'll never be lonely in your home (1 Corinthians 13:7). And be sure to keep an open door to welcome the lonely so you can show God's love.

Lord, we thank you for our family that you made.
Fill our house with your love. Amen.

One Day in the Clouds

*For the Lord himself will come down from heaven, with
a loud command, with the voice of the archangel and
with the trumpet call of God, and the dead in Christ will
rise first. After that, we who are still alive and are left
will be caught up together with them in the clouds to
meet the Lord in the air. And so we will be with
the Lord forever.* 1 THESSALONIANS 4:16-17

Our future with Jesus starts with a great adventure! A trumpet will sound and we'll meet Jesus face-to-face in the clouds. The family of God will be together all at once—no one has to wait their turn, and nobody will be left behind. Jesus will take us all to our perfect, heavenly home full of light and joy forever.

Who gets to look forward to that exciting moment in the clouds? Those who are "in Christ." To be in Christ means you're one of God's children. You believe Jesus is God's Son who took the punishment for our sins on the cross. Just as you know he was raised to life again, you'll be raised with him to live forever. You're loved, forgiven, and made new.

Whenever we look up at the clouds in the sky, we can look forward to the glorious day when we'll see Jesus.

Lord, we love you! Thank you for the hope of meeting you
in the clouds and beginning our eternal life with you. Amen.

The Identity We Wear

*Do not lie to each other, since you have taken off your
old self with its practices and have put on the new self,
which is being renewed in knowledge in the image
of its Creator.* COLOSSIANS 3:9-10

Graduates wear a cap and gown to celebrate their degrees and diplomas. A wedding gown announces a bride is no longer single. An officer's badge shows his role of authority, and a doctor's white coat says she's trained in medicine. A superhero's costume sets him apart from ordinary people. What we wear on the outside can reveal our identity.

God says when we believe in Jesus, we put on a new self. We have been "clothed with Christ" (Galatians 3:27). We wear a "crown of beauty," a "garment of praise and salvation," and "a robe of righteousness" (Isaiah 61:3, 10). We look like Jesus as we love and live like him.

When we tell a lie, it's like taking off our new self in Christ and putting on dirty, torn clothes that are fit for the trash. We cover up our new identity as God's children by our deceitfulness. If we make a habit of lying, we can feel bound up by layers of ugly sin. Yet if we confess our sin and turn to God, he will make us clean and new. He will set us free from the lies and make us shine.

Lord, make us honest and true so we can show we are yours. Amen.

Passing the Test

Remember how the LORD your God led you all the way in the wilderness these forty years, to humble and test you in order to know what was in your heart, whether or not you would keep his commands. He gave you manna to eat in the wilderness ... to humble and test you so that in the end it might go well with you. DEUTERONOMY 8:2, 16

In school, you were tested to see if you learned to solve math problems or memorized your spelling list. A doctor will order a blood test to test if you're sick or well. A runner has to run a qualifying race to compete in a marathon. Tests are a way to measure our strength, our abilities, and our health.

Would you agree, though, that tests are a challenge? It takes hard work to prepare. We have to focus and concentrate. Sometimes they can even hurt. But in the end, we know if we've succeeded or failed to reach our goal.

Our hearts need testing, too. God uses our troubles and fears to test our faith. Will we follow Jesus or go our own way? Will we trust he's still good when times are bad? Are we working to care for ourselves, or do we depend on the Father? Do we listen to the world's point of view, or do we believe the Word? Through testing, we learn what's in our hearts.

Are we wandering through a wilderness today? If we stay faithful to love and obey, we'll pass the test.

Lord, may we trust you in the wilderness. Amen.

Choices and Consequences

*"I have the right to do anything," you say—but not everything
is beneficial. "I have the right to do anything"—but not
everything is constructive. No one should seek their
own good, but the good of others.*
1 CORINTHIANS 10:23-24

As an adult, I make a lot of my own rules. I can eat what I want, whenever I like. In the car I could drive as far and fast as I please. I can stay up late and watch every channel. I choose how to spend my money. Yet just because I have the right to make my own choices, it does not mean everything is helpful or good.

If I eat only sugar, I'll feel sick. If I drive too fast, I'll get hurt or in trouble. Staying up too late makes me exhausted. Not every show or movie is wholesome for my spirit. If I waste my money, I can't buy what I need. My choices have consequences for me and everyone in my life.

Do you wish you could be your own boss? Do you want the right to do whatever you like? God tells us that rights come with responsibility. We should ask, "What is the most loving thing to do? Will my choice help or hurt other people? How can I honor God with my decision?" We lay down our rights so we can love others like Jesus.

Lord, make us wise and loving in all we do. Amen.

Turn in the Opposite Direction

Repent! Turn away from all your offenses; then sin will not be your downfall. Rid yourselves of all the offenses you have committed, and get a new heart and a new spirit. EZEKIEL 18:30-31

If a marble on a table kept rolling in the same direction, it would fall right off the table. If we're heading down the wrong path, we'll fall too. One little lie leads to more as we cover our tracks. Lazy habits make us so behind in our work, we might never catch up. Mean words, gossip, and arguments push friends so far apart, they don't know how to come back together. A stubborn heart that won't listen or obey becomes hard and cold. If we continue down the road of sin, we travel farther away from God.

In God's kindness, it's never too late to repent. We can repent—or turn in the opposite direction—to go back to God. "If we confess our sins, he is faithful and just and will forgive us our sins and purify us from all unrighteousness" (1 John 1:9). When we turn to God, he wipes out our sins and brings "times of refreshing" to our spirits (Acts 3:19). Our guilt and shame are gone.

When we repent, God gives us power to change. The Spirit bears fruit like love, kindness, and goodness in our lives. We receive a new heart and spirit as we turn to him.

Lord, let us turn to you and know your love. Amen.

Some Things Are Priceless

In the temple courts [Jesus] found people selling cattle, sheep and doves, and others sitting at tables exchanging money. So he made a whip out of cords, and drove all from the temple courts ... he scattered the coins of the money changers and overturned their tables. To those who sold doves he said, "Get these out of here! Stop turning my Father's house into a market!" JOHN 2:14-16

A toy store makes money when a customer buys a game or a doll. A baker earns a living selling loaves of bread. A cab driver is paid mile by mile on the road. Through buying and selling, companies stay in business and people prosper.

It's different with God. He invites us to "Come ... you who have no money, come, buy and eat! Come, buy wine and milk without money and without cost" (Isaiah 55:1). Money won't buy a ticket to heaven. The abundant life he gives cannot be bought or sold. It was purchased by Jesus' life on the cross.

Because of this, Jesus was angry when the temple was turned into a market. People seeking to worship God were cheated out of their money. The sellers were exploiting God's house to make money for their own houses.

God's Word is priceless. His love and mercy are given, not earned. The good news of the gospel is not a product to be bought and sold. Our church is not a place of business—it's a sanctuary of love and healing for everyone.

Lord, thank you for the free gift of eternal life. Amen.

Cracking under Temptation

"Watch and pray so that you will not fall into temptation.
The spirit is willing, but the flesh is weak." MARK 14:38

If you push, bump, or tap an egg, it will crack open and make a mess. For you and me, we can feel pushed by stress. We bump into difficult people who test our patience. We're tapped on the shoulder to do more work and give more help. We feel worried. Stressed. Tired and worn down. Our spirit wants to love and obey Jesus, but our flesh is weak.

When we give in to temptation, we "crack." Ugly words fly out of our mouths. We run away instead of facing our fears. We pick up devices instead of God's Word. Trying to make it on our own, we forget to pray for help.

What is Jesus asking us to do today? You may need to forgive those who hurt you, but you're still angry. I should stop and help someone, but I feel too busy. He could ask you to reach out to a lonely neighbor, but you're nervous or shy. Our flesh says "no" while our spirit says yes.

With care, we can squeeze an egg without cracking it open. If we're careful to stay in God's hand, we stay whole and strong. He will give us all we need to love him, love others, and obey him in everything.

Lord, we're willing. Give us strength to do what's right. Amen.

Growing Our Blessings

"It will be like a man ... who called his servants and entrusted his wealth to them. To one he gave five bags of gold, to another two bags, and to another one bag ... The man who had received five bags of gold went at once and put his money to work and gained five bags more ... But the man who had received one bag went off, dug a hole in the ground and hid his master's money." MATTHEW 25:14-18

God gives every kind of blessing and each is meant to grow. Money can increase if we save and invest wisely. We can build our health if we eat well and exercise. Friendships grow stronger as we care for people around us. Skills expand if you make the most of your schooling. God's blessings grow as we use them.

God has given the great gift of serving him. Everything we do to love and obey brings a reward in heaven. We hold treasure in our hands—the good news of salvation—and we're meant to live it and share it!

Will we hide our spiritual gifts instead of serving others? Will we stay silent or tell others about Jesus? Will we settle for an easy life or invest in God's kingdom? Let's choose to love and obey so we can hear, "'Well done, good and faithful servant! You have been faithful with a few things; I will put you in charge of many things. Come and share your master's happiness!" (Matthew 25:23).

Lord, we're tempted to bury your gifts instead of building your
kingdom. Make us your good and faithful servants. Amen.

Signs of the Messiah

"Fellow Israelites, listen to this: Jesus of Nazareth was a man accredited by God to you by miracles, wonders and signs, which God did among you through him, as you yourselves know ... Therefore let all Israel be assured of this: God has made this Jesus, whom you crucified, both Lord and Messiah." ACTS 2:22, 36

We trust what's in a package will match what's on the label. Yet we must see, touch, and taste what's inside to prove the label is true.

God sent Jesus into the world from heaven. His people had been waiting for a messiah to come for generations. When Jesus was born and lived among them, they struggled to believe he was the Savior they were hoping for.

Jesus proved himself to be God's Son by the miracles, wonders, and signs he performed. He healed little children and raised them from the dead. The blind could see and the lame could run and dance. Stormy seas were quieted by just one word. Thousands of hungry families were fed with just a few loaves of bread and fish. Jesus walked on water and took authority over evil spirits. He conquered death on the cross. No one has ever seen a man with such awesome power.

We can have confidence that Jesus truly is the Lord and Messiah. God exalted him with the "name that is above every name," so everyone will know he is the Lord.

Lord, we thank you for Jesus, our Savior and King. Amen.

God Will Grant You Justice

" ... *there was a widow in that town who kept coming to [a judge]
with the plea, 'Grant me justice against my adversary.' For some
time he refused. But finally he said to himself, 'Even though
I don't fear God or care what people think, yet because this
widow keeps bothering me, I will see that she gets justice, so
that she won't eventually come and attack me!'"* Luke 18:3-5

Life can be unfair. We feel picked on or pushed away. After working hard, we don't always get the reward we deserve. We're accused of wrong even if we're innocent. Our problems grow bigger than we can handle. Desperate for help, we wonder if God hears our prayers.

It's easier to simply ask for a drink than to dig a deep well for water with our own two hands. In the same way, God doesn't make us work to get his attention. All we have to do is ask and he'll listen to our prayers. He loves us too much to ignore our cries for help.

Do you feel mistreated or let down today? Go to our loving Father and know he is ready to help. "And will not God bring about justice for his chosen ones, who cry out to him day and night? Will he keep putting them off? I tell you, he will see that they get justice, and quickly" (Luke 18:7-8).

Lord, we know you're listening. Bring us the justice
we need today. Amen.

October

OCTOBER 1

Renew Your Strength

*Even youths grow tired and weary, and young men stumble
and fall; but those who hope in the LORD will renew
their strength. They will soar on wings like eagles;
they will run and not grow weary, they will walk
and not be faint.* ISAIAH 40:30-31

Even young people get tired and discouraged. It's hard to get up every morning for school or work. No matter how hard you work, you can't always achieve what you're working for. Even when you try to be a good friend, you feel lonely. How do we recover when we're worn out? If we feel like giving up, how do we keep trying? When it seems nothing will ever change, where does hope come from?

We have a God who promises to give us strength and energy—so much, we feel like we can fly! In his love, he invites us to pray. He wants us to cast the heavy burden of our worries on him so he can take care of us (Psalm 55:22). Perhaps we've been too proud to admit we need help. We can "humble [ourselves], therefore, under God's mighty hand, that he may lift [us] up in due time" (1 Peter 5:6). God brings healing and comfort, courage and strength if we put our hope in him.

Lord, it's hard to put one foot in front of the other.
We need your love and power to renew our strength. Amen.

Completing the Puzzle

Taking the five loaves and the two fish and looking up to heaven, he gave thanks and broke the loaves. Then he gave them to his disciples to distribute to the people. He also divided the two fish among them all. They all ate and were satisfied, and the disciples picked up twelve basketfuls of broken pieces of bread and fish. MARK 6:41-43

How many times have you worked on a puzzle, only to find you're missing a piece at the end? The empty space leaves the picture incomplete. Sometimes we feel that way about our life. We run out of time for all we want to do. We feel lonely and wish for more friends. Our budget is too tight to buy new things. Our strength is small, but our problems feel huge. Worries and troubles steal our peace.

God knows we have limits and he cares about our needs. No matter how big our struggle, he can take the little we have and make it more than enough. He is so powerful and so good, he can satisfy us in every way.

What do you need today? Take your little bit of faith and run to your big, big God. Trust him to take care of you. In his love, he'll provide and bring peace to your heart.

Lord, you are more than enough for us. Grow our faith
as you give us all we need. Amen.

Delicate Like Sugar

As a father has compassion on his children,
so the LORD has compassion on those who
fear him; for he knows how we are formed,
he remembers that we are dust. PSALM 103:13-14

The sweetness of sugar is part of almost every celebration. We place candles on birthday cakes, we decorate colorful Christmas cookies, and we fill our Easter baskets with candies and chocolate. Yet the sugar we taste is fragile. Its tiny grains are like dust—easily spilled or brushed away. It quickly dissolves in water, and it will scorch if heated. But no matter how delicate, a little taste of sugar can make us smile.

God loves you and *likes* you so much more than sweets! Psalm 149:4 says, "The Lord takes delight in his people." He says we are precious. Honored. Loved (Isaiah 43:4). Because we are so special to God, he has a compassionate heart for us.

He knows we're only human. Our bodies get hurt or sick. Our minds become confused or struggle to understand what's true. In our spirits we worry and doubt. We become tired and discouraged. Sometimes we have to learn lessons the hard way. Even when we try our best, we make mistakes. Through it all, God is patient and kind. He knows how we're fragile and weak.

God calls us to follow Jesus. When we struggle along the way, he's ready to forgive and keep us going.

Lord, you know our limits. Make us stronger in Jesus every day. Amen.

OCTOBER 4

Be Patient

*Be completely humble and gentle; be patient, bearing
with one another in love. Make every effort to
keep the unity of the Spirit through
the bond of peace. EPHESIANS 4:2-3*

It takes hard work to get along! It's hard to slow our pace to match the one who's lagging behind. It's tough to be a good sport when a referee makes bad calls. When a friend backs out of the special plans you've been anticipating for weeks, the frustration is real. We find ourselves hurt or let down, even by those who love us most.

How do we keep a broken promise from breaking up a friendship? Does a wrong word, a mistake, or a sin have to tear us apart? God says the glue that keeps us together is a patient spirit.

If we're patient, we know others need time to grow at their own pace. We remember how we struggle so others have room to struggle, too. We forgive like God forgave us. We choose to love the unlovable, always trusting and hoping God is doing his work in their lives (1 Corinthians 13:7).

Do you feel a little aggravated today? Are you tired of waiting for someone to change? God is faithful to give what we need. With his patience in our hearts, he will bind us together for always.

Lord, make us patient so we love each other no matter what. Amen.

Rekindle Your Hope

*May the God of hope fill you with all joy and peace as you
trust in him, so that you may overflow with hope
by the power of the Holy Spirit.* ROMANS 15:13

Does it seem like everything is going wrong? You feel lonely and frustrated, tired and discouraged. The world offers all kinds of advice to stir a little hope in your heart:

If you believe it, you can achieve it.

Follow your heart.

Just be yourself.

Keep your chin up.

Just believe in yourself.

Quitters never win and winners never quit.

Fake it 'til you make it.

We're told hard work and positive thinking can take us wherever we want to go. The world says to put hope in ourselves and our own strength. But following that advice is like trying to catch the waves at the seashore. In our darkest night, we need real hope to hold on to.

God offers true joy, peace, and hope in any situation. We can trust him completely because he holds unlimited power to change everything. Instead of depending on our own strength, we rely on him. He's always here and he loves us too much to let us fall. His Spirit will fill us with hope as we put our faith in him.

Lord, today we put our trust in you. Fill us with peace
and joy by your Spirit. Amen.

OCTOBER 6

The Awesome Fire

" ... Fill four large jars with water and pour it on the offering and
on the wood. Do it again ... Do it a third time," he ordered ...
The water ran down around the altar and even filled the trench.
Then the fire of the LORD fell and burned up the sacrifice,
the wood, the stones and the soil, and also licked up
the water in the trench. 1 KINGS 18:33-35, 38

God is called "a consuming fire." Nothing can stand before him. When God does the impossible—burning up, breaking down, or clearing out—he proves he is the one true God.

In the end, he will destroy all evil once and for all. "That day will bring about the destruction of the heavens by fire, and the elements will melt in the heat. But in keeping with his promise we are looking forward to a new heaven and a new earth, where righteousness dwells" (2 Peter 3:12-13).

God is also "a refiner's fire." Just as silver is melted in the fire to make it shine, God allows us to feel the heat of trouble. He uses our struggles to purify us from sin and strengthen our faith.

A consuming fire destroys what's evil. A refining fire creates beauty and perfection. Our God is loving and good—his glory burns brightly forever.

Lord, you are an awesome fire. We trust you to make all things new,
whether in the world or in our own hearts. Amen.

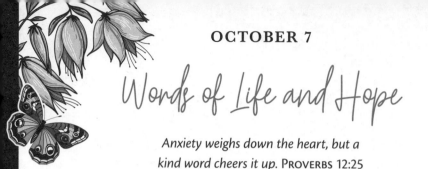

Words of Life and Hope

Anxiety weighs down the heart, but a
kind word cheers it up. PROVERBS 12:25

When we're feeling anxious, it can seem like the weight of the world rests on our shoulders. We worry and wonder if we'll finish our work on time. What if we fail? What if people don't like us? What if we don't have what we need? What if we get in trouble? What if we can't handle what's coming our way? We even worry if we can't stop worrying! When we struggle with anxiety, it's hard to hold on to hope and joy in Jesus.

We have a powerful way to keep our spirits up—talking and sharing with our spiritual "family." If we're feeling overwhelmed with too much to do, we can say to each other, "I'm here to help." If we're scared we're going to lose or fail, we can tell each other, "I love you no matter what." When we're feeling lonely or insecure, we can remember we're each other's favorite people. If you're afraid to admit your mistakes, we'll always say, "I forgive you." When we're scared of tomorrow, we can speak the Word of God to remember he's with us wherever we go.

Our words are able to breathe life and hope into one another. No matter what we're going through, let's keep each other's spirits up with kindness and encouragement every day.

Lord, your kindness gives us hope for tomorrow. You tell us
we're loved in so many ways. Teach us how to cheer
each other up when we're feeling down. Amen.

Be a Blessing

*"So in everything, do to others what you would
have them do to you, for this sums up the
Law and the Prophets."* MATTHEW 7:12

In God's Word he gave his Law—his commandments that teach us right from wrong. God created his Law so the whole world could see what his love looks like. Whenever we treat others as we want to be treated, we're showing the same kind of love we've been given from God.

Just as we like to receive presents and help with hard things, we can be generous to others. It feels good to hear compliments and encouragement, so we also build others up with our words. We know the hurt of feeling left out or pushed away, so we make sure everyone around us feels welcome. Our own sins and mistakes leave us with guilt and regret—we offer friends and family the same forgiveness we find in Jesus.

We're called to bless others as we've been blessed. God has poured out his love on us without holding back one good thing. Every time we show kindness, respect, compassion, and care to others, we're living the perfect law of God's love.

Lord, we know how we want to be treated, and you love us
best of all. Teach us to love like you. Amen.

The Lessons in the Struggle

*Consider it pure joy, my brothers and sisters, whenever you
face trials of many kinds, because you know that the
testing of your faith produces perseverance.
Let perseverance finish its work so that you
may be mature and complete,
not lacking anything.* JAMES 1:2-4

If we placed eggs, flour, and sugar in the oven, they wouldn't turn to cake once we shut the door. The ingredients must be cracked open. Beaten and stirred. Poured out, and placed under intense heat. Yet after those preparations, the batter transforms into a delicious treat.

You and I are becoming something new as well. God is working so we become more fully like Jesus. What does God use to do this work? His Word teaches about his love and plan for salvation. Other believers motivate us to serve and obey. The Spirit gives wisdom to guide our steps. Yet one of God's most powerful tools is our trials.

Without difficult people and problems, how would we learn patience? Without needs, how would we learn that God will provide? Without weakness, how would we know God's strength? Suffering moves us to pray and invite God into our pain. We learn to trust him most when he's all we have left.

When troubles come our way, we might complain or try to get them over with. Instead, let's welcome the lessons God is teaching in the struggle. Let's trust he's in control. In the end, we'll know more of God's love than we could imagine.

Lord, help us to find joy in our trials. Amen.

Hidden in a Basket

Then Pharaoh gave this order to all his people: "Every Hebrew boy that is born you must throw into the Nile, but let every girl live." … a Levite woman … gave birth to a son. When she saw that he was a fine child, she hid him for three months. But when she could hide him no longer, she got a papyrus basket for him and coated it with tar and pitch. Then she placed the child in it and put it among the reeds along the bank of the Nile. Exodus 1:22, 2:1-3

Children are a blessing and reward from God. From the moment that tiny bundle was placed in your arms, you've wanted to keep her happy, well, and safe. You do all you can to protect your children. Nothing would feel more sad or scary than knowing your children are in danger.

Yet parents have limits. You can use sunscreen, but you can't keep the sun from shining. We buckle up in the car, but you can't control traffic or icy roads. You can teach kindness at home, but you can't help stop mean kids at school. If you focused on all the dangers you can't control, you'd spend every moment stressed and upset.

Peace is found by placing your children in God's hands. He knows every threat they face. Nothing takes him by surprise. You can claim his promise to "be with you wherever you go" (Joshua 1:9). "The one who is in you is greater than the one who is in the world" (1 John 4:4).

Lord, you love every child. Protect our family by your power. Amen.

Be a Credible Witness

"Do not spread false reports. Do not help a guilty person by being a malicious witness. Do not follow the crowd in doing wrong." EXODUS 23:1-2

In court, the judge needs to hear the truth. Was a crime committed? Did anyone see what happened? Who is guilty or innocent? The judge listens to each witness to learn the facts. What if a witness tells a lie? A criminal could go free and hurt someone else. Or, an innocent person could suffer. Words are powerful and we can't take them back once they're spoken.

You and I are witnesses every day. You know who accomplished their tasks or forgot them. You watch drivers break the speed limit. You see customers cutting in line at the store. You're proud when you witness your child finishing every page of their homework. Whether at home or out in the world, we see both right and wrong.

Are we truthful when we tell what we see? Are you tempted to lie so your friend stays out of trouble? If you're angry, do your accusations aim to hurt someone's reputation? Do I let others take the blame for my mistakes? Do I ignore the wrong in front of me instead of standing up for what's right?

The Bible says Jesus is the truth. We're called to be truth-tellers, too. We are honest witnesses who protect the innocent and stand for justice.

Lord, give us courage to tell the truth. Amen.

Willing to Be Sharpened

Better is open rebuke than hidden love. Wounds from a friend can be trusted, but an enemy multiplies kisses. As iron sharpens iron, so one person sharpens another. PROVERBS 27:5-6, 17

Sometimes, the truth hurts. It's hard to be confronted with our mistakes. We feel shame or embarrassment to find we let someone down. Our pride avoids criticism or correction. We don't want to hear we failed. It's easier to stay as we are without having to change.

Yet just as love means giving and helping, it means telling the truth. Like a doctor's medicine can cure sickness, a friend's truthful words can bring healing to our life. Hearing about our sin allows us to face it, confess it to God, and find forgiveness and freedom. A godly friend is able "to open [our] eyes and turn [us] from darkness to light, and from the power of Satan to God, so that [we] may receive forgiveness of sins and a place among those who are sanctified by faith in [Jesus]" (Acts 26:18).

Today, are we willing to grow and change? Do we have humility to let others sharpen us? Will we take good advice to heart? Can we receive hard truth as a gift of love from those who care for us? Let's trust God that the "wounds" of correction will bring healing and life in the end.

Lord, we're not perfect. Make us humble to listen
so we can learn and grow. Amen.

Don't Be like the Pharisees

*"Woe to you, teachers of the law and Pharisees, you hypocrites!
You clean the outside of the cup and dish, but inside they are
full of greed and self-indulgence. Blind Pharisee! First clean
the inside of the cup and dish, and then the outside
also will be clean".* MATTHEW 23:25-26

In Jesus' day, religious leaders called "pharisees" cared a lot about looking good on the outside. They were in charge, and they made everyone follow strict rules about what to eat, how to dress, and who to spend time with. All that strenuous effort to look perfectly right just filled them with pride. They were such good rule-followers, they thought they were better than everybody else.

But Jesus could see their hearts. No matter how many rules they followed, they were ugly and sinful inside. They didn't love God or anybody else but themselves.

God wants us to obey him from the inside out. If we love God and his Word, it will show in everything we say and do.

Lord, keep us from pride that tries to impress everyone
by following the rules. Let all we do and the words
we speak come from your love in our hearts. Amen.

Working with All Your Heart

Whatever you do, work at it with all your heart, as working for the Lord, not for human masters, since you know that you will receive an inheritance from the Lord as a reward. It is the Lord Christ you are serving. COLOSSIANS 3:23-24

If we're honest, we often avoid hard work. Chores feel frustrating, because the dishes we wash today have to be washed all over again tomorrow. Paperwork and bills are stressful and tiring after a long day at work. It's a challenge to clock in early at a job when we'd rather sleep in. We're tempted to do the bare minimum instead of working with all our hearts.

God drops an amazing promise into the middle of our struggle with work. If we give it our all—as if the Lord is our teacher or boss—he's pleased. He offers rewards in heaven much greater than the paycheck, admiration, and tidy home we might earn today.

We need to ask who we're serving. Are we working for more money or success? Do we want to please our boss and impress our colleagues? Is it our goal to look good, with the most impressive house on the block? Jesus invites us to turn away from selfish gain to work out of love and obedience to him.

Let's look at our jobs and responsibilities with fresh eyes today. With God's help, we can work hard with the joyful hope of heavenly rewards to come. We're serving the One who knows us, loves us completely, and never leaves our side.

Lord, teach us what it means to work for you. Thank you for the promise of an inheritance that lasts forever. We love you. Amen.

Overcoming Gossip

*Like a fluttering sparrow or a darting swallow, an undeserved
curse does not come to rest.* PROVERBS 26:2

Have your friends ever talked about you behind your back? Lies and gossip make us feel embarrassed and angry. Mean comments make us feel unwanted. Rude remarks are disrespectful and say we're not important. Friendships are divided when ugly words come between them.

When people speak negative words that aren't true, it's not just our feelings that get hurt. We worry the lies will "stick" and damage our reputations. We're afraid people will believe what they hear. We don't want to lose their trust and respect.

God knows the stress we feel from others' words. He says if our conscience is clear, we don't have to be afraid. Gossip and false words will fall away if we're loving and living like Jesus. Strong character breaks the fragile, empty bubbles of false words.

Are you worried about your reputation today? We can depend on God like his Son Jesus when he was accused: "When they hurled their insults at him, he did not retaliate; when he suffered, he made no threats. Instead, he entrusted himself to him who judges justly" (1 Peter 2:23). Let's keep doing what's right and trust God to take care of us.

Lord, protect us so mean words and lies don't hurt
our reputation. Help us to do what's right. Amen.

Recharging Your Batteries

In peace I will lie down and sleep, for you alone,
Lord, make me dwell in safety. Psalm 4:8

Sleep is a gift from God. It recharges our batteries so we have energy for a new day. The hours we sleep are a break from work and worry each night. Our beds are a warm, relaxing place to think, pray, and rest. It's a relief to know sleep is waiting for us at the end of every busy day.

Yet sometimes sickness, anxiety, or scary dreams steal your sleep. Dark shadows or strange sounds stir up your imagination. You feel alone as you wait for the morning's light. Your bed can seem like a place of fear and loneliness instead of comfort. You miss out on the gift God had in mind for us at night, and you wake up tired in the morning.

Tonight, make a list of the worries or struggles that keep you awake. Pray and ask God to take care of you. Remember he is loving, mighty and powerful, and close to you all night long. Because he's your protector, you can lie down and sleep in peace. Ask for help to trust him all the time.

Lord, you never slumber or sleep. You're watching over us every night.
Help me rest peacefully and quietly as I trust you. Amen.

OCTOBER 17

Get Back on Your Feet

He lifted me out of the slimy pit, out of the mud and mire;
he set my feet on a rock and gave me a firm place
to stand. He put a new song in my mouth,
a hymn of praise to our God. PSALM 40:2-3

Sometimes we walk ourselves into a mess, don't we? We lie and try to cover our tracks. We break a promise or let people down. After joining in gossip, we regret what we heard and said. We disobey and become caught in all kinds of trouble. We feel guilty and embarrassed. We're stuck—unable to climb out of the pit of shame and regret.

God knows how we sin and fail. While we're slipping and sliding into trouble, God is holding out his hand. He reaches out to save us. We can confess what we've done and know we're forgiven. We'll be washed clean from a guilty conscience (Hebrews 10:22). He'll set us on our feet so we can begin again.

Do you feel like you're losing your footing? Is it hard to do what's right? Do you feel tired, afraid, or alone? Take God's hand so he can place your feet on a rock. Stand on the Word that says you're loved. Let God teach you his ways so you don't slip and fall. When we stand with him, we're strong. He fills us with joy that we can't hold inside.

Lord, set our feet on your rock so we stand firm in you. Amen.

Cool Your Temper

An angry person stirs up conflict, and a hot-tempered person commits many sins. PROVERBS 29:22

"In your anger do not sin": Do not let the sun go down while you are still angry, and do not give the devil a foothold. EPHESIANS 4:26-27

God created us to feel all kinds of emotions. Sadness, excitement, anger, and joy move through us all the time. Feelings aren't good or bad—they're simply a response to what's happening around us.

Anger isn't always wrong. It can motivate people to work for justice and help the innocent. However, we can feel angry for selfish reasons. We might want our own way. We're frustrated when we have to wait. We don't like others pointing out our mistakes or telling us what to do. That kind of anger can lash out with ugly words and actions.

God says if we give in to our temper, we're going to sin. We'll hurt people and do things we regret. If anger keeps burning, it gives power to Satan to harden our hearts. Our reputations and relationships can be ruined by the way we act on our angry feelings.

The answer is a humble heart that's willing to patiently obey. We can pray for God's help to calm down. We can go to bed every night at peace with him and each other.

Lord, keep our anger from burning out of control. Teach us how to handle our strong feelings. Fill our home with love and peace. Amen.

A New Mind, Heart and Life

*You were taught, with regard to your former way of life, to put
off your old self, which is being corrupted by its deceitful
desires; to be made new in the attitude of your minds;
and to put on the new self, created to be like God in
true righteousness and holiness.* EPHESIANS 4:22-24

In the beginning, God created mankind in his image. People shared his creative imagination. His purity. His wisdom. They shared his presence, as Adam and Eve walked with God in the garden. When sin came into the world, it destroyed the perfect beauty of all God made. The human race still bears God's image, but it's corrupted, deceived, and separated from God.

You and I see this in ourselves. We struggle with bad attitudes. We want our own way, and we hurt others to have it. What's good can seem bad, and what's wrong seems right. We need the rescue of a Savior to give us a new mind, heart, and life.

By God's great love, he sent Jesus. When we believe in him we're changed from the inside out. He makes us holy like we were created to be from the beginning. We love instead of hate. Give instead of take. Know and tell the truth instead of lies. The wrong in us is made right. "Therefore, if anyone is in Christ, the new creation has come: The old has gone, the new is here!" (2 Corinthians 5:17).

Lord, make us new so we can be like you. Amen.

A Wall of Self-control

Like a city whose walls are broken through is a person who lacks self-control.
PROVERBS 25:28

A wall offers protection from dangerous enemies. It's a shelter from damaging storms. A wall keeps vulnerable little ones from wandering away. It holds the good in, and it keeps the bad out.

Self-control is like a wall around our life. It protects us from the shame and regret of giving in to temptation. It keeps our bodies from getting hurt by foolish risk-taking. It spares us the embarrassment of saying the wrong thing at the wrong time. Self-control shields us from breaking rules and getting into trouble. It guards our reputation as we do what's right. Self-control gives strength to keep going when we want to quit.

How is your wall of self-control standing today? Are you able to think before you speak? Can you tackle a challenge without giving up? Do you need others to keep you in line? Is it hard to keep big feelings like anger, fear, or excitement from running away with you? Are you the kind of person who others can trust and depend on?

Self-control brings blessings from God like peace. Respect. Confidence. Success. A clean conscience. Friendship. Safety. Freedom. Let's ask God to build strong walls of self-control around ourselves and our family today.

Lord, we need self-control to think clearly and live like Jesus.
Help our "walls" to stand firm by the Spirit's power. Amen.

Our Generous God

*"I have no need of a bull from your stall or of goats from
your pens, for every animal of the forest is mine,
and the cattle on a thousand hills. I know
every bird in the mountains, and the insects
in the fields are mine".* PSALM 50:9-11

It's hard to share the things that are mine. I worry and wonder, *What if they get lost or broken? What if they're used up and I don't have what I need? What if I'm unappreciated or taken advantage of? If I share with others, how do I know they'll share with me too?* I'm tempted like a little child to say, "Mine!" and keep all I have for myself.

God, on the other hand, has no worries. He owns everything he has created. God has no use of our money or possessions to fill his stomach or meet his needs. Because of his great love, he shares generously with you and me.

How has God provided for our family today? Are we awake and alive? Warm and safe? Do we have food in our kitchen and clothes in our closets? Do we have friends and loved ones to share our days? Are we able to work, learn, and enjoy the beauty outdoors? When God opens his hand, we are satisfied with good things (Psalm 104:28).

Because God is generous to us, we can share with others. Let's love and give like him.

Lord, all things are yours. Thank you for your generous love. Amen.

OCTOBER 22

An Essential Part

*Just as a body, though one, has many parts, but all its many parts
form one body, so it is with Christ. But in fact God has placed
the parts in the body, every one of them, just as he wanted
them to be. Now you are the body of Christ, and each one
of you is a part of it.* 1 CORINTHIANS 12:12, 18, 27

If we blindfold our eyes, our hands struggle to find what we're reaching for. Without a mouth, we would grow hungry and weak. Our feet let us travel and our lungs take in air we need to breathe. God created every part of our bodies so we can think, move, and live to the fullest.

When you belong to Jesus, you're part of his body—the church. You're an essential part of the kingdom family he designed. When you do your part along with the rest of the body, the whole church looks and loves like Jesus.

Your part may be teaching the truth of the Bible. Perhaps you're the most "you" when you're giving or helping. Maybe you have a heart for the sick or want to share Jesus with the lost. No matter which gift we hold from the Spirit, "we are God's handiwork, created in Christ Jesus to do good works, which God prepared in advance for us to do" (Ephesians 2:10).

Lord, thank you for creating a special place for us in your church.
Show us how to serve and love the body. Amen.

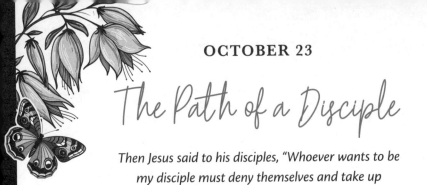

OCTOBER 23

The Path of a Disciple

*Then Jesus said to his disciples, "Whoever wants to be
my disciple must deny themselves and take up
their cross and follow me."* MATTHEW 16:24

Becoming a disciple starts with believing in Jesus. We celebrate our salvation. We receive the Holy Spirit as our helper. From the moment we first believe, we're forgiven. The power of sin is broken. God opens his spiritual treasure chest to give us peace, joy, and wisdom. We have hope, knowing we'll be with Jesus forever in heaven.

Yet believing in Jesus doesn't just change how we think. It changes how we live. Disciples follow Jesus wherever he leads. He takes us to wonderful places of blessing, but he also calls us to do hard things.

He might want us to give our money to help others. We offer our time and energy to serve and build his kingdom. Instead of working for praise and attention, we make his name great. We obey his Word instead of going our own way. Even our bodies are no longer our own since we were bought at a price (1 Corinthians 6:20).

Not everybody will understand why we follow Jesus. If people don't trust, obey, or love him, they won't always love us, either. It takes courage and faith to follow Jesus without turning back. Can we follow him no matter what it costs?

Lord, you gave your life so we could be saved. Help us to give you
our lives in return and follow you forever. Amen.

Apologies and Prayers

"Therefore, if you are offering your gift at the altar and there remember that your brother or sister has something against you, leave your gift there in front of the altar. First go and be reconciled to them; then come and offer your gift." MATTHEW 5:23-24

Nobody's perfect. When a bunch of imperfect people share a home, we will make mistakes. Kids disobey and parents lose patience. We hurt each other's feelings. We argue and fight, complain and grumble. When we sin against each other it pushes us apart.

If we sin against each other, we're sinning against God as well. He reminds us that we can't draw close to him if we're far from each other. Before we bring our worship, thanks, and prayers to God, we should make things right between each other.

Let's apologize every time we hurt each other. We can humble our hearts to admit the ways we're selfish or unkind. God promises if you confess your sins to each other and pray for each other, your family will be healed. (James 5:16). Every time you say you're sorry and choose to forgive, it's a gift of love to God and your family.

Is hurt or anger dividing your home? Forgive and make a fresh start today.

Lord, we want to be close to you and each other. Thank you for teaching us the power of forgiveness. May the love in our home be a gift of love to you. Amen.

Tomorrow's Worries

"So do not worry, saying, 'What shall we eat?' or 'What shall we drink?' or 'What shall we wear?' But seek first his kingdom and his righteousness, and all these things will be given to you as well. Therefore do not worry about tomorrow, for tomorrow will worry about itself. Each day has enough trouble of its own." MATTHEW 6:31, 33-34

Yesterday, we didn't know all the people we would talk to or pass on the street. We worried about what might happen today, and those worries either came to pass or disappeared. We didn't know if this day would bring bad news or a fantastic surprise. The only thing we knew for certain was that the future is UN-sure.

Even though we can't know what the next hour, month, or year will hold, God knows. He says our times are in his hand (Psalm 31:15). Even before we were born, he planned all our days and wrote them in his book (Psalm 139:16). We can hope, dream, and plan for the future, but God is the One who determines where we go (Proverbs 16:9).

We don't have to be scared about tomorrow because God is already there, full of power and love for us.

Lord, we have lots of plans and hopes for tomorrow. We're also scared of bad things that might happen. Help us to trust you, since you know the future and will be with us every day. Amen.

OCTOBER 26

The Best Gift

In the course of time Cain brought some of the fruits of the soil as an offering to the LORD. And Abel also brought an offering— fat portions from some of the firstborn of his flock. The LORD looked with favor on Abel and his offering, but on Cain and his offering he did not look with favor. GENESIS 4:3-5

Can you think of the best gift you've ever received? Was it something you wanted for a long time? Was it rare or expensive? Did it take time, effort, or creativity to prepare it for you? How did it feel to hold it in your hands for the first time? We know the offering of a gift can bring great joy.

A gift or offering is meant to say, "You're important to me." Offerings to God are an act of worship and obedience. They are to be chosen from the first and best we have, not the scraps or leftovers. The heart behind a gift to God is gratitude and humility. It's given out of what God has generously provided for us.

Before we give an offering, let's look at our hearts. Do we give God's way or our way? Do we give to impress other people? Are we trying to buy God's favor? Do we give the bare minimum? God looks at our hearts and he loves a cheerful giver (2 Corinthians 9:7). Let's offer him our love and our lives.

Lord, you are worthy of the best we have to give. We love you. Amen.

Are You Ready?

*"Therefore keep watch, because you do not know on what day
your Lord will come. But understand this: If the owner of the house
had known at what time of night the thief was coming, he would
have kept watch and would not have let his house be broken into.
So you also must be ready, because the Son of Man will come
at an hour when you do not expect him."* MATTHEW 24:42-44

Do you like surprises? It's exciting to wake up to no school or work on a snow day. Money or gifts show up in our mailbox. Family or friends arrive to celebrate our birthday. We find out we made the team, got the job, or won the prize. Surprises make us wonder what each new day could bring.

The best surprise of all is coming. We are waiting "for the blessed hope—the appearing of the glory of our great God and Savior, Jesus Christ" (Titus 2:13). When Jesus went to heaven, he promised he would come back. Someday, we'll "be caught up together...in the clouds to meet the Lord in the air. And so we will be with the Lord forever" (1 Thessalonians 4:17).

How do we get ready for Jesus? We believe he is the Son of God. We trust his death on the cross paid for our sins. We believe his Word is true. We believe and keep believing until we see his face.

Lord, make us ready for Jesus to come. Amen.

Helping Others to Jesus

Some men came carrying a paralyzed man on a mat and tried to take him into the house to lay him before Jesus. ... because of the crowd, they went up on the roof and lowered him on his mat through the tiles into the middle of the crowd, right in front of Jesus. When Jesus saw their faith, he said, "Friend, your sins are forgiven." LUKE 5:18-20

We know friends and family who need Jesus. Some are sick and suffer pain every day. Some are disappointed by dreams that never come true. Others struggle to make ends meet. Some feel bitter and angry. Guilt and regret steal the peace from their hearts. They're stuck in their troubles and wonder if there's hope.

Sometimes people feel too weak to get to Jesus on their own. We can love them by helping them see Jesus. First, we can pray. We can ask for healing and rescue. We can pray God will "fill [them] with all joy and peace as [they] trust in him, so that [they] may overflow with hope by the power of the Holy Spirit" (Romans 15:13).

Next, we can love and care. We can show them Jesus by helping and give what they need. As they struggle, we can stay close and encourage them along the way. Finally, we can introduce them to Jesus. We can share the Bible and the good news of salvation. Let's do all we can to bring people to the One they need most.

Lord, show us who needs your love so we can love them too. Amen.

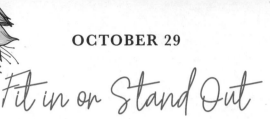

Fit in or Stand Out

Am I now trying to win the approval of human beings,
or of God? Or am I trying to please people? If
I were still trying to please people, I would
not be a servant of Christ. GALATIANS 1:10

Everywhere we go, we're surrounded by pressure to fit in. People are quick to let us know if our clothes are out of style. They tell us if we're not as smart or talented as others. We put a lot of effort and work into becoming our best. We want to feel we're accepted and belong.

Sometimes we do the wrong thing to be part of the crowd. It's tempting to break the rules or go along with sin to feel like we fit in. We might even give up loyal friends to join a more popular group. When we feel pressure to join in, we're faced with a choice: Will we please the people around us or stay faithful to God?

The only way to grow closer to God is to walk away from peer pressure. We turn away from the world's ways and "repent, then, and turn to God" (Acts 3:19). We obey his Word and do what's right no matter what anybody says. God gives strength and courage to live for him wherever we go.

Lord, we feel pressure to please people instead of you.
Help us to love you faithfully as you love us. Amen.

Crystal Balls and Tarot Cards

*Let no one be found among you who sacrifices their son or daughter
in the fire, who practices divination or sorcery, interprets omens,
engages in witchcraft, or casts spells, or who is a medium or spiritist
or who consults the dead. You must be blameless before
the LORD your God.* DEUTERONOMY 18:10-11, 13

We serve a powerful God. Psalm 147:5 tells us, "Great is our Lord and mighty in power; his understanding has no limit." Is there an enemy God cannot conquer? A question he's too confused to answer? An emotion his heart can't understand? Can we find a single hiding place in the universe where he won't find us? (Psalm 139:7-10). If we ever doubt his might, we remember his words: "I am the LORD, the God of all mankind. Is anything too hard for me?" (Jeremiah 32:27).

Since God is all-knowing, all-powerful, holy and perfect, then he's the only one we need. Turning to fortune tellers or horoscopes to predict the future denies that God plans our lives and holds each day in his hands. Witchcraft is an evil substitute for prayer, where we take our needs and questions to God and trust him to answer.

Playing with the supernatural invites contact with Satan, who "comes only to steal and kill and destroy" (John 10:10). In God's love, he warns us to avoid every kind of sorcery. Our walk with God and our safety depend on it.

> Lord, keep us far from the powers of darkness.
> We want to walk in your glorious light. Amen.

OCTOBER 31

The Real Thing

[Jesus] said to them, "Why are you troubled, and why do doubts rise in your minds? Look at my hands and my feet. It is I myself! Touch me and see; a ghost does not have flesh and bones, as you see I have." LUKE 24:38-39

Jesus' friends saw him suffer and die on the cross. When he appeared to them fully alive, they couldn't believe it! They were more likely to believe they saw a ghost than a real, living Jesus. They had to look closely and touch him before they were convinced.

Today people believe in all kinds of things, like ghosts and aliens, idols, and monsters under the bed. Even so, they find it hard to trust in a real, risen Jesus who—right now—is seated at God's right hand in heaven.

God has compassion when we struggle to believe. He knows it's easier to trust in what we can see with our eyes. We weren't there when Jesus rose to life. We didn't share a meal with him or walk and talk along the road. The many people who did see him testify to the truth of his resurrection. God will give us all we need to find confidence in the truth of Jesus.

Do you struggle with doubt today? Does Jesus seem like a story instead of a real person? Come look, see, and believe.

Lord, give us faith in Jesus that's never shaken.
Thank you for the life we find in him. Amen.

November

No Greater Joy

It gave me great joy when some believers came and testified about your faithfulness to the truth, telling how you continue to walk in it. I have no greater joy than to hear that my children are walking in the truth. 3 John 3-4

As parents there is no greater joy than knowing your children have put their trust in God. That they know following Jesus leads to every kind of blessing. Knowing that when they believe and live by his ways, they will be a good friend.

They will persevere to accomplish hard things. Their attitude is thankful and hopeful for tomorrow. Integrity earns them respect. A clean conscience gives them peace of mind. Their identity is secure as a child of God. They can say with confidence, "Surely your goodness and love will follow me all the days of my life, and I will dwell in the house of the Lord forever" (Psalm 23:6).

Pray for your children and remind them of God's promises. Remind them that He will set them free from the power of sin. That he'll fill them with courage since he never leaves their side. What a thrill it will be to see them discover their gifts from the Spirit and serve God with their whole heart. You will have no greater joy than to hear they're walking in the truth.

Lord, may I have the wonderful joy of knowing my children are in Christ. Amen.

Forgiveness and Peace

Make every effort to live in peace with everyone and to be holy;
without holiness no one will see the Lord. See to it that no one
falls short of the grace of God and that no bitter root grows up
to cause trouble and defile many. HEBREWS 12:14-15

It's hard to live at peace with everyone. In this broken world, we're going to be insulted. Cheated. Ignored. Betrayed. Disappointed. When we find ourselves offended or hurt, God calls us to answer with grace instead of demanding payback. He teaches us to forgive like he's forgiven us for all we've done wrong.

If we refuse to forgive, bitterness will grow in our hearts. This makes trouble in our relationship with God and each other. If we have a closed heart toward others, we can't have an open heart toward God. A bitter spirit will hold back your prayers, your joy, and your peace.

Has someone made you angry or hurt your feelings? Did they take what's yours? Did they tell your secret or break their promise? Do you keep thinking about what they said and did to you? Are you secretly wishing they'll "get what they deserve"? If so, it's time to ask for God's help to forgive. His Spirit can heal your heart and fill it with love again.

Lord, you know all about our anger and hurt. Help us to forgive
and keep bitterness out of our hearts. Amen.

Playing Favorites

My brothers and sisters, believers in our glorious Lord Jesus Christ must not show favoritism. If you show special attention to a man wearing fine clothes and say, "Here's a good seat for you," but say to [a] poor man, "You stand there" or "Sit on the floor by my feet," have you not discriminated among yourselves and become judges with evil thoughts? JAMES 2:1, 3-4

We say we believe in equality, but we see favoritism all around us. The popular kids get more attention at school. Favorite employees get better work and pay. Wealthy people hold the most power and influence. Racism divides communities as freedoms and privileges are not the same for all. Favoritism splits people into the wanted or unwanted, respected or put down, heard or ignored.

As God's children, we're called to love everyone. We show as much generosity to strangers as to our best friends. We respect those who serve as much as those in charge. Instead of stepping on others to get ahead, we tackle life's challenges together.

The cure for favoritism is seeing others with God's eyes. "The LORD does not look at the things people look at. People look at the outward appearance, but the LORD looks at the heart" (1 Samuel 16:7).

Lord, you love us just the way we are. Work in our hearts
so we care for others just like Jesus. Amen.

NOVEMBER 4

Payback vs Justice

Do not take revenge, my dear friends, but leave room for God's wrath,
for it is written: "It is mine to avenge; I will repay," says the Lord.
On the contrary: "If your enemy is hungry, feed him; if he is thirsty,
give him something to drink … " Do not be overcome by evil,
but overcome evil with good. ROMANS 12:19-21

You know how it feels to be treated badly. Someone has been nice to your face, but mean behind your back. You've been put down and made to feel small. An enemy will hurt you, take from you, and break their word. They refuse to admit what they've done and make it right.

When we face an enemy, anger boils up inside our hearts. We want payback to get what's fair. We imagine what we could say and do to take revenge. We want our enemy to get what they deserve.

God tells us to go to him with our anger and frustration. Instead of fighting our enemies, we can put them in his hands. God promises to deal with their sin at the right time and in the right way. While we wait for God's justice, we choose to love. We give and help. We're kind and respectful. When evil comes our way, we meet it with good.

Are you boiling mad on the inside today? Pray for good for your enemy. Pray for justice, and pray for God's love in your heart.

Lord, help us to overcome evil with good. Amen.

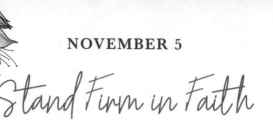

NOVEMBER 5

Stand Firm in Faith

Moses answered the people, "Do not be afraid. Stand firm and you will see the deliverance the LORD will bring you today. The Egyptians you see today you will never see again. The LORD will fight for you; you need only to be still." EXODUS 14:13-14

If we have a problem, we try to fix it. We keep a supply of glue, tape, and tools to repair what's broken. Our rags and broom are ready for messy spills. A quick internet search finds a mechanic for our car or a pill for a headache. When we fight, we apologize and talk it out until we're close again. We tackle our problems until the job is done.

Yet some enemies are too powerful to overcome. Not every sickness has a cure. We're kind and friendly, but still find ourselves alone. Replacing what's been lost might be too expensive. We can work with all our might, but still fall short of our goal. Overwhelmed, we either panic or quit trying altogether.

God offers another way. In his love, he gives strength, power, and help. If we put our trust in him, we can stop trying to rescue ourselves. He gives courage when we're afraid. Peace when we're upset and angry. Wisdom in our confusion. If we stand firm and wait for God, he will fight for us.

What problem are you trying to fix today? Pray and ask God to quiet your heart. He'll give you faith to wait for him.

Lord, calm our hearts as we trust in you. Amen.

Caretakers of His Works

You made them rulers over the works of your hands;
you put everything under their feet: all flocks and
herds, and the animals of the wild, the birds in
the sky, and the fish in the sea, all that swim
the paths of the seas. PSALM 8:6-8

God gave us the authority and responsibility to care for the living things he created. In the beginning of time, he called the fish, birds, and animals "good" as he made them (Genesis 1). The very first man, Adam, was given the wonderful assignment to name the animals God made. Each one has been designed to show the brilliant creativity of God, who made them all.

When we're diligent to care for our pets, help a lost or injured creature, or keep our property free of litter and harmful chemicals, we're obeying God's call to "rule over the works of his hands." We can support companies who prevent damage to animal habitats. Local animal shelters would welcome our donations of food and supplies. Our daily choices can help or hurt the natural world God made.

Each time we visit a zoo or spend time outdoors, let's celebrate the variety of living things God created. Each one is a gift from him to make this beautiful world we enjoy.

Lord, thank you for making all living things. We are
in awe of your creativity. Show us how to care
for the creatures around us. Amen.

NOVEMBER 7

Saying Nothing At All

*Even fools are thought wise if they keep
silent, and discerning if they hold
their tongues.* PROVERBS 17:28

Have you felt embarrassed for calling out the wrong answer in a study group?
Have you talked about someone when they were standing right behind you? In
a theater or library, have you been scolded for making too much noise? Have
you jumped into the middle of someone's conversation without being invited?
Has your temper made you say things you regret? When we talk too loudly,
too quickly, or with too much pride, we make ourselves look foolish.

God's Word says we look wise by saying nothing at all! If a loved one is
hurting, we can offer a listening ear. In a class or meeting, we respectfully stay
quiet and pay attention. If our friends start a fight, we let them make peace
without interfering. We hold our advice until others ask for it. Wisdom tells us
when to speak and when to be still.

Is it hard to be quiet in this noisy world? In silence, we can show wisdom
and love. And when we do speak, our words will matter.

Lord, give us wisdom in our words and our silence. Amen.

Lighten Their Load

*Carry each other's burdens, and in this way you will fulfill the
law of Christ. Let us not become weary in doing good,
for at the proper time we will reap a harvest
if we do not give up.* GALATIANS 6:2, 9

All of us have burdens we carry each day. Work feels stressful and hard. Our things become broken or lost, costing too much money to fix. Mean words hurt our feelings. Sickness or injuries keep us from working or having fun. We can feel weighed down by troubles and worries.

In our life together with our family, we can lighten the load for each other. Jesus says to "do good" every chance we get. Let's encourage one another if we're sad or afraid. Offer to help when somebody has a big job to do. Be polite and kind with our words and actions. Share and take turns. Pray every day that God will take care of us. If we stick together and choose to love, our burdens will grow lighter. And everyone who sees us will see the love of Jesus.

Lord, give us strength to serve each other without
getting tired or giving up. Thank you for hearing
our prayers and lightening our load every day. Amen.

A Thriving Fruit Tree

"No good tree bears bad fruit, nor does a bad tree bear good fruit. Each tree is recognized by its own fruit. People do not pick figs from thornbushes, or grapes from briers." LUKE 6:43-44

We're pretty good at making excuses for our behavior. We say, "He didn't really mean it." "She was just tired or stressed." "I forgot." "My temper got the best of me." "You know what I meant." "It really wasn't that bad." We tell ourselves if someone breaks a promise, they meant well. If they're rude or selfish, they didn't know better. If they stubbornly refuse to obey, they have a bold personality. We taste the "bad fruit" of others' choices and it hurts.

Everybody fails to do the right thing at all times. Yet if we love God and trust in Jesus, we feel sorry. We confess and ask for forgiveness. We do all we can to make it right. We pray and learn God's Word. Over time, we grow in obedience. We love our family, friends, and neighbors more and more. We see God keeping his promise to make us new.

Are we like healthy trees, bringing "good things out of the good stored up in [our] heart"? (Luke 6:45). Do we speak kind, loving words that build each other up? Let's pray for God to bear good fruit in us.

Lord, grow your love and goodness in our hearts. Amen.

NOVEMBER 10

Talking to God about Everything

Is anyone among you in trouble? Let them pray. Is anyone happy?
Let them sing songs of praise. Therefore, confess your sins
to each other and pray for each other so that you may
be healed. The prayer of a righteous person is powerful
and effective. JAMES 5:13, 16

At the end of the day, we love to hear what's going in the lives of our family members. We ask how it went at school. The kids share about their day and express their fears and excitement. You share about your day with your spouse and listen to what he has to say. You tell each other you love each other. Through talking together, you stay close and share your lives.

God loves the sound of your voice, too. He invites you and me to pray and tell him everything. He wants us to share our worries and ask for help with any problem, big or small. He wants to celebrate our victories and hear thanks for all his gifts each day. When we sin, we can tell him what we've done and find forgiveness. If others are in pain or struggling to do what's right, we can pray for God to help. Our prayers are powerful and make a difference.

Let's stay in constant conversation with God because he loves and listens every time.

Lord, teach to pray about every detail of our lives. Amen.

God's Ambassadors

*And he has committed to us the message of reconciliation.
We are therefore Christ's ambassadors, as though God were
making his appeal through us. We implore you on Christ's
behalf: Be reconciled to God.* 2 CORINTHIANS 5:19-20

God loves you with his whole heart and never wants you to be distant or divided from him. Yet when sin entered the world, every person became separated from him. The world was broken and doomed to die apart from him. God loved the people he created too much to leave them lost and alone. He sent Jesus to be "the way and the truth and the life" so everyone can be united to our Father God (John 14:6).

This is the greatest news the world has ever known! You and I are called God's ambassadors—his messengers of peace. We're sent out with the good news so others can draw close to him. We carry God's invitation to repent and believe. Through our message, the world can know his love.

Lord, thank you for sending Jesus to make a way to you.
Show us how to be your ambassadors so others
can know your love. Amen.

A Mirror for Your Heart

*Do not merely listen to the word, and so deceive yourselves.
Do what it says. Anyone who listens to the word but does
not do what it says is like someone who looks at his face
in a mirror and, after looking at himself, goes away and
immediately forgets what he looks like.* JAMES 1:22-24

A glance in the mirror lets us know if we're ready to head out the door. By its reflection, we can see if we need to floss our teeth. If we have a spot on our shirt. If we've brushed our hair or put on our glasses. A mirror shows if our clothes are wrinkled or mismatched. We can see how we truly appear in others' eyes.

God says the Bible is a mirror for our heart. We can hold it up to our character and see what we're like. It will show if we're selfish with our things or ready to share. It exposes a quick temper or a patient spirit with our family. We can recognize if we're foolish and impulsive or wise and careful. The Word shines a light on the secret sins and habits we've been keeping in the dark.

God gives us his "mirror" as a gift of love. If we look and listen, we can repent and be made new. Today, let's be humble to let the Word do its work in you and me.

Lord, use your Word to make us look like Jesus.
We want to listen and obey. Amen.

The Coming Paradise

Now the LORD God had planted a garden in the east, in Eden;
and there he put the man he had formed. The LORD God made
all kinds of trees grow out of the ground—trees that were
pleasing to the eye and good for food. In the middle of
the garden were the tree of life and the tree
of the knowledge of good and evil. GENESIS 2:8-9

Can you imagine a perfect place like Eden? Nobody felt sick, scared, or sad. Delicious fruit was ripe for the picking. God himself came to walk and talk in the cool of the day. Caring for the garden and animals made life full of fun and purpose. It was very, very good.

Yet in the middle of that beautiful garden, Adam and Eve were tempted. They believed the lie that "very good" wasn't good enough. By disobeying God and eating the fruit he'd forbidden, they traded his blessings for a curse. The garden was no longer their home. They became separated from God and doomed to die.

The good news is, that's not the end of the story! God will restore this broken world. He sent his only Son, Jesus, to give life and make us new. He made a way to be with God forever. All of God's people will eat "from the tree of life, which is in the paradise of God" (Revelation 2:7).

Lord, we love you as the Creator of all things. Thank you
for your promise to make all things new. Amen.

Safe in Stormy Waters

For forty days the flood kept coming on the earth, and as the waters increased they lifted the ark high above the earth. Every living thing on the face of the earth was wiped out; people and animals and the creatures that move along the ground and the birds were wiped from the earth. Only Noah was left, and those with him in the ark. GENESIS 7:17, 23

The Bible tells the same kind of story over and over through its pages. We see that sin and evil lead to destruction. Faith and love bring life in the waters.

God sheltered Noah and his family in the ark. He carried baby Moses in a basket in the river. God sent a fish to rescue Jonah from drowning. Jesus calmed the storm so his disciples could cross the sea in safety. He kept Peter from sinking beneath the waves. No matter how the waters rise, God saves the ones who love and trust him.

Do you feel like you're drowning in your problems? Are you all alone as you believe and follow Jesus? Have courage—God is with you. He'll do whatever it takes to put your feet on dry land. The same One who commanded the floods to rise made the seas as smooth as glass. He'll prove his power as he carries you, helps you, and loves you every day.

Lord, it feels like we're flooded with troubles and worries. Give us peace as we trust you to carry us through. Amen.

Love That Makes No Sense

*"But to you who are listening I say: Love your enemies, do good
to those who hate you, bless those who curse you,
pray for those who mistreat you."* LUKE 6:27-28

It's easy to connect with those we like and trust. With friends and family, we're glad to share hugs, presents, and special occasions. We're eager to share both our happiest news and our hardest days. If a loved one is hurting, we stop to pray and help without a second thought.

It's a different story with our enemies. It's hard to be polite to someone who's rude every time they speak. We don't like to give when we'll receive nothing in return. It hurts to offer friendship knowing we might just be rejected. We wonder, *Why should I care for them if they don't care about me?*

God tells us to love our enemies because that's what his love looks like. Jesus didn't wait for us to love him first. "But God demonstrates his own love for us in this: While we were still sinners, Christ died for us" (Romans 5:8). Every time we offer kindness, forgiveness, and prayers for people who don't love us back, we look just like Jesus.

Love like that makes no sense to the world. Loving the unlovable gets attention! It's one way we shine the light of God so they can see him too.

Lord, give us courage to love our enemies. Put your love
in our hearts for everyone. Amen.

Choosing the Lord

"We gave you strict orders not to teach in this name," [the high priest] said ... Peter and the other apostles replied: "We must obey God rather than human beings!" Acts 5:28-29

Since the church was born over two thousand years ago, enemies of Jesus have tried to stop it. Believers around the world are persecuted for owning Bibles and worshiping God. They experience violence and prison. They pay expensive fines or lose their jobs. God's people are often rejected, insulted, and laughed at for putting faith in him.

To follow Jesus we have to make a choice. Will we give in to pressure from people or obey him no matter what? This might mean staying home if friends are making bad choices. We may have to sacrifice popularity to show kindness to the outcast. While others are striving to get rich, we choose to give money to help those in need. If we're pushed to cheat or lie, our integrity might keep us from getting ahead. If we love God, we obey him.

Who is discouraging you from obeying the Lord today? Do you feel embarrassed to say you believe in Jesus? Is it hard to do the right thing when you're the only one who cares? Let's build each other up so we can say, "But as for me and my household, we will serve the LORD" (Joshua 24:15).

Lord, we want to be faithful and obey you always. Amen.

Seeing through Tricks and Lies

But I am afraid that just as Eve was deceived by the serpent's cunning, your minds may somehow be led astray from your sincere and pure devotion to Christ. 2 CORINTHIANS 11:3

Just because something looks delicious, it doesn't mean it's good for our mouths or our stomachs. An exciting movie preview can pass off a poorly-made film as great entertainment. Until we taste or take a closer look, we can be misled or deceived.

Our enemy, Satan, is tricky. God calls him "a liar and the father of lies" (John 8:44). He'll do all he can to make sin and evil appealing so we fall to temptation. Just as he twisted God's words to Eve in the garden, he'll try to make you doubt God's truth in the Bible. He wants to shake our trust in God's perfect love, wisdom, and goodness.

How do we know if we're swallowing a truth or a lie? We compare the words we hear to the Word of God. It will teach us right from wrong. It describes the kind of trustworthy leader to follow. God reminds us all through the Bible that love, forgiveness, and mercy are free gifts for everyone who believes. We should test what we hear before we're led away from Jesus.

Lord, teach us to recognize Satan's lies so we live by your truth.
Keep us close to you, always. Amen.

Close to Him

Rejoice always, pray continually, give thanks in all circumstances;
for this is God's will for you in Christ Jesus. 1 THESSALONIANS 5:16-18

If we tried to list all the ways God cares for us, we'd run out of paper and ink! Our food and clothes, cozy beds and warm house are gifts from his hand. He provides friends and family to love us. School and work to give purpose to our days. Forests, beaches, and mountains to explore. He gives us goals and dreams and the strength to go after them. In him, we "lack nothing" and our "cup overflows" (Psalm 23:1, 5).

If God never stops loving and giving, we can thank him all the time. When we get up in the morning, we can praise him for a new day. As we share our meals, we thank him for our food. As we work and learn, we remember our talent, strength, and skill is from him. Even while we're sick or sad, we can praise him for never leaving our side.

Praying and thanking God through the day keep our hearts close to him. It makes us notice God's touch on every part of our lives. We grow in our love. Joy, hope, and peace fill our minds. We trust him more and more. We are ready to tell everyone about our good Father.

Lord, fill us with thanks and praise every moment. Amen.

Always Greedy for More

Then he said to them, "Watch out! Be on your guard
against all kinds of greed; life does not consist
in an abundance of possessions." LUKE 12:15

Greed is always hungry. It shops and spends and shops some more. It's jealous of others' gifts and blessings. Greed is the opposite of gratitude. It complains and whines for more and more. It's easily bored and never has enough. Greed searches for life but never finds it.

Is greed whispering in your ear today? Is it telling you if you could have this or do that, you'd be completely happy? God knows the danger of listening to those lies. He wants you to find true joy that money can't buy. He wants to satisfy your heart with love that lasts when all our possessions pass away. To God, you're not just a consumer. You're his own child with spiritual gifts and a calling to live for him.

Let's watch out for greed in our lives. With God's help we can find joy in what truly matters. He'll teach us what it means to be content. We can become thankful, generous individuals who count our blessings. Through Jesus, we "may have life, and have it to the full" (John 10:10).

Lord, we're tempted to be greedy for more than you've given.
Let us find our life in you alone. Amen.

NOVEMBER 20

One Big Family

*They devoted themselves to the apostles' teaching and to fellowship,
to the breaking of bread and to prayer. All the believers were
together and had everything in common. They sold property
and possessions to give to anyone who had need.
They broke bread in their homes and ate together
with glad and sincere hearts, praising God and enjoying
the favor of all the people.* ACTS 2:42, 44-47

How do we know you're part of a family? You share a name and an address. You are busy together from morning until night. You celebrate your most important moments with each other. If one is hurt or sad, the rest do all they can to help. You love each other through thick and thin.

Jesus said when we believe in him, we're his brothers and sisters. That makes all God's people one big family! As family, we're to fellowship together all the time. God's family prays, celebrates, helps, laughs, and cries together. We support each other in hard times. We open our homes to each other, sharing meals and making memories. The best part is that when we love our brothers and sisters in Jesus, the world gets to see what God's love looks like.

Lord, thank you for adopting us into your family. Show us
what it means to fellowship with our brothers and sisters.
We want to love your people like you love us. Amen.

Kindness for the Unkind

*"And if you do good to those who are good to you, what credit
is that to you? Even sinners do that. But love your enemies,
do good to them, and lend to them without expecting
to get anything back. Then your reward will be great,
and you will be children of the Most High, because he is
kind to the ungrateful and wicked."* Luke 6:33, 35

When you love someone, you bless them. You offer gifts on their birthdays and holidays. You respect and speak well of them to other people. When they're feeling down, you give encouragement and loving words. If they have a problem, do all you can to help. Loving someone means reaching out to care.

Loving our friends and family like that feels simple. It's a lot harder to love our enemies who hurt us. Who lie and cheat. Who break promises or steal from us. Our enemies make us want to fight back or run in the opposite direction.

Why should we love our enemies? God says we were once his enemies, too. We didn't believe in him or obey his Word. Even so, "While we were still sinners, Christ died for us" (Romans 5:8). God loved us first, before we knew and loved him too.

We're called to love all people, whether they love us back or not. God holds a great reward if we love like him. How can we show kindness and care for our enemies today?

Lord, teach us to love and help our enemies. Amen.

Our Heavenly GPS

Your word is a lamp for my feet, a light on my path. PSALM 119:105

*When Jesus spoke again to the people, he said,
"I am the light of the world. Whoever follows me
will never walk in darkness, but will have
the light of life." JOHN 8:12*

A GPS can navigate the route to new places. Its illuminated screen provides step-by-step instructions to reach your destination. By its guidance, you can travel with confidence you'll get where you need to go.

God knows we need help on our journey through life as well. Tough questions and problems make us feel as if we're walking in darkness. We wonder, *How can I make good friends? Should I join a club or start volunteering? Which career move is right for me? How can I feel brave? What if I make a big mistake? How do I handle temptation? Who can I trust? What does it mean to follow Jesus?* Questions and struggles can stop us in our tracks.

God gave his Word to help us find our way through life. Its wisdom shows us what to do. It calms our fears and gives courage to do what's right. The Bible is like a light shining on our path so we can walk without stumbling. If we live by the Word, we can follow God wherever he leads.

Lord, let us trust your Word as our light, our guide,
and our help every step of the way. Amen.

NOVEMBER 23

Beating the Odds

That same day Pharaoh gave this order to the slave drivers and overseers in charge of the people: "You are no longer to supply the people with straw for making bricks; let them go and gather their own straw. But require them to make the same number of bricks as before; don't reduce the quota." EXODUS 5:6-8

A cold, heartless master will set you up to fail. They demand you know what you've never been taught. They expect you to perform perfectly without the chance to practice. You're expected to produce without enough resources or supplies. It's like you're put on the front lines of a battle with no armor or weapons. You're defeated before you begin.

When the odds are stacked against you, it's overwhelming. You feel hurt and betrayed. It's just not fair. Yet the God we serve is loving and kind. "As a father has compassion on his children, so the LORD has compassion on those who fear him; for he knows how we are formed, he remembers that we are dust" (Psalm 103:13-14).

When God calls us to obey, he gives his Spirit to help us do it. He gives us strength and power to do whatever he asks. We never have to face anything on our own because he's with us.

Lord, you lead us with love and compassion. Thank you
for giving us rest when we're tired and the work feels
too hard. Help us to trust you to provide all we need
to live for you. Amen.

Worthy of All Praise

Praise the LORD, my soul, and forget not all his benefits—who forgives all your sins and heals all your diseases, who redeems your life from the pit and crowns you with love and compassion, who satisfies your desires with good things so that your youth is renewed like the eagle's. PSALM 103:2-5

God wants to know we remember all he's done. He forgives our sins and shows mercy and patience when we're slow to learn and grow. He heals our pain and helps in our trouble. He gives strength to overcome temptation. God makes us new, filling us with his Spirit so we can love like him. He gives the desires of our hearts (Psalm 37:4) and proves himself as our generous provider. God is worthy of all our praise forever.

How can we praise God today? We can thank him in our prayers. We can "sing and make music to the LORD" (Psalm 27:6). We can tell of his power and kindness in our lives. Because of his love, we can bless him in all we do and say.

Lord, we praise your name for your love to us. Amen.

NOVEMBER 25

Resisting Temptation

No temptation has overtaken you except what is common to mankind. And God is faithful; he will not let you be tempted beyond what you can bear. But when you are tempted, he will also provide a way out so that you can endure it. 1 CORINTHIANS 10:13

What kinds of temptations did you and I face today? Maybe we wanted to grab dessert before eating our vegetables. Our fingers were itching to pick up a good book instead of working. We wanted to throw out insults or sarcasm instead of listening and showing respect. Moment by moment, we make choices to give in or do what's right.

Yet, some temptations feel impossible to resist. Our best friend asks us to lie to keep them out of trouble. We've been hurt so badly, we want to hold a grudge and get revenge. The world's kind of fun seems irresistible, even though we know it's wrong. When bad things happen, we start to worry and complain instead of trusting in God's love. The temptation is bigger than our willpower—how can we do what's right?

No matter how we struggle with sin, God will make a way out. He'll provide what we need. He'll tell us when to run to safety. He'll send a godly friend to help us stand firm. We have the Word, the Spirit, and prayer to change our heart and mind.

Lord, rescue us from temptation so we obey you always. Amen.

There Are No Foolish Questions

If any of you lacks wisdom, you should ask God, who gives generously to all without finding fault, and it will be given to you. JAMES 1:5

If we're honest, it's hard to ask for advice. You want to build your project on your own. If I lose my way, I don't want to stop and ask for directions. As a kid you might have attempted your homework without asking your teacher for help. You might put off going to the doctor as long as you can. We want to feel smart. Independent. Strong. We think asking questions will make us look weak or helpless.

God knows life is too complicated to figure out on our own. We face tough decisions and don't know what to do. What if we make the wrong choice? What if by trying to make something better, we make it worse? What would the Bible say? Who can I trust? We need the perfect wisdom only God can offer.

God hears your prayers and mine. To him, there is no such thing as a foolish question. When we ask him for wisdom, it says, "I trust in your love. I believe your power and knowledge are greater than my own. I am your child, and I need you."

Are you looking for answers today? Do you feel worried or confused? Are you stuck, not knowing which way to go? Ask the Lord and he'll give all the wisdom you need.

Lord, teach us to depend on your wisdom. Amen.

NOVEMBER 27

A Welcoming Smile

Do not forget to show hospitality to strangers,
for by so doing some people have shown hospitality
to angels without knowing it. HEBREWS 13:2

Hospitality offers a friendly hello, a space at the table, and a listening ear. When we show hospitality, we make room in our lives for others who need a friend.

We can show a warm welcome wherever we go. We can offer a seat to a stranger on the bus or hold the door for guests at church. In the lunchroom, we can invite new faces to sit beside us. We can step across the street to greet our neighbors and offer a helping hand. As we hear of needs in our community, we can share our food, clothes, money, and time with those who struggle.

It takes courage to be friendly. We can pray for confidence to look others in the eye and start conversations. The Spirit will open our eyes to recognize people who feel lonely and left out. As we offer our lives and our homes to God, he'll teach us to show hospitality more and more every day.

> Lord, you made us welcome in your kingdom. You sent Jesus
> to invite us to know your love. Teach us to show kindness
> and hospitality in your name. Amen.

God Has No Limits

"Ah, Sovereign LORD, you have made the heavens and the earth by your great power and outstretched arm. Nothing is too hard for you." JEREMIAH 32:17

We know our own limitations. Without a minimum of food, water, and sleep, we won't make it through the day. We don't know the answers to every question. We can't afford to buy all we'd like or travel everywhere we'd like to see. Our limits are the most painful when we crash into a problem we can't solve. Some kinds of sickness, struggles, and enemies are too big to overcome on our own.

Unlike you and me, God has no limit to his power. He knows and understands all things. His strength is greater than any force in heaven or earth. He planned yesterday, today, and tomorrow, so nothing is outside his control. Those impossible problems we face are no match for the power of God.

What feels too hard for you today? Does someone refuse to get along or treat you right? Have doctors and medicines left you feeling sick and tired? Have you run out of money for what you need? Go to God in prayer, believing he is enough. In Him, we can "be strong in the Lord and in his mighty power" (Ephesians 6:10).

Lord, nothing we face is too difficult for you. Amen.

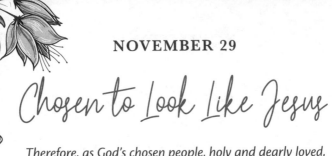

NOVEMBER 29

Chosen to Look Like Jesus

Therefore, as God's chosen people, holy and dearly loved,
clothe yourselves with compassion, kindness, humility,
gentleness and patience. COLOSSIANS 3:12

We are hand-picked by God to look like Jesus. He chose us to be his very own. We used to wear selfishness that only cared about ourselves. A me-first attitude didn't care what others wanted or needed. The Spirit helps us to take off that ugly sin to be dressed in compassion and kindness.

Before we knew Jesus, we were proud. We wanted the last word in every argument. Our way was the best way, and we wouldn't take no for an answer. The Spirit dresses us up in humility that respects other people. We give and help, listen and obey. Our humble hearts love others as we love ourselves.

The Spirit helps us take off the hurrying and worrying that make us so impatient. We put on faith that quietly trusts in God to provide. Our quick tempers give way to mercy. We bear with each other, just like God is patient with us as we grow. We become people of peace in every situation.

Are we well-dressed like God's chosen people? Are we wearing compassion, kindness, humility, gentleness, and patience? Do we see the love of Jesus all over each other? God is ready and willing to make us new. In him, we can "put on the new self, created to be like God in true righteousness and holiness" (Ephesians 4:24).

Lord, we thank you for choosing us to be your own.
You've changed the attitudes of our hearts and you
show us what love looks like. Amen.

Respecting the King

To the LORD your God belong the heavens, even the highest heavens,
the earth and everything in it. For the LORD your God is God
of gods and Lord of lords, the great God, mighty
and awesome, who shows no partiality and
accepts no bribes. DEUTERONOMY 10:14, 17

Serve the LORD with fear and celebrate his rule with trembling. PSALM 2:11

Our God is more powerful than any force of nature. All through the Bible we read we're to "fear" him. This doesn't mean God is scary and mean—it means he deserves our total respect, worship, and obedience.

We show our fear of God through our words. We speak his name respectfully as we talk to him or about him. When we pray, we remember we're talking to the "King of kings and Lord of lords" himself (Revelation 19:16).

We also fear God through our actions. As we face choices and temptations, we give up our own way for God's way. Every time we give, love, serve, and show integrity, we honor him.

We can even fear God in our thoughts. We read the Bible so God will put his laws in our minds and write them on our hearts (Hebrews 8:10). We let God fill us with his truth.

Lord, we want to worship you like you deserve. Show us what
it means to fear you and love you in every way. Amen.

December

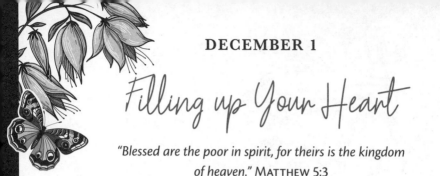

DECEMBER 1

Filling up Your Heart

"Blessed are the poor in spirit, for theirs is the kingdom of heaven." MATTHEW 5:3

An empty drawer can hold plenty of clean, new clothes. Our loved ones can seat the vacant chairs around the table for a meal. An empty box can be filled with a gift, wrapped, and given away as a blessing. A blank sheet of paper is ready for a story to be written. Sometimes, what's most empty can receive the best of all.

God knows our hearts are empty, too. Every person tries to fill up their heart in this world. Some try money and success as their ticket to happiness. Others believe friends and loved ones will keep heartache away. Helping the poor and following the rules might make you feel like a good person. Yet no matter how we try, we can't find the peace and joy our spirits are longing for.

If we're humble, we'll see how far we fall short of God's glory (Romans 3:23). We need forgiveness for our sins. Apart from God, we can't do anything (John 15:5). If we bring our empty hearts to God, he will fill them up. We'll receive the spiritual riches of mercy, salvation, and love. "The poor will eat and be satisfied; those who seek the LORD will praise him—may your hearts live forever!" (Psalm 22:26).

Lord, we are poor in spirit without your love. Fill us today. Amen.

Good Role Models

Join together in following my example, brothers and sisters,
and just as you have us as a model, keep your eyes on those
who live as we do. PHILIPPIANS 3:17

A builder needs blueprints to construct a solid house. Young dancers imitate the form and grace of accomplished ballerinas. A coach will show players exactly how to control a soccer ball on the field. Teachers demonstrate math problems on the board so students can master new skills. To learn and grow, we need the example of experts who know how to do it right.

It's the same for believers who want to grow in faith. How do we know what obedience looks like? What does it mean to love our neighbor? How do we understand the Bible? God gives us the example of mature Christians who live like Jesus.

Whose example are you following today? Who is motivating you to bravely face your fears and trust God? What habits do you admire most in those around you? Who is speaking words of wisdom and encouragement into your life? How do others cope with trouble and temptation? Pray for eyes to recognize the models of faith and love God has given.

Lord, teach us to keep our eyes on those who love you,
obey you, and look like Jesus. Amen.

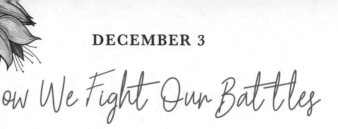

DECEMBER 3

How We Fight Our Battles

David said to the Philistine, "You come against me with sword and spear and javelin, but I come against you in the name of the LORD Almighty, the God of the armies of Israel, whom you have defied. All those gathered here will know that it is not by sword or spear that the LORD saves; for the battle is the LORD's, and he will give all of you into our hands." 1 SAMUEL 17:45, 47

We know our enemies don't give up without a fight! Abusers, liars, and gossips rarely change their ways overnight. We feel pulled in two directions—do we do the right thing or give in to temptation? Tough challenges wear down our strength and determination. We can feel like we're fighting giants who are too big and powerful to beat.

Who or what is coming against you today? Are you scared or ready to quit? Do your "weapons" feel useless against the enemy you face? You can have hope in knowing God fights for you in your battles.

Go to God in prayer and tell him all about your struggle. Ask him to protect you from your enemies. Call on him for rescue and help. Let his Spirit fill you with courage and hope as you trust him for victory.

Lord, our problems are too big to solve on our own. Rescue us from trouble and hurt by your great power and love. Amen.

DECEMBER 4

Rewards in Heaven

*"Blessed are you when people insult you, persecute you
and falsely say all kinds of evil against you because of me.
Rejoice and be glad, because great is your reward in heaven,
for in the same way they persecuted the prophets
who were before you."* MATTHEW 5:11-12

Jesus was popular when he gave the crowds what they wanted. A full stomach for free? He was the best. Healing from a painful disease? Go, Jesus! Deliverance from an evil spirit? Start the show! Yet when Jesus obeyed God by speaking the truth, they didn't like what they heard. When he made friends with the poor and the outcasts, he was rejected too. When Jesus chose to love instead of hate, he was hated himself.

If we do what's right, the world will call it wrong. They'll say our looks matter more than our character. We should work for money and fame. They'll say we should step on others to get ahead—honesty and a humble heart will only slow you down. People will think if we obey God, we're judging their choices. The more we look like Jesus, the less we look like the world. And the world won't like that one bit.

It hurts to be insulted and turned away. Our hope is found in God's promises. The evil we suffer now brings great rewards in heaven. When we see Jesus' face, it will be worth it all.

Lord, give us courage to face persecution in your name. Amen.

DECEMBER 5

Cherish Your Elders

*Gray hair is a crown of splendor; it is attained
in the way of righteousness.* PROVERBS 16:31

*"Stand up in the presence of the aged, show respect for the elderly
and revere your God. I am the LORD."* LEVITICUS 19:32

These days, older people get little respect. Their clothes and words seem old-fashioned. They don't use the latest technology. Slow movements, poor hearing or eyesight, and low energy can make them feel hard to understand. In our busy, hurried days it seems they can't keep up. We can become so caught up in our own lives that we leave them behind.

God takes a different view of the elderly. He describes them like royalty, with gray hair for a crown. God calls us to show great respect and honor every time they're in the room. He knows the wisdom, experience, and knowledge of God they've gained in their many years of life. If we take time to sit and listen carefully to their words, we'll learn so much and grow closer, too.

Let's think of ways to cherish the older people in our lives. Whether it's through gifts of help, time and attention, or presents, let's do all we can to love God by loving the elderly.

Lord, we want to obey your Word and care for the elderly
in the way you teach us. Show us how to love, give,
and serve them in your name. Amen.

DECEMBER 6

Worn Out

Elijah was afraid and ran for his life. "I have had enough, Lord,"
he said. "Take my life; I am no better than my ancestors."
Then he lay down under the bush and fell asleep. The angel
of the Lord came ... and said, "Get up and eat,
for the journey is too much for you." 1 Kings 19:3-5, 7

When the heat is on, we can feel like we're melting under the pressure. Our work can feel too hard. People let us down or refuse to get along. We're put down for doing the right thing. Our hopes feel just out of reach. We can become so tired and overwhelmed, we just want to quit.

Is God angry or disappointed when our strength runs out? No, he is full of compassion and love all the time. The Bible says "he knows how we are formed, he remembers that we are dust" (Psalm 103:14). He knows our energy has limits, and he shows mercy when we're discouraged.

When we feel we can't go on, it's time to pray. We can ask for help. Comfort. Wisdom. Protection. "He gives strength to the weary and increases the power of the weak" (Isaiah 40:29). He'll give us whatever we need so we have enough to stand up and face what's ahead.

Lord, sometimes we're so worn out, we just want to quit.
We trust you are enough. Give us strength and hope
to keep going as we depend on your love. Amen.

DECEMBER 7

It Slipped My Mind

"But when all goes well with you, remember me and show me kindness; mention me to Pharaoh and get me out of this prison ... I have done nothing to deserve being put in a dungeon." The chief cupbearer, however, did not remember Joseph; he forgot him. GENESIS 40:14-15, 23

If we're late and rushing out the door, it's easy to forget a lunchbox or library book. When we feel tired or sick, an appointment might slip our minds. How many times have we shopped for groceries, only to come home without the one thing we needed most? With our full and busy days, we simply can't remember it all.

It's one thing to forget where we put the keys, but forgetting our friends and family is another. Busy schedules can distract us from caring for others. Grandparents might feel lonely but we forget to write or call. We run off with our friends instead of including a new coworker. A pet's food dish can sit empty while we head out to run errands. We become so caught up in our own concerns, we leave others behind.

Jesus said, "Never will I leave you; never will I forsake you" (Hebrews 13:5). His kind of love never forgets! With his help, he'll make us faithful people who remember to love like him.

Lord, we're always on your mind. Help us to remember who needs our love and kindness every day. Amen.

Let Your Inner Beauty Shine

*Your beauty should not come from outward adornment, such
as elaborate hairstyles and the wearing of gold jewelry or
fine clothes. Rather, it should be that of your inner self,
the unfading beauty of a gentle and quiet spirit, which
is of great worth in God's sight.* 1 Peter 3:3-4

We often use our outsides to tell people about our insides. We can wear clothes to say, "I'm successful, I've got style and status, and I fit in," without saying a word. The way we slouch, strut, or skip across the room communicates our mood and attitude. People use hair color, makeup, tattoos, and jewelry to get noticed. Yet it's not our outside appearance that makes us special—it's our inner spirit that matters most.

Instead of spending hours in front of the mirror to look just right, we can spend time in prayer and worship. Rather than searching for the latest and greatest shoes at the store, we can search the Scriptures for God's truth. Instead of trying to "dress to impress," God calls us to please him through our love for other people.

The Spirit allows us to see with God's eyes, "For the Lord sees not as man sees: man looks on the outward appearance, but the Lord looks on the heart" (1 Samuel 16:7). Gentleness and kindness look good on you. Patience and peace are beautiful. Let's dress up our hearts in the love of God every day.

Lord, give us the beauty of gentle and quiet spirits
that never fade away. Amen.

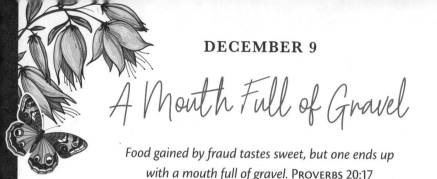

DECEMBER 9

A Mouth Full of Gravel

*Food gained by fraud tastes sweet, but one ends up
with a mouth full of gravel.* PROVERBS 20:17

Cheating might give you an edge in your boss's eyes at work. It might help you win a competition or put a little extra money in your pocket. But tomorrow, you'll miss out on the rewards and pride of a job well done.

Pretending to share the same worldview or values as others might help you fit in today, but tomorrow you'll feel lonely because no one will appreciate you for who you truly are. Burying a pile of bills might preserve your bank balance a little longer. Yet eventually you'll have a bigger pile of debt on your hands than when you started.

We're all tempted to cheat to get what we want. We bend the truth to avoid work or stay out of trouble. Yet in the end, a fake or a fraud is disappointed. The happiness we hope for stays out of reach.

If we have a goal, let's work hard to achieve it. If we have a need, let's take it to God in prayer and depend on him to provide. Let's put every hope and dream in his hands, trusting him as the giver of all good things. His blessings are better than anything we could take on our own.

Lord, teach us to be honest in all we say and do. Be our source
of joy and happiness. Amen.

Turning Back to God

*"But the father said to his servants, 'Quick! Bring the best robe
and put it on him. Put a ring on his finger and sandals
on his feet. Bring the fattened calf and kill it. Let's have
a feast and celebrate. For this son of mine was dead
and is alive again; he was lost and is found.'
So they began to celebrate."* LUKE 15:22-24

The sin in our hearts can send us in the wrong direction. We turn away from God to go our own way. His blessings are ignored in hopes of something better in the world. We find out the hard way that sin just leads to heartbreak and disappointment.

When we realize how far from God we've traveled, we can feel scared. We wonder, *Is God mad at me? Will he listen if I pray? Is he waiting to punish me for what I did? Why should God forgive me at all?* Our fears can keep us from running back to him, so we stay stuck in our guilt and shame.

Do you feel like your choices and attitudes have taken you down a road away from God? No matter what, he loves you. It's never too late to run to God and find his love and forgiveness waiting for you. Every time you turn back from your sin and turn to God, he celebrates! He wants to be your Father forever.

Lord, our sin can lead us far away from you. Help us to know you,
love you, and stay with you forever. Amen.

Obey the Rules

Let everyone be subject to the governing authorities, for there is no authority except that which God has established. The authorities that exist have been established by God. Consequently, whoever rebels against the authority is rebelling against what God has instituted, and those who do so will bring judgment on themselves. ROMANS 13:1-2

For a game to work, we must obey the rules. In life we also need signs, rules, and leaders so our home and community can work well together. Imagine if cars could drive wherever they liked at any speed.

What would happen if your child could walk out the door to recess in the middle of a lesson? How healthy would you be if you ignored your doctor's directive to eat right and take your medicine? How would your career suffer if you refused to follow company policy or show up each day? Laws and limits are put in place to help us stay happy, secure, and well.

God says he puts leaders and authority figures in place for our good. Every time we obey the rules and follow the laws of our land, we're obeying God himself. Sometimes it might be hard to obey, but know that rules are there for our benefit.

Lord, thank you for giving us limits and leaders to keep us safe
and secure. Give us willing hearts to obey
so we can obey you, too. Amen.

Put It All in His Hands

Do not be anxious about anything, but in every situation, by prayer and petition, with thanksgiving, present your requests to God. And the peace of God, which transcends all understanding, will guard your hearts and your minds in Christ Jesus. PHILIPPIANS 4:6-7

Everybody has stress and anxiety. We wonder, *Will I get my work done? Am I going to feel better? Will I get along with my friends? Can my problem be fixed? Am I good enough?* No matter what we might be struggling with today, God invites us to bring it to him in prayer.

Ask God for help with your relationships, responsibilities, and work. If you're tired and overwhelmed, pray for strength and rest. When you run out of time, money, or supplies, ask him to provide what's needed. If you're confused about what to do next, seek him for wisdom and direction. He cares about you so much that he wants to help with every detail of your life.

When you put all your concerns in God's hands, he puts his peace in your heart and mind. His peace will protect you from negative thinking, doubt, and discouragement. He'll fill you with hope and joy beyond anything we can understand. He loves you!

Lord, you know our fears and troubles. Please help us
and give us what we need today. Fill us with your peace
so our hearts and minds trust in you completely. Amen.

DECEMBER 13

Too Busy for God

> *[Martha] had a sister called Mary, who sat at the Lord's feet listening to what he said. But Martha was distracted by all the preparations that had to be made. "Martha, Martha," the Lord answered, "you are worried and upset about many things … Mary has chosen what is better, and it will not be taken away from her."* LUKE 10:39-42

Our days are full and busy! Learning, working, caring for our loved ones, serving our community, and pursuing our goals keeps us on the move. While we fill our days with good things, sometimes we're so busy we forget to take a break. We miss out on rest and quality time. Our stress goes up and our energy goes down as we go, go, go.

The most important thing we miss when we're too busy is time with God. He knows we need quiet moments alone to pray. We won't read and meditate on his Word unless we unplug and sit still with him. It's hard to commit to church and worship if we're worn out every Sunday morning. A full calendar can lead to an empty heart.

Have we become so busy and distracted that we've left no room for him? If we're "worried and upset about many things," let's choose "what is better" and turn toward Jesus.

> Lord, open our eyes to see what's distracting us from you.
> Show us what to set aside so we can draw close to you.
> We love you and want to sit at your feet every day. Amen.

DECEMBER 14

Living Wisely

Be very careful, then, how you live—not as unwise but as wise ...
Do not get drunk on wine, which leads to debauchery.
Instead, be filled with the Spirit, speaking to one
another with psalms, hymns, and songs
from the Spirit. EPHESIANS 5:15, 18-19

If people drink too much alcohol, take medicine for the sick when they're healthy, or use illegal drugs, they can't think clearly. Their minds become blurry and confused. They won't be able to hear God's wisdom, so they will make bad choices and disobey his Word. The words they speak will be foolish and wrong instead of truthful and loving.

God loves us so much, he wants to give us wisdom and guide our steps. He doesn't want anything we eat or drink to keep us from hearing his voice. Instead of using drugs or alcohol to try to feel happy, his Spirit can fill us with real joy that lasts.

If we love God, he gives us the Spirit. He fills us with joy that overflows through what we say and sing. Do you want the Spirit to fill our hearts and our home with God's love? We can pray and ask for more wisdom, more joy, and more strength to obey. He'll fill our house with singing and joy.

Lord, teach us how live in your wisdom. Fill us with your Spirit
so we obey and sing your praises every day. Amen.

Limits and Consequences

*"... the Lord disciplines the one he loves, and he chastens
everyone he accepts as his son." No discipline seems
pleasant at the time, but painful. Later on, however,
it produces a harvest of righteousness and peace
for those who have been trained by it.* HEBREWS 12:6, 11

Nobody likes limits. We'd rather scroll through social media than work or go to bed on time. It's easier to say and do what we like than obey who's in charge. We'd rather spend money on our wants than our needs. If we go out of bounds, limits and discipline put a lid on our behavior. They help us stay healthy, meet our goals, and get along with others.

One way God shows his love is through limits and consequences. He'll expose our secret sins to help us do what's right. He'll pair us with difficult people to practice patience and grace. He'll give a tough challenge so we learn to trust and depend on him. He'll let us lose or fail to deal with our pride. God does what it takes to help us grow.

Are we willing to accept God's discipline and teaching right now? If we do, we'll grow to love and look more and more like Jesus.

Lord, it can be hard to accept discipline. Make us willing to learn
and grow. We trust you know what's best for us all the time. Amen.

DECEMBER 16

Sharing Stored Blessings

Seven years of great abundance are coming throughout the land of Egypt, but seven years of famine will follow them. They should collect all the food of these good years that are coming and store up the grain under the authority of Pharaoh, to be kept in the cities for food. This food should be held in reserve for the country, to be used during the seven years of famine ... GENESIS 41:29-30, 35-36

Everyone is hungry for something. Lonely people crave friendship and a warm welcome. The sick want to find healing and comfort. Those in danger are desperate for safety and peace. Sadly, some families are unable to provide for basic needs like food, clothing, and shelter. God loves everyone, and he shows that love by sending helpers to those in need. He allows us to store up blessings in good times so we can share with others in hard times.

God says we act as his hands and feet to serve others. His plan all along has been for us to make a difference. With our feet, we walk toward those who suffer. With our hands, we reach out with comfort and help. "For we are God's handiwork, created in Christ Jesus to do good works, which God prepared in advance for us to do" (Ephesians 2:10).

Lord, you know who is suffering through a season of hunger
and pain in this world. Show us how to give and help
for your name's sake. Amen.

DECEMBER 17

Accepting Burdens and Blessings

For three days they traveled in the desert without finding water. When they came to Marah, they could not drink its water because it was bitter ... So the people grumbled against Moses, saying, "What are we to drink?" EXODUS 15:22-24

Your hungry stomach wants dinner, now! The trip in the car is taking forever. You have too much paperwork to do. You gave it your all at work, but you couldn't land the sale. Again. Your favorite shirt is still in the laundry. It can feel like everything and everyone is determined to spoil your day.

Are we grumbling more than we're grateful? How do we handle setbacks and disappointments? Are we taking our struggles to God in prayer, or do we worry and complain? Can we accept the burdens along with the blessings that each day brings?

If everything came easy and we always had our way, we'd never learn to wait. We would never know God as our provider and helper. Our faith would stay small and weak, and our prayers would go silent. We wouldn't discover that the hundreds of promises in the Bible are true. God uses hard things to teach us to trust him. He proves he's loving and faithful every time.

Lord, forgive us for grumbling when we face a problem.
Give us hearts that love you, trust you, and depend
on you for all we need. Amen.

Knock on His Door

"Ask and it will be given to you; seek and you will find;
knock and the door will be opened to you. For everyone
who asks receives; the one who seeks finds; and to the
one who knocks, the door will be opened." MATTHEW 7:7-8

God calls himself our heavenly Father. He's always ready to answer if you knock on his door. You can talk to him and ask for whatever you need. He offers forgiveness for your sins and mistakes. He holds wisdom to help you know what to do. If you're tired or worried, he offers strength and help with your problems. When you're lonely and sad, he stays right by your side.

God loves you. He'll never hide from you, turn his face away, or ignore you. He's waiting with arms open wide for you to run to him. Knock on his door today.

Lord, we thank you for your love. Move us to seek you
with all our hearts. We want to find you and receive
all you've promised to give. Amen.

Grant Me Diligent Hands

Lazy hands make for poverty, but diligent hands bring wealth. He who gathers crops in summer is a prudent son, but he who sleeps during harvest is a disgraceful son. PROVERBS 10:4-5

Hard work can feel like hard work! If we had our way, we might choose to relax and have fun all the time. Can you imagine a life of sleeping in and doing whatever we like, whenever we like? We might enjoy ourselves for a while, but the consequences of choosing play over work would be no fun at all.

Refusing to cook or clean would leave us hungry, dirty, and miserable. Skipping school or job responsibilities would mean a failed report card or an angry boss. We'd lose our health, our reputation, and our money. Our goals for the future would come to a stop.

Work is a gift from God. Our jobs provide income to buy what we need. School develops kids' talents and skills for the future. Taking care of our home creates a comfortable, happy space to share life together. God designed work to bring wonderful rewards that we'd miss if we quit.

Let's change our point of view so our jobs, chores, and responsibilities are a blessing instead of a burden.

Lord, we're tempted to quit our work before it's done.
Inspire us to give our best effort so we can receive
the rewards you have in store. Amen.

He Hears When We Call

Know that the LORD has set apart his faithful servant for himself;
the LORD hears when I call to him. If I had cherished sin in my heart,
the LORD would not have listened; but God has surely listened
and has heard my prayer. PSALM 4:3, 66:18-19

When you love someone, you listen to all they have to say. You laugh at their jokes and funny stories. You answer their questions. If they're sad or afraid, you look for ways to help. You take their thoughts and opinions seriously. Loving means listening.

God loves you and wants to hear your voice. You can tell him you're stressed and ask for his peace. You can thank him for all the ways he cares for you. When you sin and disobey, you can ask him to forgive and make you clean. If you struggle to understand his Word, you can bring him your tough questions. He promises to listen whenever you call for help.

The only thing that keeps God from listening is our own hard hearts. If we're determined to sin on purpose, we cherish our sin more than our Father in heaven. A stubborn heart will silence our prayers. The moment we choose to confess and repent, God opens his arms to listen and forgive.

Pray with confidence today. If you seek God, you will find him. If you ask, he will give you good things. If you knock, he will open his door to you (Matthew 7:7). You are loved!

> Lord, you hear us when we call on you.
> Thank you for love that listens. Amen.

DECEMBER 21

The Universe's Best Dad

As God has said: "I will live with them and walk among them,
and I will be their God, and they will be my people."
And, "I will be a Father to you, and you will be my sons and
daughters, says the Lord Almighty." 2 CORINTHIANS 6:16, 18

When a man becomes a father, he's given the priceless gift of a child. That child needs protection. Hugs and laughter. Food, clothes, and a home. Kids need strong arms to pick them up and hold them close. They need comfort when they're hurt and courage when they're scared. When a dad loves his child, it's a taste of the limitless love of Father God for all his children.

Not every child has a father—he's passed away or gone away and they're no longer together. God knows the place in the heart of every person that longs for a father's love. God is able to fill that place better than any human dad ever could.

God is a father who never leaves. He knows what you need before you ask him. He teaches what's right and shows which way to go. He protects you from danger and battles your enemies. His ears are always open to your prayers, and he never takes his eyes from you. When you're adopted into God's family, you're his child forever. No one can snatch you from his hand.

Lord, in you we find a Father's love. Thank you
for calling us your children. Amen.

Guardian Angels

*For he will command his angels concerning you to guard you
in all your ways; they will lift you up in their hands, so that
you will not strike your foot against a stone.* PSALM 91:11-12

Did you know God assigns guardian angels to watch over you? People are sometimes confused about what angels are. Some believe that people transform into angels when they die. But angels are actually God's unique creations from before he made the earth. They serve him as warriors, messengers, and helpers who care for God's children.

In the Bible we see angels described in many ways. We see them as mighty warriors. They brought food and comfort. They rolled away the stone from Jesus' tomb. Angels would often come in the form of ordinary men. When they display the glory of God, they are so bright and awesome people that fall down on the ground! God sends them as his powerful servants who are ready and willing to help.

God promises to watch over you and stay with you all the time. While he helps you in all kinds of ways, his angels are one part of his plan to protect and keep us from harm.

Lord, thank you for sending powerful angels to keep us safe.
Help us to trust you to take care of us every day. Amen.

True Peace of Mind

*"Peace I leave with you; my peace I give you. I do not give to you
as the world gives. Do not let your hearts be troubled
and do not be afraid."* JOHN 14:27

In our busy days, can you remember what peace and quiet feel like? We live by
the clock as we run from morning to night. Pressure to keep up can wear us
down. We want to feel peaceful and calm. How can we move from "doing" to
simply "being"?

The world's answer says to stay organized in every detail. They tell us that
money can buy peace of mind. If we're social and popular, we won't feel alone.
If we strive to reach our goals, success will be worth the price. The world's
peace leaves us more anxious than when we started.

God's peace is the real thing. It's not based on our performance. It can't be
bought at the store. Peace from God doesn't depend on happy circumstances
or a full bank account. We find God's peace when we trust him for everything
we need.

Are you stressed and worried today? Are you exhausted, with no rest in
sight? Take everything to God in prayer. Ask for strength and help. Read the
Bible to hear how much he loves you. Remember his promise that says, "You
will keep in perfect peace those whose minds are steadfast, because they trust
in you" (Isaiah 26:3). God will give us peace that nothing can take away.

Lord, help us to find our peace in you alone. Amen.

A Special Baby

"Today in the town of David a Savior has been born to you; he is the Messiah, the Lord. This will be a sign to you: You will find a baby wrapped in cloths and lying in a manger." LUKE 2:11-12

For to us a child is born, to us a son is given, and the government will be on his shoulders. And he will be called Wonderful Counselor, Mighty God, Everlasting Father, Prince of Peace. ISAIAH 9:6

Babies are tiny and helpless. They have no voice—no money, power, or authority—to influence the world. Yet when they are brought into a family, everyone is filled with love and joy. A family has never been the same after a new bundle of joy arrives.

Jesus came into this world as a baby. He not only changed the lives of Mary and Joseph, but his birth changed the whole course of history. He left his throne in heaven so people could see the face of God himself. They heard God's message of love and salvation with their own ears. As Jesus grew up, he brought teaching and healing like the world had never known before. He was born so he could die for us and give us life forever. Since he came into the world, he made a way to God the Father for all who believe.

Jesus was the one baby who still changes lives today. Let's thank God for his birth right now.

Lord, thank you for sending Jesus into this world as a baby.
In him we find peace and life forever. Amen.

Who Is Jesus to You?

[Jesus] asked his disciples, "Who do people say the Son of Man is?" They replied, "Some say John the Baptist; others say Elijah; and still others, Jeremiah or one of the prophets." "But what about you?" he asked. "Who do you say I am?" Simon Peter answered, "You are the Messiah, the Son of the living God." MATTHEW 16:13-16

Jesus asked the most important question of all: "Who do you say I am?" It is the most important question of all time. When we discover who Jesus truly is, it changes our lives forever.

Jesus is the one and only Son of God, given as a gift of his love. (John 3:16)

He is the way, the truth, and the life. He's our only way to the Father. (John 14:6)

Jesus is our Savior, bearing our sins in his body on the cross. By his wounds we are healed. (1 Peter 2:24)

He is Immanuel—God with us—who came down from heaven. (Matthew 1:23, John 6:51)

Jesus is the creator of all things. (Colossians 1:16)

He is King of kings and Lord of lords. (Revelation 17:14)

He is our blessed hope. (Titus 2:13)

If we believe in Jesus, we are saved. We receive forgiveness and life forever. Adopted as God's children, we receive freedom and power now and heaven in the future. "But what about you? Who do you say Jesus is?" (Matthew 16:15).

Lord, thank you for Jesus. We want to know him and love him more every day. Amen.

DECEMBER 26

Eager to Give and Serve

We were not idle when we were with you, nor did we eat anyone's food without paying for it. On the contrary, we worked night and day, laboring and toiling so that we would not be a burden to any of you. ... we gave you this rule: "The one who is unwilling to work shall not eat." 2 THESSALONIANS 3:7-8, 10

No matter whether it's a family, a classroom, or a team, all goes well when everybody does their part. If one person chooses to give up or sit out, it makes the load heavy for everyone.

The church needs us, too. The responsibility of teaching, giving, and helping is meant to be shared. Every time we volunteer to serve or support missionaries in sharing the good news of Jesus, we're doing our part to build God's kingdom. It's exciting to know that when we join in God's work it makes a difference forever.

Is it tempting to sit back and let others do the work? Would we rather receive than give? Let's pray for God to set us free from idleness so we can serve him better.

Lord, you invite us to join in your work of loving the world.
Make us eager to give and serve every day. Amen.

DECEMBER 27

Sparkling New

*"Come now, let us settle the matter," says the LORD.
"Though your sins are like scarlet, they shall be as white as snow;
though they are red as crimson, they shall be like wool."* ISAIAH 1:18

Think about your favorite thing to wear. It's the first thing you grab from the laundry. It's comfortable and fits perfectly. You love the color. Everybody says it looks great. When you wear it, you feel like "you." It would be hard to give up if it were badly stained or torn. Yet even with mending or washing, it would never be the same.

In God's eyes, you're the one. He chose you to be his "treasured possession" (Deuteronomy 14:2). You're the "apple of his eye" (Psalm 17:8). His beloved creation. His child. You are so precious to God, he sent his own Son to seek you and save you forever.

Yet we're born with the stain of sin that we can't wash away. This sin makes us stubborn and rebellious. We're blind to what's true and right. We feel guilt and shame for what we've done. Sin separates us from our God.

Through Jesus we can be clean and new. When we believe in him, we're washed as white as snow. We're made righteous and holy. We're given his Spirit. Instead of guilt and fear, we have life and joy forever.

Lord, forgive us of our sins and make us white as snow. Amen.

Watch Who You Follow

But there were also false prophets among the people, just as there will be false teachers among you. They will secretly introduce destructive heresies, even denying the sovereign Lord who bought them— bringing swift destruction on themselves. 2 PETER 2:1

If my friend gave false directions, I'd get lost on the road. If your daughter copied her classmate's spelling list instead of the teacher's, she might fail her test. A recipe lists correct amounts of flavoring—if you added any seasoning you liked, it could taste terrible. We depend on true information to stay happy and well.

False teachers threaten our faith. They say God doesn't care about sin, or they burden us down with rules he never made. False teachers make God look small—they deny his power. His wisdom. His authority. If we listen to them, we can lose our way.

How do we spot a false teacher? We look for Jesus to show in their life. Are they loving, kind, and patient? Are they gentle and peaceful, or is their anger out of control? Are they honest, humble, and pure?

Godly teachers love and obey the Bible. They praise Jesus as the King. Instead of turning us away from God, they encourage us to follow him faithfully. Their life is blameless.

God warns us to watch who we follow. False teachers try to break our trust in his Word. They say bad is good, and good is bad. If we close our ears and turn away, our faith can remain safe and sound.

Lord, protect us from false teachers who deny the truth
and love of Jesus. Amen.

Freed From Guilt

Let us draw near to God with a sincere heart and with the full assurance that faith brings, having our hearts sprinkled to cleanse us from a guilty conscience and having our bodies washed with pure water. Let us hold unswervingly to the hope we profess, for he who promised is faithful. HEBREWS 10:22-23

God made a way to set us free. Instead of hiding in shame, we can accept his invitation to get close to our Father. If we pray and confess our sins, he promises to forgive.

He'll make us clean and new. We'll have the joy of a clean conscience. He'll give the hope of a fresh start.

We stay trapped in our guilt if we doubt God's love. Today, let's remember he is faithful. He'll never turn us away. Jesus' work on the cross covers every sin we commit.

By faith, let's offer him a "broken and contrite heart" that he will not despise (Psalm 51:17). He will fill us with joy and peace that never ends.

Lord, you take away our sins and wash us clean. Set us free from our guilt and shame as we put our faith in you. Amen.

Through It All

[Job] said: "Naked I came from my mother's womb, and naked I will depart. The LORD gave and the LORD has taken away; may the name of the LORD be praised." In all this, Job did not sin by charging God with wrongdoing. JOB 1:21-22

This year held every kind of blessing. We met wonderful friends. We grew in mind, body, and spirit. Our families created memories as we shared life together. God gave much to be thankful for.

Yet this year also brought losses. We said painful goodbyes. Some hopes and dreams failed to come true. We were blindsided by trouble we couldn't see coming. Some of our hurts have yet to fully heal. Blessings slipped through our fingers and are gone.

Can we see God in the good and the bad? Was he here when we struggled? Did he care about our pain? Yes, he loved us through it all.

God has never left our side. He will use what was taken to give us good things. Even now, our troubles are making us "mature and complete, not lacking anything" (James 1:4). We know more of prayer, trust, and hope than we ever knew before.

Let's claim his promise for the year ahead: "And the God of all grace, who called you to his eternal glory in Christ, after you have suffered a little while, will himself restore you and make you strong, firm and steadfast" (1 Peter 5:10).

Lord, in the end, you restore what we've lost. Amen.

God Is Faithful Forever

*For the word of the LORD is right and true; he is faithful
in all he does. The LORD loves righteousness and justice;
the earth is full of his unfailing love.* PSALM 33:4-5

Can you name your hopes for the year ahead? Where might you like to travel? What is something new you'd like to try? Who do you hope to meet or get to know better? Do you have a goal you want to accomplish? The coming months are full of possibilities.

Yet for all the good we know is coming, we will face challenges. We'll feel sick or tired at times. Special things will be lost or broken. We'll be overwhelmed by the stress of busy days. We'll struggle with our limitations. We don't know the troubles coming our way.

What we do know is that God is faithful. He watches over every moment of our life (Psalm 121:7). He knows all our needs and will provide (Matthew 6:32). God will listen to every prayer when we're afraid and cry out to him. No matter where we go and what we do, we'll be wrapped closely in his love (Psalm 139:5).

Nothing we do can change God's faithfulness. If we sin, he forgives. If we fall down in failure, he picks us up again. If we walk away, he seeks until he finds us again. "If we are faithless, he remains faithful, for he cannot disown himself" (2 Timothy 2:13).

Let's start the new year full of hope. Our God is faithful forever.

Lord, we trust you with our lives. Your love never ends. Amen.

Scripture Index

About the Author

Joanna Teigen and her husband, Rob, have been married for 25 years and are loving life with two sons, three daughters, and a beautiful daughter-in-law. As founders of their ministry, Growing Home Together, they believe that their vows are for always, children are a gift, and prayer is powerful.

The Teigens currently live in West Michigan and are passionate to help people experience the power of God in their families. The couple have authored several books including *Mr & Mrs: 366 Devotions for Couples*, *101 Prayers for My Daughter* and *101 Prayers for My Son*.